From the Local to the Global

From the Local to the Global

Key Issues in Development Studies

Second Edition

Edited by
GERARD McCANN and STEPHEN McCLOSKEY

PlutoPress
www.plutobooks.com

First published 2003
Second edition published 2009 by Pluto Press
345 Archway Road, London N6 5AA and
175 Fifth Avenue, New York, NY 10010

www.plutobooks.com

Distributed in the United States of America exclusively by
Palgrave Macmillan, a division of St. Martin's Press LLC,
175 Fifth Avenue, New York, NY 10010

British Library Cataloguing in Publication Data
A catalogue record for this book is available from the British Library

ISBN   978 0 7453 2843 0   Hardback
ISBN   978 0 7453 2842 3   Paperback

Library of Congress Cataloging in Publication Data applied for

This book is printed on paper suitable for recycling and made from
fully managed and sustained forest sources. Logging, pulping and
manufacturing processes are expected to conform to the environmental
standards of the country of origin.

10   9   8   7   6   5   4   3   2

Designed and produced for Pluto Press by
Chase Publishing Services Ltd, Sidmouth, England
Typeset from disk by Stanford DTP Services, Northampton
Simultaneously printed digitally by CPI Antony Rowe in England, UK
and Edwards Bros in the United States of America

CONTENTS

ACKNOWLEDGEMENTS

A publication of this nature would not have been possible without the support and encouragement of our respective institutions, and the organisations that each of the contributors is associated with. We would like to thank the Centre for Global Education and St Mary's University College for their full support and co-operation in the compilation of this text. We have benefited from the support of colleagues and access to invaluable resources in both institutions. We thank the various non-governmental organisations who have supported this research and provided both incentive and material. Without their work this type of endeavour would be impossible. We would also like to thank Roger van Zwanenberg and his team at Pluto Press for encouraging the idea of a second edition and managing the production of the text with great professionalism.

The contributors to this text deserve our thanks for working to such difficult deadlines and delivering quality manuscripts. This made our role as editors much easier. Together with the contributors we relied on the support of a great many individuals who diligently and patiently went through various aspects of the text, offered specialist advice and gave us encouragement throughout. We thank all who have made this edition possible. Of course, as editors, we take full and ultimate responsibility for the content of this publication.

Gerard McCann
Stephen McCloskey
August 2009

ABBREVIATIONS

AAA	Accra Agenda for Action
ADB	African Development Bank
AFTA	ASEAN Free Trade Area
AIDS	Acquired Immune Deficiency Syndrome
AMF	Asian Monetary Fund
AMICC	American NGOs Coalition for the ICC
APEC	Asia-Pacific Economic Co-operation
ARV	AIDS-Associated Retrovirus
ASEAN	Association of Southeast Asian Nations
AU	African Union
BME	Black and Minority Ethnic organisations
CAP	Common Agricultural Policy
CBI	Confederation of British Industry
CEDAW	Convention on the Elimination of All Forms of Discrimination against Women
CET	Common External Tariff
CFSP	Common Foreign and Security Policy
CICC	Coalition for an International Criminal Court
CIT	Countries in Transition
CMI	Chiang Mai Initiative
COMESA	Common Market for Eastern and Southern Africa
CPA	Country Programmable Aid
CPD	Continuing Professional Development
CSO	Civil Society Organisation
CTT	Currency Transaction Tax
DAC	Development Assistance Committee
DAF	Development Awareness Fund
DAWN	Development Alternatives for Women in a New Era
DDCI	Debt and Development Coalition Ireland
DEA	Development Education Association

DEEP	Development Education Exchange in Europe Project
DERC	Development Education Research Centre
DERN	Development Education Research Network
DFA	Department of Foreign Affairs (Ireland)
DfID	Department for International Development (UK)
DNGO	Development Non-governmental Organisation
DRC	Democratic Republic of Congo
EAC	East African Co-operation
EBA	'Everything but Arms' Initiative
EBRD	European Bank for Reconstruction and Development
EC	European Community (EEC, EU)
EC	European Commission
ECA	Economic Commission for Africa
ECOWAS	Economic Commission of West African States
EDF	European Development Fund
EE	Environmental Education
EEC	European Economic Community (EU, EC)
ELI	Export-Led Industrialisation
EMU	Economic and Monetary Union
ENDD	European Network on Debt and Development
ERT	European Round Table of Industrialists
ESAF	Enhanced Structural Adjustment Facility
ESD	Education for Sustainable Development
EU	European Union
EURODAD	European Network on Debt and Development
FAO	Food and Agriculture Organisation
FARC	Colombian Revolutionary Armed Forces
FDI	Foreign Direct Investment
FfD	Financing for Development
FOCUS	Focus on the Global South
FSO	Fund for Special Operations
FTA	Free Trade Agreement
FTAA	Free Trade Area of the Americas
G20	Group of Leading Financial Powers
G8	Group of Leading Industrial Powers

GAD	Gender and Development
GATS	General Agreement on Trade in Services
GATT	General Agreement on Tariffs and Trade
GAVI	Global Alliance for Vaccines and Immunisation
GBS	General Budget Support
GDF	Global Policy Forum
GDP	Gross Domestic Product
GFI	Global Financial Integrity
GMP	Genetically Modified Product
GNI	Gross National Income
GNP	Gross National Product
GRZ	Government of the Republic of Zambia
HDI	Human Development Index
HDR	Human Development Report
HIPC	Heavily Indebted Poor Countries
HIV	Human Immunodeficiency Virus
H-O	Heckscher–Ohlin model
IBRD	International Bank for Reconstruction and Development
ICT	Information and Communication Technology
ICTFY	International Criminal Tribunal for the Former Yugoslavia
IDA	International Development Association
IDB	Inter-American Development Bank
IFC	International Finance Co-operation
IFG	International Forum on Globalisation
IFI	International Financial Institution
IGAD	Intergovernmental Authority on Development
IGO	International Governmental Organisation
ILO	International Labour Organisation
IMF	International Monetary Fund
IPCC	Intergovernmental Panel on Climate Change
ISI	Import-Substitution Industrialisation
IT	Information Technology
ITO	International Trade Organisation
JAS	Joint Assistance Strategies
JDC	Jubilee Debt Campaign

LAFTA	Latin American Free Trade Association
LDC	Least Developed Country
MAI	Multilateral Agreement on Investment
MDG	Millennium Development Goal
MDRI	Multilateral Debt Relief Initiative
MFN	Most Favoured Nation
MNC	Multinational Corporation
MST	Landless Rural Workers Movement
NAFTA	North American Free Trade Agreement
NAMA	Non-Agricultural Market Access
NATO	North Atlantic Treaty Organisation
NCDE	National Committee for Development Education
NDP	National Development Plans
NGO	Non-Governmental Organisation
NIC	Newly Industrialised Country
ODA	Overseas Development Assistance
OECD	Organisation for Economic Co-operation and Development
OPEC	Organisation of Petroleum Exporting Countries
PCA	Partnership and Co-operation Agreement
PEPFAR	President's Emergency Plan for AIDS Relief
PRGF	Poverty Reduction and Growth Facility
PRSP	Poverty Reduction Strategy Papers
SADC	Southern African Development Community
SAFTA	Southern African Free Trade Area
SAP	Structural Adjustment Programme
SAPRI	The SAPRI Report
SDI	Spatial Development Initiative
SGA	Strategic Grant Agreement
SIVE	Integrated System of External Vigilance
STABEX	Stabilisation of Export Earnings from Products
SWIFT	Society of Worldwide Inter-bank Financial Telecommunications
TNC	Transnational Corporation
TRIM	Trade-Related Investment Measure
TRIP	Trade-Related Intellectual Property Right
TWN	Third World Network

UK	United Kingdom
UN	United Nations
UNAIDS	Joint UN Programme on HIV/AIDS
UNCED	United Nations Conference on Environment and Development
UNCTAD	United Nations Conference on Trade and Development
UNDSD	United Nations Decade on Sustainable Development
UNFPA	United Nations Population Fund
UNHCHR	United Nations High Commissioner for Human Rights
UNHCR	United Nations High Commissioner for Refugees
UNIFEM	United Nations Development Fund for Women
UNRISD	United Nations Research Institute for Social Development
UNSC	United Nations Security Council
US	United States (of America)
USA	United States of America
WDM	World Development Movement
WEDO	Women's Environment and Development Organisation
WID	Women in Development
WIDE	Women in Development Europe
WRI	World Resources Institute
WSF	World Social Forum
WSSD	World Summit on Sustainable Development
WTO	World Trade Organisation

Part I

Development Discourse and Definitions

1

INTRODUCTION: RECASTING DEVELOPMENT IN A CHANGING GLOBAL ECONOMY

Stephen McCloskey

Since the publication of the first edition of this book in 2003, a number of global issues have converged to place immense strain on the structures and policies underpinning international development. Over the past six years, climate change, rising food and fuel prices and, more recently, a significant contraction in the global economy have both challenged the progress of international development and reinforced the need for a more sustained and enhanced commitment to development by the world's leading economies. The economic downturn, like all of the factors that undermine development, most severely impacts on the poor, who are most vulnerable to the vagaries of the global economy and least well equipped to withstand the cold wind of recession. With the imperative of addressing the causes and effects of the global recession has come a questioning of the validity of the neoliberal model of development and the need to restore good governance and democratisation to the stewardship of the global economy. To this extent, there is the possibility of opening up a debate on how we should develop at national and global levels in the context of sustainability and prioritising the needs of the poor.

This chapter considers the prospects for international development in the context of the changing global economy. As the global recession begins to bite, there has emerged the possibility of changes in global financial governance, proposed by development non-governmental organisations (NGOs) aiming to democratise and stabilise the regulation of the international economy. This chapter also signposts the reader to the main issues considered in the text, beginning with a consideration of some definitions of development.

What is Development?

Defining development is important in setting out the parameters of our discussion, but also in characterising the methods and ultimate goal underpinning the development process. Definitions of development can be contentious, as they can also determine how we measure success or failure in arriving at the 'developed' state. The World Bank, for instance, has traditionally measured development in the context of national wealth calculated on the basis of gross domestic product (GDP) and gross national income (GNI) expressed in per capita terms. Of course, what the per capita figure does not tell us is how national wealth is distributed within society, both among its citizens and social institutions, to maximise societal well-being. The United Nations (UN) *Human Development Report* (HDR) takes a more rounded view of development:

> Human Development is a development paradigm that is about much more than the rise or fall of national incomes. It is about creating an environment in which people can develop their full potential and lead productive, creative lives in accord with their needs and interests. People are the real wealth of nations. Development is thus about expanding the choices people have to lead lives that they value. And it is thus about much more than economic growth, which is only a means – if a very important one – of enlarging people's choices. (http://hdr.undp/org/en/humandev)

Definitions of development can point to the economic philosophy underpinning them. Thus, a free-market definition of development is likely to emphasise the wealth creation possibilities arising from unfettered trade and unrestrained markets. A state interventionist definition is likely to emphasise the enlarged human choices, improved lifestyles and standard of living that could result from a rights-based approach to development. While the laissez-faire approach assumes that the market will distribute wealth across society without state intervention, the Keynesian method believes that the guiding hand of the state is needed as a social safety net for those excluded from wealth creation and distribution. In assessing the two approaches Kingsbury suggests that development means

> the material advancement of people, especially the world's poor. But material advancement, especially if understood as simple economic growth, is not enough by itself, and, indeed may not even be realized without other components of development which include the capacity to ensure adequate distribution of the benefits of such growth, ecological sustainability in the way growth is achieved, and the governance to ensure that the processes to achieve such growth are agreed in a politically inclusive manner and operate under the rule of law. (Kingsbury et al. 2008, p.11)

If we accept that development in its fullest form represents more than material advances and economic growth, then the measurement of development needs to reflect this broader definition. The *Human Development Report* endeavours to measure development through a Human Development Index (HDI). The HDI is calculated on the basis of 'three dimensions' to human development: first, a *long and healthy life*, measured by life expectancy at birth; second, *knowledge*, measured on the basis of adult literacy rates and the combined gross enrolment ratio for primary, secondary and tertiary schools; third, a *decent standard of living*, measured by GDP per capita. On the basis of these indices, the United Nations Development Programme (UNDP) ranks countries according to their development performance in high, medium and low development categories.

Because the indices go beyond the realm of economic performance, the countries heading the Human Development Index are those with strong social indicators in health, education and welfare. Thus the 2008 index is headed by Iceland and Norway, with the United States in just 15th position despite its economic wealth (http://hdr.undp.org/en/statistics). However, critics of the HDI suggest that the index is not sophisticated enough to provide qualitative data on the delivery of education or health care within nation states, which are crucial to their assessment. The HDI is therefore an improvement on a purely economic conceptualisation of development in recognising the importance of the social pillars of development, especially health and education; but it is limited in its capacity to identify regional variations in development, which could reveal persistent levels of poverty and social need in specific areas, masked by national statistics. Some social scientists and development practitioners go further in their criticism of the HDI by suggesting that the paradigm of development in which the index operates is fundamentally flawed and intended to perpetuate Western dominance over the developing world (Storey 2003). By measuring development in the context of a Western conceptualisation of the term, the global North is imposing the flawed and unsustainable model of development implemented in the developed world on the poorer countries in the global South.

Just as the measurement and practice of development is contested, so are its theoretical underpinnings. The two dominant theories of development regard it as either a matter of historical progress or a process of modernisation. McGillivray suggests that development as human progress 'refers to the unfolding of human history, over a long period of time, in a manner thought to be progressive' (2008, p.23). Modernisation, on the other hand 'is a process whereby societies move through a fundamental, complete structural transition from one condition to another, from a starting point to an end point' (ibid.). This process is most directly associated with industrialisation and the transition from the late eighteenth century onward from a high dependency on agriculture to urban-based manufacturing. The influential political scientist Samuel Huntington described modernisation as 'a process in which societies have more control over their natural and social environment due to the use of superior scientific and technical knowledge' (ibid.). Huntington also argued that as societies modernise they become more complex and disordered, a process that requires political institutions capable of managing the stress of modernisation. Modernisation and historical progress have also been considered in the works of Rostow who analysed the implications of economic development to wider society and social relations. Rostow (1960) discussed the evolution of society through stages of development from traditional society to an 'age of high mass consumption'. The more recent discourse on development – with its focus on the process of globalisation and economic meltdown – in many ways reflects an older tradition which considered global economic shifts in terms of crises, the division of labour and class struggle. Marx too saw society as progressing through stages of development, but his developmental process culminated with the creation of a revolutionary class that would overthrow the owners of private property.

In the aftermath of the Cold War, the ideas underpinning the Marxist analysis of capitalism appeared to be politically redundant given their association with command economies in the former Eastern bloc. Neoliberalism and its version of development have been in the ascendancy since the late 1970s, supported by right-of-centre governments across Europe – Margaret Thatcher's British administration from 1979–90 was a prime example – and North America. However, the ideological debate on economic development has been reignited by the global economic downturn in 2008. The next section considers the prospects for development in the context of the global recession.

Capitalism in Crisis

According to the World Development Movement (WDM), in 2008 global capitalism 'entered a fundamental crisis of legitimacy, triggered by a "perfect storm" of the banking meltdown, rising energy costs and a spike in world food prices' (WDM 2008). The financial crisis had its origins in the sub-prime property market in the United States of America (USA), where banks and mortgage lenders operated in a financial bubble of low interest rates and risky and/or fraudulent mortgage lending that exposed the banks to bad debt and mortgage holders to repossessions. No less a figure than Alan Greenspan, the former chair of the USA Federal Reserve for 18 years, admitted 'that he had put too much faith in the self-correcting power of free markets and had failed to anticipate the self-destructive power of wanton mortgage lending' (*New York Times* 2008). During his tenure as chair of the 'Fed', Greenspan developed a reputation for prudence and wise stewardship of the economy, with the business sector hanging on to his every syllable. However, a humbled Greenspan told a (USA Congressional) House Committee on Oversight and Government Reform that 'those of us who have looked to the self-interest of lending institutions to protect shareholders' equity, myself included, are in a state of shocked disbelief'. He added, 'I have found a flaw [in my ideology]. I don't know how significant or permanent it is. But I've been very distressed by that fact' (ibid.).

The depth of the crisis became clearer when Lehman Brothers Investment Bank, one of the USA's biggest institutions, went into bankruptcy and the Federal Reserve refused to provide a bailout (*The Times* 2008). The Lehman collapse followed the USA government's effective nationalisation of the mortgage giants Fannie Mae and Freddie Mac, which were found to have liabilities of $5 billion – this extraordinary debt would now be shouldered by the American taxpayer (*Guardian* 2008a). As if to highlight the global dimensions of the crisis, the British government had to nationalise Northern Rock in February 2008 and absorb £25 billion of the bank's emergency borrowing, a debt that would also be passed on to the tax payer (*Guardian* 2008b). These extraordinary interventions in the economy by governments ideologically wedded to neoliberalism reflected their concerns at the depth of the economic crisis and their desperation to shore up the financial sector.

The contagion of financial crisis has not been confined to these sectors and has also gripped national economies, with the so-called 'credit crunch' necessitating an emergency bailout of Hungary. The International Monetary Fund (IMF) provided emergency assistance in the form of a $15.7 billion loan over a 17 month period in November 2008, and this followed similar loans to Iceland ($2 billion) and Ukraine ($16.5 billion) (IMF 2008). But it is the economies of lower- and middle-income countries that have been hardest hit hard by the global recession. These countries have already had to contend with fluctuating food and fuel prices, with the former causing riots and unrest across the developing world. The Food and Agricultural Organisation (FAO) of the United Nations estimated the number of undernourished people in the world at 923 million in 2007, an increase of more than 80 million since 1990–92. In a 2008 report, the FAO found that '[h]igh food prices are driving millions of people into food insecurity, worsening conditions for many who were already food insecure and threatening long-term global food security' (FAO 2008, p.4).

The FAO found that high food prices have a particularly devastating effect on the poorest citizens in both urban and rural areas, as well as on the landless and female-headed households. Regionally, the FAO estimates that rising food prices have plunged 'an additional 41 million people in Asia and the Pacific and another 24 million in sub-Saharan Africa into hunger' (FAO 2008, p.7), with real food prices in 2008 a massive 64 per cent above their 2002 levels. Food prices started to rise in 2002 after four decades of largely declining trends, and in 2007 there was a sharp spike in prices. In identifying the causes of the increase, the FAO points to a long-term growth in demand for food outstripping supply, with food production hampered by increases in petroleum prices which in turn have tripled the price of fertiliser and doubled transportation costs (FAO 2008, p.10). The emergence of the biofuel market – designed to mitigate the use of fossil fuels – has also impacted on food prices as an estimated 100 million tonnes of cereals (4.7 per cent of global production) has been designated for biofuel production.

In identifying possible measures to address problems in food production, the FAO has called for the implementation of safety nets and social protection programmes for small farmers who are most vulnerable to increases. Small farmers need to boost food production and require access to resources like seeds, fertilisers and animal feed that have often been priced beyond their reach. The FAO has criticised the measures implemented by some countries to offset the effects of high food prices, such as price-capping and limiting exports, which it suggests will further stifle food supply and damage trade relations. Small farmers need support to increase the production and supply of food at a time of financial contraction. Although fuel costs subsided in mid 2009, it is likely that the demand for biofuels and cost of fertiliser and transportation, along with the demand for food, will remain high for the foreseeable future. In this context, small farmers and vulnerable rural communities will need maximum support to sustain food production.

The striking turbulence besetting the global economy at present – in the form of a banking and mortgage crisis that has spilled over into other sectors, such as the auto industry in the USA and the retail sector in the UK, combined with rising food and fuel prices – raises the question: Are we witnessing the death throes of capitalism? Seumas Milne suggests that the economic crisis has certainly 'exposed deregulated capitalism as bankrupt and its ruling elites as greedy and inept. But it is the free market model, not capitalism that is dying' (2008). Milne adds that it is not Marx 'who has been rehabilitated in short order, but John Maynard Keynes, out of dire necessity' (ibid.). Keynes was a British economist who advocated state intervention in the form of fiscal and monetary measures to mitigate the adverse affects of the unregulated market. Milne argues that the current crisis could renew enthusiasm for Keynesian interventionism and public ownership to protect those most vulnerable to the recession 'rather than make them pay the price for it' by way of house repossessions, unemployment, higher tax and subsistence costs, etc. If, knowing that the economic implosion has already forced Western governments into taking private stock into public ownership, we accept that neoliberalism has been discredited, then we now have an opportunity to reshape the economic system. The next section considers proposals for change recommended by the development non-governmental sector in the context of the economic crisis.

International Development and the Economic Crisis

In November 2008, 20 leaders of United Kingdom (UK) civil society organisations, including leading development agencies, the

Muslim Council of Britain, and the Trade Union Congress (TUC), wrote to the British prime minister, Gordon Brown, in respect of the growing economic crisis. Their letter describes the 'failed policies' of the 'institutions that govern the world economy' and suggests that the United Nations (UN) 'should lead a process of comprehensive reform'. It goes on to propose financial regulation, 'democratisation of international economic institutions', and 'a major recovery plan that puts people and the environment at its heart' (letter to Gordon Brown, November 2008). The World Development Movement put flesh on this agenda with a five-point plan for addressing key international development concerns in the context of the current crises. These proposals are summarised as follows:

1. *Steer globalisation on course for a low-carbon future*: to de-link economic development from the high carbon consumption of fossil fuels that causes global warming and threatens the natural environment.
2. *Get capital to serve the needs of society and the environment*: to ensure that the banking system serves the wider public interest, particularly those institutions in public ownership. This would also involve clamping down on corporate tax havens.
3. *Ensure democratic and accountable global financial institutions*: the IMF and the World Bank must be restructured to be democratically accountable bodies.
4. *Bring the food system in line with new energy and climate realities*: to move away from dependency on fossil-fuel-based technology, corporate control, and prices set in distant, volatile markets.
5. *Develop trade deals based on co-operation rather than exploitation*: the European Union is aggressively pushing a series of trade deals which will oblige poor countries to open their financial markets to the very same banking institutions that have wantonly abused deregulated markets in the UK. These proposals need to be replaced with trade deals based on mutual co-operation instead of corporate exploitation. (WDM 2008)

Interestingly, the WDM and other leading development agencies stopped short of calling for the mandates of the IMF and the World Bank to be withdrawn, despite these organisations' association with the disastrous debt crisis in the developing world and their complicity with Western governments and corporations in the deregulation of global markets. They opted instead for 'comprehensive reform' and greater democratisation in global financial governance. The next section considers the likely economic impact on the developing countries arising from the economic crisis.

The Cost of the Crisis

The development agency ActionAid put a price on the cost to developing countries resulting from declining growth and higher food, commodity and fuel prices. It estimated that developing countries would lose $180 billion by the end of 2009 and $400 billion within three years. ActionAid suggested that the international financial institutions (IFIs: the IMF, the World Bank and the World Trade Organisation) could support those developing countries most vulnerable to these economic pressures by cancelling debt, using gold reserves and refinancing (ActionAid 2008). While the projected losses of developing countries are immense, they dwindle in comparison to the cost of bailing out the global economy, which has been estimated at between $2 and $4 trillion ($2,000 – $4,000 billion). To put this expenditure in perspective, the Stern Report on climate change (2006) estimated that 1 per cent of global gross domestic product (GDP), or $540 billion, would contain greenhouse gas emissions to avoid the worst effects of climate change. WaterAid estimates that £37.5 billion could provide clean water and sanitation to the 2.5 billion people currently lacking a safe supply of water. And the FAO estimates that $30 billion would feed the 862 million people who go hungry every day (*Guardian* 2008c).

Developing countries will have contrasted the urgency and rapidity with which Western governments released staggering levels of finance to bail out the global economy with the tardiness and unfulfilled pledges that have characterised aid contributions to the developing world. In 1970, the United Nations General Assembly agreed a resolution (UN General Assembly Resolution 2626, 24 October 1970) that committed wealthy countries to contributing 0.7 per cent of gross national income (GNI, the total value produced within a country) to overseas development assistance (ODA). Almost 40 years later, just five countries have reached the 0.7 per cent target – Norway tops the list at 0.95 per cent of GNI followed by Sweden, Luxembourg, Denmark and the Netherlands. The United Kingdom's overseas aid contribution currently stands at 0.36 per cent of GNI while the USA provides proportionately the lowest contribution to ODA at just 0.16 per cent of GNI (OECD 2008). There remains real concern within developing countries that overseas aid budgets will fall victim to the current recession if it bites deeply into economies in the global North over a sustained period. Aid is an easy target for reduced spending when a national economy is under the cloud of recession. Moreover, should ODA be reduced and the global economy continue to contract then the prospects for achieving the United Nations' millennium development goals (MDGs) – the global framework for international development policy and practice – will be further undermined.

The millennium development goals comprise eight targets agreed by the United Nations in 2000 to tackle the underpinning causes of poverty and inequality in the developing world. The overarching aim of the goals is to reduce by half the number of people living in extreme poverty by 2015. The eight MDGs break down into 18 quantifiable targets that are measured by 48 indicators focusing on issues such as health, infant mortality, HIV, gender equality, environmental sustainability and universal primary education (www.undp.org/mdg). In an interim assessment report on progress toward the MDGs, the UN secretary-general, Ban Ki-moon, stated:

> We have made important progress towards all eight goals, but are not on track to fulfil all our commitments ... We face a global economic slowdown and a food security crisis, both of uncertain magnitude and duration. Global

warming has become more apparent. These developments will directly affect our efforts to reduce poverty; the economic slowdown will diminish the incomes of the poor; the food crisis will raise the number of hungry people in the world and push millions more into poverty; climate change will have a disproportionate impact on the poor. (UN 2008, p.3)

The UN has regularly pointed to the differential progress achieved by countries and regions in respect to achieving the MDGs, with some economies underperforming and falling short of anticipated progress needed to achieve the goals by 2015. A UN report published in 2007, *Africa and the Millennium Development Goals*, suggested that Africa 'is not on track for achieving any of the goals'. It added:

Although there have been major gains in several areas and the Goals remain achievable in most African nations, even the best governed countries on the continent have not been able to make sufficient progress in reducing extreme poverty in its many forms. (http://unstats.un.org/unsd/mdg/ resources/static/Products/Africa/Africa-MDGs07.pdf)

Given that some of the poorer regions and countries in the developing world, particularly sub-Saharan Africa, were already in difficulty with regard to achieving the MDGs prior to the global financial crisis, it is likely that many of the UN targets will not be met. The UN outlined some of the main obstacles to achieving the goals as including the 'lack of employment opportunities for young people, gender inequalities, rapid and unplanned urbanisation, deforestation, increasing water scarcity, and high HIV prevalence' (www.un.org/Pubs/chronicle/2007/ issue4/0407p14.html). These challenges will be more difficult to address in the current financial climate. The next section considers some of the factors that have underpinned global solidarity and the ethos and values underpinning this text.

Global Solidarity

In the 1840s Ireland experienced a humanitarian disaster when a failure of the potato crop combined with colonial misrule induced a famine that claimed over 1 million lives and forced more than 2 million others to seek refuge overseas. The famine (1845–49) became known as An Gorta Mór (the great hunger) and in 1847 inspired a moving humanitarian effort by the Choctaw Indian nation when they collected a donation of $710 and sent it to help starving Irish men, women and children. By today's standards this donation would be close to $1 million, but even more significantly it came just 16 years after the Choctaw suffered forced removal from their lands, starvation and many deaths on what became known as the 'Trail of Tears' from Mississippi to southern Oklahoma. Around one-third of the Choctaw were removed in successive years from 1831 to 1833 and of the '6,000 Choctaws who had started out from Mississippi in the fall of 1831, only slightly more than 4,000 remained alive' (*Bishinik*, November 1978, pp.8–9, at www.tc.umn.edu). In 1988, the NGO Action from Ireland (Afri) started commemorating 'a journey of horror' during the Irish famine when starving and desperate local people walked from Louisburgh to Delphi Lodge in County Mayo on the night and morning of 30–31 March 1849. Twenty people died on this ten-mile walk, which was undertaken by hundreds so that they could be certified as paupers 'entitling them to a ration of three pounds of meal' (Afri 2008); an 'unaccounted number' died later in their homes. Gary White Deer of the Choctaw Nation was among the first to lead the Afri Commemorative Walk in Mayo (Kinealy 1997) in remembrance of those who died on the 'trail of tears' and those who perished on the walk to Delphi Lodge. His presence was also a reminder of the staggering generosity of the Choctaw in 1847.

This episode of great suffering and solidarity from the Irish famine reminds us that actions resonate through generations and throughout history. The sense of empathy and solidarity that informed the Choctaw donation has been mirrored in the work of civil society groups across the world involved in campaign, solidarity, aid and awareness-raising activities addressing the causes of poverty and inequality in local and global contexts. This impulse for social justice has also informed the compilation of this text, which aims to support learning and to encourage human agency in the area of international development.

The Irish famine experience helped to shape Ireland's subsequent engagement with the developing world on the basis of shared elements in their historical development. In addition to famine, migration and emigration, Ireland has been subject to colonialism, conflict and economic underdevelopment. These collective experiences have informed multiple and sustained relationships between Irish civil society groups and government bodies with partners in the developing world. Many of the contributions to this book speak to, or result from, these relationships and offer insight, analysis and experience in their treatment of development issues.

About the Book

This revised, updated and expanded text retains core issues within development discourse, such as aid, debt and trade, and adds chapters on new and topical issues that have become a central part of the debate on international development. The additional topics include that of climate change, which has become increasingly integrated into the work of governments and development agencies around the world. While climate change was an issue that initially appeared to be the sole domain of the environment sector, it has become the focus of development campaigns and collaborative working by environment and development NGOs on joint strategies for advocacy, education and sustainable development. In Chapter 7, 'Climate Change and Development', Satish Kumar considers the impact of global warming on developing countries and the potential outcomes of the Stern Report on climate change for governments and NGOs alike.

The revised text also addresses the emergence of new popular movements and progressive governments in Latin America, which have challenged and forced into retreat the ideological hegemony and influence of the USA. In Chapter 11, 'Voices of Popular Power in Latin America', Ronaldo Munck assesses the significance of these developments for the region as it endeavours to steer its own course to development. Countries in Latin America and other regions in the global South are working toward the achievement of the UN millennium development goals by 2015 and, in Chapter 9, on the MDGs, Chrispin Matenga provides an interim assessment of progress toward the goals from a Southern perspective. Another new topic in this edition is that of asylum seekers, and in Chapter 12 Anna Morvern considers how the terms 'refugee' and 'asylum seeker' have been devalued by institutions and the media to create a framework of distrust and suspicion around those individuals who claim asylum, particularly in the United Kingdom.

The four-part structure of the book is intended to navigate the reader toward related issues, although each chapter can be used on a standalone basis as an introduction to the issue it addresses. Part I is labelled 'Development Discourses and Definitions' and includes Andy Storey's chapter on 'Measuring Human Development' (Chapter 2), in which he considers the question: Who gains from the very act of measuring development? This part also includes Paul Hainsworth's contribution (Chapter 3) on the International Criminal Court and its implications for the globalisation of justice.

Part II of the book examines the 'Economics of Development'; it includes chapters on the closely integrated issues of aid (Joanne McGarry, Chapter 4), trade (Denis O'Hearn, Chapter 5) and debt (Nessa Ní Chasaide, Chapter 6). These chapters have been fully updated to include recent changes of policy. The authors consider the effectiveness of aid in the context of the unjust debt burden carried by the majority of developing countries. Chapter 5 on trade discusses economic theory and current approaches to policy given the increasing influence of emerging economies in the developing world on trade negotiations. The three chapters collectively provide a solid foundation in the impact of global financial governance on developing countries.

Part III discusses 'Development Policy' and includes the chapters by Kumar (7) on climate change and Matenga (9) on the millennium development goals. This part also includes Gerard McCann's analysis of the role of the European Union as an aid provider to, and trading partner with, countries in the global South (Chapter 8). The chapter details the emergence of EU development policy and its key strategic interventions in developing regions, from the comparatively progressive Lomé Agreement to the more neoliberal Cotonou Agreement. This section concludes with Maeve Taylor's account of 'Gender and Development' (Chapter 10), which argues that an understanding of the structures that perpetuate gender inequality and the processes through which such inequality is manifested is critical for the formulation of development policies and programmes.

Part IV concentrates on 'Human Development' and includes Madeleine Leonard's chapter (13) on the complex issue of child labour. She considers the underlying reasons why children work and the need to listen to children in formulating policies governing young people in the workplace. In addition to chapters from Morvern (12) and Munck (11), this section also includes an analysis of development education (Chapter 14), which considers the theory and practice of Brazilian educator Paulo Freire, who conceived of education as a means of empowerment, self-esteem, community development and social transformation. This chapter examines how Freire's conception of education was introduced in the global North and continues to influence contemporary educational practice. Gerard McCann's conclusion (Chapter 15) questions the legitimacy of neoliberalism in the context of the current global financial crisis. He suggests that the global recession provides an opportunity for political leaders to redesign development policies away from the neoliberal model toward a process aimed at genuine global development strategies.

Target Groups and Terminology

The book is aimed at tertiary-level students, academics, teachers, development NGOs and civil society groups interested or involved in development work. The text will provide a useful introduction to development issues for the uninitiated, but will also provide enough new material to support the work of the most experienced development activist. The contributors to the book are a mix of activists and academics – committed individuals with direct experience through research or campaigning of the issues they are addressing. You will find appended to each chapter a list of useful websites that will support further reading on the issues discussed in the book. Many of these sites will also suggest actions that can be taken to effect positive change in the field of development.

The contributors to the book use various terms to describe what is often labelled the 'First' and 'Third' Worlds. Alternative terms include 'developed' and 'developing' countries, the global South and global North, and the 'majority' and 'minority' worlds. All of these terms are considered equally valid and acceptable to the editors; they all have their merits and demerits and would afford an interesting discussion in their own right. The main aim is not to prescribe specific terminology, but to engage the reader in a debate on development that will encourage greater interest in and activism on the issues discussed. The esteemed American author Alice Walker said that 'activism is my rent for living on this planet', and this book is an education tool toward informing that activism.

References

ActionAid (2008) 'The Global Financial Crisis: Poor Countries Could Suffer Poverty Catastrophe', 14 November.

Afri (Action from Ireland) (2008). www.afri.ie/pdf/famine_walk_2008.pdf

FAO (Food and Agricultural Organisation) (2008) *The State of Food Insecurity in the World 2008: High Food Prices and Insecurity – Threats and Opportunities*, United Nations, Rome.

Guardian (2008a) 'US Mortgage Giants Freddie Mac and Fannie Mae Taken into Public Ownership', 7 September. www.guardian.co.uk/business/2008/sep/07/freddiemacfanniemae

Guardian (2008b) 'Northern Rock Reclassified as Public Company', 7 February. www.guardian.co.uk/business/2008/feb/07/northernrock.economics

Guardian (2008c), 'What Would the Bank Bail-out Money Buy for the Environment?' 17 October. www.guardian.co.uk/environment/2008/oct/17/marketturmoil-climatechange

IMF (International Monetary Fund) (2008), October. www.imf.org/external/pubs/ft/survey/so/2008

Kinealy, Christine (1997) *A Death Dealing Famine: The Great Hunger in Ireland*, Pluto Press, London.

Kingsbury, Damian, John McKay, Janet Hunt, Mark McGillivray and Matthew Clarke (2008) *International Development: Issues and Challenges*, Palgrave Macmillan, Basingstoke.

Letter to Gordon Brown (2008), signed by 20 civil society organisations, November. www.choike.org/bw2/

McGillivray, Mark (2008) 'What is Development?' in Kingsbury et al. (2008), pp.21–51.

Milne, Seumas (2008) 'Not the Death of Capitalism, but the Birth of a New Order', *Guardian*, 23 October.

New York Times (2008) 'Greenspan Concedes Error on Regulation', 23 October. www.nytimes.com/2008/10/24/business/economy/24panel.html

OECD (2008) 'Aid Targets Slipping out of Reach?', Organisation for Economic Co-operation and Development. www.oecd/dac/stats

Rostow, W. (1960) *Stages of Economic Growth*, Cambridge University Press, Cambridge.

Stern, Nicholas (2006) *Stern Review on the Economics of Climate Change*, HM Treasury, Cabinet Office, London, October. www.hm-treasury.gov.uk/sternreview_index.htm

Storey, Andy (2003) 'Measuring Development', in G. McCann, and S. McCloskey (eds) *From the Local to the Global: Key issues in Development Studies*, 1st edn, Pluto Press, London and New York.

The Times (2008) 'Lehman Brothers Collapse Sends Shockwaves Around the World', 16 September. www.business.timesonline.co.uk/tol/business/industry_sectors/banking_and_finance/article4761892.ece

UN (2008) 'The Millennium Development Goals Report 2008', United Nations, New York. http://www.un.org/millenniumgoals/reports.shtml

WDM (World Development Movement) (2008) 'Responding to the Crisis: Five Ideas for a New World Order', November. www.bond.org.uk/data/files/wdms_five_point_plan_for_kidtronic.pdf

Websites

ActionAid	www.actionaid.org
Action from Ireland	www.afri.ie
BOND	www.bond.org.uk
Centre for Global Education	www.centreforglobaleducation.com
Christian Aid	www.christian-aid.org.uk
Concern Worldwide	www.concern.net
Debt and Development Coalition	www.debtireland.org

Dochas	www.dochas.ie
Millennium Development Goals (MDGs)	www.undp.org/mdg/
OECD	www.oecd.org
Oxfam	www.oxfam.org
Jubilee Debt Campaign	www.jubileedebtcampaign.org.uk
Trade Justice	www.tjm.org.uk
Trócaire	www.trocaire.org
United Nations Development Programme	www.undp.org
World Development Movement	www.wdm.org.uk

2

MEASURING HUMAN DEVELOPMENT

Andy Storey

Underdevelopment is shocking: the squalor, disease, unnecessary deaths, and hopelessness of it all! No man [sic] understands if underdevelopment remains for him a mere statistic reflecting low income, poor housing, premature mortality or underemployment. The most empathetic observer can speak objectively about underdevelopment only after undergoing, personally or vicariously, the 'shock of underdevelopment'. This unique culture shock comes to one as he is initiated to the emotions which prevail in the 'culture of poverty'. The reverse shock is felt by those living in destitution when a new self-understanding reveals to them that their life is neither human nor inevitable ... The prevalent emotion of under-development is a sense of personal and societal impotence in the face of disease and death, of confusion and ignorance as one gropes to understand change, of servility toward men whose decisions govern the course of events, of hopelessness before hunger and natural catastrophe. Chronic poverty is a cruel kind of hell, and one cannot understand how cruel that hell is merely by gazing upon poverty as an object. (Goulet, quoted in Todaro 2000, p.15)

Measuring development presupposes being able to define what development entails. Therefore, this issue of definition is first addressed in this chapter before moving on to an examination of the most commonly used measures of economic development – notably gross domestic product (GDP) and gross national product (GNP). These remain the standard international measures of economic development but, arguably, encompass only a very limited understanding of how development affects the way in which people actually live. One example of this limitation that has attracted special attention in recent years is the attempt on the part of economic analysis to incorporate the impact of climate change – the difficulty of measuring that impact illustrates many of the problems of economic measurement of development.

As a method of measuring development the best known alternative to the economic indices is the Human Development Index (HDI), which relies upon multiple (not solely economic) criteria and which is partly based on the work of the Indian economist Amartya Sen. There are also concepts of development and underdevelopment that point towards the impossibility of quantitatively measuring development (or its absence) at all; indeed, according to some commentators, the very *attempt* at measurement may result in, or reinforce, Western domination of the so-called 'Third World'. However, the attractions of quantifiable measurement remain strong and partially underpin the recent emergence of the millennium development goals (MDGs) as a new means of measuring development progress. But there are problems with the MDGs also, and the chapter concludes by emphasising the necessarily inconclusive and open-ended nature of this topic.

Defining Development

Measures of development are inextricably linked to definitions of development, highlighting the need for a better understanding of what development is before seeking to measure it. For many years this understanding seemed fairly unproblematic. For most economists and policy analysts, development was seen as equivalent to economic growth, of which growth of GNP – discussed in detail below – served as the main indicator. This was (and still is) usually expressed in 'per capita' (per person) terms, i.e. the gross, or total, national product was divided by a country's population to give an average figure for a country's level of economic development. Comparing GNP per capita from year to year provides a measure of economic growth relative to population size, and this therefore constitutes a measure of development progress, or the lack of it. This view of development still underlies much current official thinking.

For many years also, development was officially seen not only as growth in the economy, but also as a transformation or shift of the economic structure away from primary goods production (of agriculture and raw materials) towards manufacturing and service activities. This was most famously articulated by the prominent United States of America (USA) social scientist (and senior USA government adviser) Walt Rostow in *The Process of Economic Growth* (1960), in which he developed the notion of 'stages of growth'. Rostow's stages were: (1) traditional society; (2) preconditions for take-off; (3) take-off; (4) drive to maturity; (5) age of high mass consumption. Rostow saw the world in quite crude, linear terms – poor societies become 'modernised' (both economically and socially) and, ideally, would end up resembling the USA.

This approach came under increasing criticism, particularly in the 1960s and 1970s. The notion of 'growth without development' became increasingly common with reference to countries like Brazil, where impressive GNP per capita growth – and indeed a degree of Rostow-style structural transformation – seemed to coexist with growing inequality and poverty for many. As a Brazilian politician is said to have remarked, 'Brazil is doing well but its people are not'. For the British economist Dudley Seers, alternative definitions of development were required:

> The questions to ask about a country's development are therefore: What has been happening to poverty? What has been happening to unemployment? What has been happening to inequality? If all three of these have declined from high levels then beyond doubt this has been a period of development for the country concerned. If one or two of these central problems have been growing worse, especially if all three have, it would be strange to call the result 'development' even if per capita income doubled. (Seers, quoted in Todaro, p.15)

The development criteria suggested by Seers can be discerned, at least in part, in the later method of measurement introduced by the United Nations Development Programme (UNDP) in the form of the Human Development Index (HDI). As will be discussed further below, an even more important influence on the HDI was the work of Amartya Sen. The HDI encapsulates a concept of development as a process of enlarging people's choices, allowing them the opportunity to live longer, to acquire knowledge, etc. Thus, the narrow focus on economic growth and transformation is widened to embrace a variety of other (economic but also non-economic) factors. The 1980s saw a further crucial variable thrown into this definitional pot, that of environmental sustainability. In its most famous articulation, from the Brundtland Commission, 'Sustainable development is development that meets the needs of the present without compromising the ability of future generations to meet their own needs' (quoted in Martinussen 1997, p.150). The central challenge of the environmental critique of 'traditional' development is to question whether unlimited access to narrowly defined economic development is sustainable within the constraints of a finite ecosystem.

Beyond the standard measurement systems which are utilised by international agencies, there are many more contested definitional issues. Some writers, for example, see societies which have developed materially but have lost touch with traditional – itself a contested concept – spiritual or cultural values, as having 'maldeveloped' (see *European Journal of Development Research* 'special issue', EJDR 1996). Others see the absence of political freedom and democracy as invalidating any claim to development regardless of levels of economic growth (sustainable or not) and the improvement of social indicators (www.freedomhouse.org). Furthermore, a growing number of writers and activists identify development as being about the progressive realisation of human rights – the so-called rights-based approach to development, which emphasises both political and civil rights (traditionally seen as outside the remit of development) and economic and social rights, the more common 'stuff' of development (Uvin 2004).

This brief overview of how definitions of development have evolved obviously raises as many questions as it answers. These questions include: Is it possible to have unlimited economic growth without ultimately destroying the environment? And if the human rights of all people have to be fully protected at all times, can an economy or society function efficiently? And, aside from these questions of principle, there remain practical imperatives, including the desire on the part of many interested parties to know whether development is occurring or not – in other words, there is a desire to *measure* development despite its evident complexity. This ultimately may be why many commentators still seek to measure development in a narrower and less than holistic sense. It is to these narrower measurements that we now turn.

Measuring Development: Standard Economic Development Measures

A basic measure of economic activity is gross domestic product (GDP) – the total output of goods and services in an economy, measured at market prices. It is important to note that this measurement should, ideally, only include the *final* output produced and not *intermediate* production. For example, if a factory produces screws that subsequently contribute to the value of a car also produced in the same country, then only the final value of the car should be included in GDP – to count the value of the screws separately would be to double-count. GDP, essentially, measures the total productive capacity (in use) of an economy. However, it does not measure the extent to which resources are *available* in that economy, in that not all that is produced is necessarily available to the residents of that country.

In order to capture the actual level of resource availability it is necessary to adapt GDP. One way to do this is to engage in a process of addition and subtraction. One could subtract from GDP certain outflows of resources. Some of these resources are related to capital – chiefly, profits remitted out of an economy by companies (often, though not necessarily, foreign ones) operational in that economy. Other resource outflows are related to labour – such as the percentage of wage income remitted home by migrant workers resident in that economy. Because capital and labour are conventionally described as the 'factors of production', such outflows are referred to as factor outflows. Conversely, one could add to GDP certain inflows of resources. These would include capital-related flows, such as the profits remitted *into* an economy from a company operating externally – for example, in the case of the United States of America, the profits sent back to that country from a USA multinational company's operations in, say, Nigeria or Colombia. There will also be labour-related inflows, such as the portions of wages sent home to India or Mexico by workers from those countries labouring in the Gulf States or in Europe. Taken together, these are referred to as factor inflows.

For any given economy, there will be both factor outflows and factor inflows. Balancing out these different flows will yield what is called 'net factor income' – which can be either positive or negative. GDP plus net factor income generates gross national product (GNP), the most commonly used measure of economic development, especially when expressed relative to population size, i.e. per capita. The main argument in favour of using GNP per capita as a measure of development is that unless there is an increase in the availability of goods and services then development is unlikely to be occurring – that is, a rising GNP per capita is, at least, a *precondition* for development. Moreover, the method of calculating GNP is relatively well understood and reasonably widely recognised – most people know what is being measured and how. Also, all countries produce GNP estimates, so international comparison can be facilitated.

The arguments against using GNP per capita as a measure of development merit greater discussion, because they have fed into the emergence of alternative measures of development. Firstly, and fundamentally, GNP is an *economic* measurement and, by definition, does not take account of non-economic criteria. If, as discussed above, one's definition of development incorporates social, cultural or political considerations then any solely economic measurement is obviously unsatisfactory. Secondly, GNP, when expressed in per capita terms, takes no account of how resources are distributed. GNP per capita is a statistical average that bears no necessary relationship to the actual resources available to any person in a country. A society with a highly unequal distribution of resources might have a high GNP per capita while the majority of its population live in extreme poverty or even destitution. It was precisely this anomaly that prompted Seers (see above) to suggest instead an emphasis on features such as unemployment and poverty as the proper criteria of development.

Thirdly, GNP (as with GDP) is based on market prices. Non-market transactions are not necessarily covered. A variety of economic activities, especially in poorer economies, may not be included in GNP calculations. These typically include: the cultivation of food for domestic consumption; the processing and cooking of that food; the maintenance and repair of domestic equipment and clothing; the provision of household fuel and water; caring for children, the elderly and the sick; and participation in (unpaid) community activities. A common thread unites these disparate activities, namely that they are usually performed by women. Thus, GDP and GNP emerge as gender-biased indicators of development (Benería 1995, pp.1839–50). But it is not only women's work that may be undervalued or excluded from GDP and GNP. Activities taking place in the so-called 'informal' economy – perhaps involving barter or otherwise not passing through official market channels – are also usually underestimated or completely ignored by the standard measures of economic development.

Fourthly, market prices – the foundation stones of GDP and GNP – may not reflect the real social value or cost of producing an economic resource. For example, a chemical factory may produce and make available a drug valued at a certain market price which is included in GDP/GNP on that basis. But this production may simultaneously generate considerable pollution and, strictly speaking, the cost of that should be reflected in the market price of the drug. In practice this is unlikely to be the case, and the pollution remains what economists call a 'negative externality', which should somehow be factored into any true measure of overall societal development but is often excluded under existing conventional practice.

Measuring Environmental Destruction

Still related to this fourth point, it is in the area of the environment that some of the problems posed to conventional economic measurement of development are most starkly revealed (Daly 1997, pp.121–5; Kovel 2007). There is, in fact, no guarantee that the economic activity comprising GDP/GNP is really a positive contribution to society at all. If a production activity comprises serious environmental depletion and damage, then it might be more accurately considered a hindrance to society's development, whereas the GDP/GNP measure will automatically regard the marketed output as a boost to development. This point is underlined in the extreme example of a country that cut down all its trees, sold them for wood and then gambled the proceeds: GNP per capita would register a significant increase, whereas real societal development would clearly have been seriously impaired.

In order to counter this sort of extreme distortion, some commentators have sought to develop environmentally adjusted measures of economic development. One such is 'green GDP' – an aggregate measure of conventional GDP minus depletion of environmental assets and minus the costs of environmental degradation. But how does one accurately value the environment? Economists may try to use the 'willingness to pay' criterion – asking people what they would be willing to pay in order to protect or guarantee the environment. But this assumes that people have accurate information on which to base such preferences, and it is also likely that poor people may undervalue the environment as they are probably faced with more pressing needs (food, health care, shelter, etc.) that they will prioritise over environmental concerns.

Some of the difficult issues of how one might go about attaching a value to the environment (and its possible destruction) were comprehensively discussed in the Stern Report on the economics of climate change (Stern 2006). This report makes the crucial observation that most economic analysis is concerned with assessing marginal changes, whereas climate change is a vast (and vastly uncertain) domain potentially involving catastrophic declines in well-being and threats to species survival. At one level, the issue of climate change is a classic 'negative externality': the producers of global warming are imposing costs on others but are not facing the full consequences of their actions. But the standard economic response – typically the imposition of a tax on the offending firm or country according to the 'polluter pays principle' – is difficult to organise in the absence of a global governance system. More fundamentally, there is no guarantee that such technical responses would be sufficient to tackle the problem because it may well be the case that the risks are not yet fully understood and, potentially, simply incalculable. If that is the case, then the Stern Report and others have raised the question of whether a 'precautionary principle' should be adopted and all risks should simply be eliminated or minimised regardless of their estimated cost. For the purposes of our present discussion, this means that the risk of getting the measurement of economic development wrong is so great that all normal consideration of costs and benefits should, arguably, be abandoned, and combating climate change should be prioritised regardless of what it means for conventional GDP/GNP.

The issues of resource distribution and the environment have been tied together in the pithy observation of Edward Goldsmith that 'GDP growth is the rate at which the powerful are expropriating the resources of the weak to create garbage' (with the added element that they may also be producing, through climate change, the erosion or elimination of the ecosystem itself) (Goldsmith, quoted in Starr 2000, p.1). Of course, it remains the case that GDP or GNP growth *could* still represent improved welfare for the poor and the production of socially useful and ecologically sustainable goods and services. But the potential dangers of a crude reliance on such indicators are obvious, and the desirability of alternative measures of development equally apparent.

Sen and the Human Development Index

Amartya Sen first became famous for his work on famine, in which he argued that whether one had food or not did not depend on its actual availability (food is usually available even in famine situations) but on whether one could exercise an 'entitlement' to food – through, for example, being able to pay for it from the proceeds of wage labour (Sen 1981). Typically, people starve because their entitlements collapse (such as when rural labourers lose their jobs) rather than because there is an absolute shortage of food.

Sen has developed his work over the years to encompass development more generally. He does not see development as being about what people *have* in terms of commodities, because such possessions may be of limited value at certain times and in certain situations – a book is of little use to a starving or illiterate person. Different people value different things, and what is most important is that each person is able to acquire those things that are important for their own self-realisation. These are not only material things but also cultural life, participation in the life of the community, etc. Sen bundles these things together into the idea of 'freedom' – the expansion of freedom (in terms of being able to acquire what one needs for the achievement of one's own concept of development) is the endpoint of development; but it is also the means to development – enhancing freedom (or choice) allows people to determine and fulfil their own visions of development (Sen 1999). How might one operationalise such a vision? The HDI is, in part, an attempt to do just that.

Since 1990 the United Nations Development Programme (UNDP) has produced an annual publication entitled the *Human Development Report*. The centrepiece of this report is the HDI, which ranks countries on the basis of developmental criteria extending well beyond economic indices. Specifically, the HDI is an amalgam of three variables for each country:

- per capita income or output;
- life expectancy;
- educational attainment – itself an amalgam of each country's adult literacy rate and the average number of years spent at school.

The three variables were chosen on the basis of their being proxies for, and/or means to achieve, other aspects of human development, thus echoing Sen's means/ends conceptualisation of freedom and development. A relatively high life expectancy is a good thing in itself but is also a measure of how much room/time a person has to achieve self-realisation (their own conception of development). Educational attainment is likewise something to be valued for its own sake, but is also a means through which people are empowered to pursue other goals – such as economic progress or cultural self-assertion. Income is itself useful and, again, is a tool through which people may pursue social objectives. Each of these variables is converted into a ranking index (from 0 to 1), facilitating the construction of an aggregate measure of development for each country.

Over the years, this classification system has helped draw attention to the fact that some countries that appear very 'developed' in GNP per capita terms fare considerably less well on the HDI ranking. This is often the result of their unequal resource distributions and correspondingly poor standards of life expectancy and educational attainment. Many of the states of the Middle East (such as Kuwait) fall into this category. On the other hand, some countries with relatively low levels of GNP per capita emerge quite creditably on the HDI scale due to their comparatively high levels of social expenditure (including on health and education) – Cuba and Costa Rica are examples in this regard. While the HDI is, like GNP per capita, a societal average, life expectancy or years spent at school cannot show income-style inequalities. A rich person will usually live longer than a poor person, and a child of rich parents will usually spend more years at school than a child of the poor, but in neither case can this be by a factor of several million – as is the case with income differentials. Thus, the HDI is much less vulnerable than GNP per capita to the problem of distortion by gross inequality – more egalitarian countries tend to do better on the HDI scale than they do on the GNP per capita league table.

However, there are still some obvious shortcomings or limitations in using the HDI as a measure of development. One is that various potential dimensions of development – political freedom, human rights, gender equality, environmental sustainability – are not covered by the core index (though each HDI does contain copious data, analysis and rankings for these other aspects). There has also been some debate about the weighting of the three variables; the UNDP assigns each an equal weight, but it might plausibly be argued that life expectancy could be accorded a greater importance than either income or education. And perennial controversy surrounds the question of data reliability – for many countries, the data available on life expectancy, let alone other indicators, are very problematic. Even where reasonably good data are at hand, information on the *quality* of, for example, education is not necessarily provided – one may know how many years, on average, children spend at school but not the pupil–teacher ratio or the standard of available resources (including textbooks) and, therefore, one does not know how much children are actually learning.

Perhaps the most serious criticism of the HDI is the charge of it being Eurocentric, or overly focused on Western conceptions of what development should constitute. Thus, average years' schooling refers to Western-type classroom schooling, implicitly devaluing other forms of education that might take place in, say, the African countryside. And while Sen's underpinning conception of freedom may appeal at many levels, it remains essentially an *individualistic* idea – the focus is on the enhancement of the individual's choices and freedoms whereas other conceptions of development (from socialist to religious) might argue in favour of greater constraints being placed on the individual for the good of society as a whole (van Staveren and Gasper 2002).

This last point raises the question of how a measure of development may become a form of oppression – by insisting that development has to consist of certain steps, such as the acquisition of Western-style education or through individual empowerment. Even the seemingly progressive HDI may contain a hint of the prescriptive modernisation ethos associated with someone such as Rostow (see above). Indeed, one group of writers has come to see all existing measurements of development as not only flawed, but as positively oppressive.

Post-development Theory: Against Measurement and Classification

For some writers, dissatisfaction with the idea of development has led to dissatisfaction with *any* attempt to measure development and indeed to a rejection of the very concept of development itself. This line of thinking can be broadly classified as the 'post-development' approach, which draws from wider currents of postmodern philosophy and also from post-colonial theory (Sylvester 1999, pp.703–21). Within this approach development is viewed as a discourse:

> This theory argues that development constitutes a specific way of thinking about the world, a particular form of knowledge. Development is ... a particular discourse which does not reflect but actually *constructs* reality. In doing so, it closes off alternative ways of thinking and so constitutes a form of power. (Kiely 1999, p.1)

What effects then does this form of power generate? According to the post-development approach, the principal effect generated by development discourse is to legitimise and reinforce Western dominance over the 'Third World', in part through its very definition or categorisation of the 'Third World' as being in *need* of Western-style development and as constituting an *object* of/for development (Hobart 1993). The 'Third World' thus becomes subject not only to the economic but also to 'the definitional power of the West. Development ... [is] a standard by which the West measures the non-West' (Zardar 1999, pp.44, 49). For example, the absence of Western forms of technology (or education) is treated as a criterion not of simple difference but of underdevelopment. 'Development discourse, from this perspective, is about disciplining difference, establishing what the norm is and what deviance is' (Munck 1999, p.68). Thus, the standard measures of development become instruments of oppression, tools whereby one group of people exercise power over others.

The essence of the argument being made by the post-development approach may be illustrated by means of a specific example. Ferguson, in his 1990 analysis of the World Bank's depiction of the economy of Lesotho, found a recurrent World Bank emphasis on certain putative features of the Lesotho economy, including the assertion that Lesotho was an 'aboriginal' economy largely unexposed to commercial markets and the money economy, i.e. that it was a classically 'underdeveloped' or 'deviant' economy by Western standards (Ferguson 1990). Ferguson shows how these alleged characteristics were wildly at variance with reality. Indeed, Lesotho had been part of a cash economy for centuries. But Ferguson argues that the World Bank's stylised portrayal of the Lesotho economy was inaccurate but not irrational, its purpose dictated by the bank's need to find a role for itself in the 'development' or 'disciplining' of that economy – through the financing of rural cattle markets, the building of rural roads, and other such 'development' projects. Lesotho was thus constructed, defined and painstakingly *measured* as 'underdeveloped' in order to legitimate, and facilitate the exercise of, Western dominance over it.

For writers within this approach, to demonstrate the measurable 'failure' of development – to reduce poverty, for example – is to miss the point, because the real purpose of the development exercise (measurement included) is to discipline and dominate. The apparent failure of development simply becomes a rationale for further, 'corrective' interventions. As Crush puts it: 'development is always the cure, never the cause' (Crush 1995, p.10); and the 'Third World' always remains objectified, its people's needs externally defined. Thus, the very act of measurement is inextricably tied to the act of domination.

In turn, the post-development approach has been extensively critiqued (Storey 2000, pp.40–46). One could, for example, query the portrayal of all attempts to measure development and under-development as being inevitably and only elements of Western power. Does not, say, a measurement of life expectancy convey something that is of concern to *all* people, rather than being a device through which poorer countries are classified as requiring external intervention? Nonetheless, the strength of the post-development school is to suggest that measurement always plays a social role – people and countries are often measured in ways that serve the interests of some and not of others. The question of who gains from the very act of measuring development is an important one, and it is one that merits being asked vis-à-vis the most recent approach to measuring development progress – the millennium development goals (MDGs).

The Millennium Development Goals

On 8 September 2000, world leaders adopted the Millennium Declaration, in which they solemnly pledged that they would 'spare no effort to free our fellow men, women and children from the abject and dehumanizing conditions of extreme poverty'. The goals are particularly significant because, as the official MDG website notes, they 'have been commonly accepted as a framework for measuring development progress' (www.un.org/millennium-goals). This point is elaborated on by Vandemoortele: 'The MDGs have moved quickly to the centre of the international development agenda, in part because they can be monitored in quantitative terms. Not only do we have an agreed agenda, we also have a measurable agenda' (Vandemoortele 2005, p.6).

Each goal constitutes a headline objective and each contains one or more specific targets that can be monitored to assess if progress is being made towards its achievement. In addition, each goal and its targets are associated with various indicators: quantitative measurements of goal and target fulfilment, or the lack of it. The match between goals, targets and indicators is not always exact: for example, Goal 1 is to eradicate extreme poverty and hunger, but the targets are only to halve income poverty and hunger by 2015; likewise, Goal 3 is to promote gender equality and to empower women, but the target is only to eliminate gender disparities in education – although the indicators encompass broader empowerment criteria, such as the proportion of parliamentary seats held by women. The full set of goals is as follows:

- Eradicate extreme poverty and hunger
- Achieve universal primary education
- Promote gender equality and empower women

- Reduce child mortality
- Improve maternal health
- Combat HIV/AIDS, malaria and other diseases
- Ensure environmental sustainability
- Develop a global partnership for development

It is not possible to have a full discussion here on the enormous array of controversial issues that have been highlighted in the ongoing debates on the MDGs. However, a major concern in recent years has been that they simply will not be achieved – most countries are 'off-track' for target fulfilment, leading to fears that this recent flagship development project will be deemed a failure and that public support for further development efforts, and for development assistance, will be eroded as a result (Martens and Debiel 2008).

But it is the emphasis on measurement – especially of a quite narrow, quantitative type – that most concerns some commentators (Trócaire 2005). For example, if a country achieves such measurable 'success' does that implicitly justify the adoption of any and all means to the end? Are undemocratic and non-participatory processes seen as legitimate if they foster MDG progress? And where do the MDGs leave the idea of development as being about people's own choices and priorities? Is a straitjacket of this sort – tick off progress under these predetermined headings and you are 'developing' – compatible with notions of self-determination and self-realisation? And, as post-development writers would argue, are the MDGs not just another way of defining the 'Third World' as different and deviant, in need of Western intervention? Finally, and closely related to this last point, the MDGs have much to say about the perceived problems of poor countries, but little about Western responsibility for these problems. It is, for the most part, the 'Third World' that is expected to demonstrate measurable progress, rather than the West being asked to reform its own policies and structures, other than to increase aid to help fund the MDGs, i.e. to adopt a largely charitable stance that neglects underlying questions of structural injustice. Once again, a measurement exercise serves certain interests over others.

Conclusion

The question of measuring development covers a very wide field. It moves from questions of how development is to be defined, through the 'nitty-gritty' of some of the more conventional measures of development, to a questioning of whether the very act of measurement contributes to the perpetuation of oppression. No single answer to these questions is possible. Much will depend on what one's own conception of development is – or should be. By way of conclusion, we might, however, bear in mind the dangers of undue attention to measurement, as humorously parodied by Robert Chambers:

> Economists have come to feel
> What can't be measured isn't real
> The truth is always an amount
> Count numbers, only numbers count.
> (Chambers 1997, p.42)

We should also always bear in mind the social context within which measurement occurs, and the social purpose which any attempt at measurement serves. There are no such things as 'mere facts': any aspect of reality that is focused on (for example, income or education) may dilute or obscure a focus on other aspects of reality, such as political freedom or human rights. Describing some countries as 'underdeveloped' according to certain criteria may divert attention from their successes in other realms. And, above all, countries do not exist in isolation. It is one thing to measure, say, the shortcomings of the educational system in Zambia, but it is quite another to understand the social meaning of that measurement and the complex national and international forces that lie behind it. We can, in part, measure *where* a country is at in certain respects – and we must bear in mind that it is only ever a partial, and indeed potentially misleading, picture – but that is relatively uninformative unless we also seek to understand *how* it arrived at that position.

References

Benería, L. (1995) 'Towards a Greater Integration of Gender in Economics', *World Development*, vol.23, no.11, pp.1839–50.

Chambers, R. (1997) *Whose Reality Counts? Putting the Last First*, Intermediate Technology Publications, London.

Crush, J. (1995) 'Introduction: Imagining Development', in J. Crush (ed.), *Power of Development*, Routledge, London.

Daly, H. (1997) 'Sustainable Growth: An Impossibility Theorem', *Development*, vol.40, pp.121–5.

EJDR (1996) *The European Journal of Development Research*, vol.8, no.2.

Ferguson, J. (1990) *The Anti-Politics Machine: 'Development', Depoliticisation and Bureaucratic Power in Lesotho*, University of Minnesota Press, Minneapolis and London.

Hobart, M. (1993) *An Anthropological Critique of Development: The Growth of Ignorance*, Routledge, London.

Kiely, R. (1999) 'The Last Refuge of the Noble Savage? A Critical Assessment of Post-Development Theory', *European Journal of Development Research*, vol.11, no.1.

Kovel, J. (2007) *The Enemy of Nature: The End of Capitalism or the End of the World?* Zed Books, London.

Martens, J. and T. Debiel (2008) 'The MDG Project in Crisis: Midpoint Review and Prospects for the Future', *INEF Policy Brief*, no.4.

Martinussen, J. (1997) *Society, State and Market: A Guide to Competing Theories of Development*, Zed Books, London.

Munck, R. (1999) 'Dependency and Imperialism in the New Times: A Latin American Perspective', *European Journal of Development Research*, vol.11, no.1.

Rostow, W.W. (1960) *The Process of Economic Growth*, Clarendon Press, Oxford.

Sen, A. (1981) *Poverty and Famine: An Essay on Entitlement and Deprivation*, Oxford University Press, Oxford.

Sen, A. (1999) *Development as Freedom*, Oxford University Press, Oxford.

Starr, A. (2000) *Naming the Enemy: Anti-Corporate Movements Confront Globalisation*, Zed Books, London.

Stern, Nicholas (2006) *Stern Review on the Economics of Climate Change*, Cambridge University Press, Cambridge.

Storey, A. (2000) 'Post-Development Theory: Romanticism and Pontius Pilate Politics', *Development*, vol.43, no.4, pp.40–6.

Sylvester, C. (1999) 'Development Studies and Postcolonial Studies: Disparate Tales of the "Third World"', *Third World Quarterly*, vol.20, no.4, pp.703–21.

Todaro, M.T. (2000) *Economic Development*, 7th edn, Addison-Wesley, Reading, Mass.

Trócaire (2005) 'More than a Numbers Game? Ensuring that the Millennium Development Goals address Structural Injustice', April. www.trocaire.org

Uvin, P. (2004) *Human Rights and Development*, Kumarian Press, Sterling, Va.

Van Staveren, I. and D. Gasper (2002) 'Development as Freedom: Contributions and Shortcomings of Amartya Sen's Development Philosophy for Feminist Economics', Working Paper 365, Institute of Social Studies. www.iss.nl

Vandemoortele, J. (2005) 'Ambition is Golden: Meeting the MDGs', *Development*, vol.48, no.1.

Zardar, Z. (1999) 'Development and the Locations of Eurocentrism', in R. Munck and D. O'Hearn (eds) *Critical Development Theory: Contributions to a New Paradigm*, Zed Books, London.

Websites

OECD	www.oecd.org
Statistics on Human Development	www.ids.ac.uk
UN Development Programme	www.undp.org
UNESCO	http://unescostat.unesco.org
United Nations	www.un.org
UN Human Development Reports	http://hdr.undp.org/en/statistics/
UNMDGs	www.un.org/millenniumgoals/
World Bank	www.worldbank.org

3

THE DEVELOPING GLOBALISATION OF JUSTICE: THE INTERNATIONAL CRIMINAL COURT AT THE CROSSROADS

Paul Hainsworth

Globalisation is Janus-faced. On the one hand, for instance, it has the potential to impoverish the life and rights of individuals in one part of the globe, via decisions made in another part. According to Susan George: 'Globalisation is a process ... [and] a system which is being pushed forward and put in place by the very largest industrial and financial transnational corporations ... it moves wealth from the bottom to the top' (George 2001, p.12). George Monbiot presents a similarly critical doomsday scenario for the future: 'The world will consist of a single deregulated market, controlled by multinational companies, in which laws to protect the environment or human rights will not be allowed to survive' (quoted in Gunnell and Timms 2001). On the other hand, and not contradicting the socioeconomic observations of these two authors, the universalising reach of globalisation can be utilised as a force of progress, international justice and societal improvement. In this sense, it is part of the process to create a cosmopolitan citizenship which endows individuals and states with broader extra-national rights and responsibilities (see Heater 1999). The quest to establish an effective international criminal court (ICC) – to prosecute perpetrators of the most heinous crimes – falls into the latter category of classification.

In this chapter, the pathway to set up an ICC is assessed initially, in order to put the court into some context. The first section, therefore, examines briefly what many observers see as the ICC's early predecessor, that is, the 1946 Nuremberg Tribunal. The next section turns to later attempts to create an international system of justice, namely the ex-Yugoslavia and the Rwanda Tribunals, set up in the 1990s. These bodies, of course, were constructed on an ad hoc basis to pursue justice in specific situations and geographical areas. Unsurprisingly, there have been calls to set up similar bodies to prosecute individuals for very serious and notorious crimes perpetrated in other places.

The debate about international justice has moved markedly away from a resort to ad hoc tribunals covering geographically limited jurisdictions or fixed time spans. The focus has turned increasingly towards setting up and putting into operation a truly global and permanent international criminal court. This, a key development issue in today's world, is the principal focus of the chapter. The campaign to establish an ICC, or *the* ICC, gathered momentum and culminated in the signing of the 1998 Rome Statute; a process of country-by-country ratification of the statute duly followed. By 2002, the ICC had ratification by enough member states to enable it to come properly into being. Following lift-off, the nascent ICC set about its business, as illustrated below.

One significant global and key player, the United States of America, has been conspicuously reticent in the construction of the ICC – a theme that is assessed in the next section. The debate about an ICC and the issue of international justice was put into a new context after 11 September 2001, following the fatal attacks on the twin towers of the World Trade Centre in New York and on the Pentagon in Washington. The penultimate section of the chapter, therefore, assesses some of the connections between these tragic events and the call for an ICC. The conclusion draws the main points of the chapter together.

Nuremberg

An immediate post-war attempt to produce an international mechanism of justice was the Nuremberg Tribunal, which was created in 1946 by the victorious Allied powers in response to serious human rights abuses committed by the Nazis during the Second World War. The Nazis were seen to have committed some of the most heinous crimes known to the world, including the 'Final Solution' of the Holocaust. The remit of the Nuremberg Tribunal was to prosecute individuals acting on behalf of a state for war crimes (committed against other nationals) and crimes against humanity (committed internally), with the death penalty serving as the ultimate punishment for those declared to be guilty. A similar body, the Tokyo Tribunal, was set up to prosecute Japanese perpetrators of serious crimes, notably General Tojo, but significantly and controversially not Emperor Hirohito.

Nuremberg was thus an important step in the process of trying *individuals*; where crimes against humanity were concerned, it prioritised international and humanitarian obligations above national ones. This principle would be resuscitated some years later in the setting up of the ex-Yugoslavia and Rwanda Tribunals and during the ICC debate. Unlike these more recent innovations though, Nuremberg was without doubt a 'victors' tribunal'. Its working procedures were marked by this reality. For instance, as Geoffrey Robertson points out, only the defeated were being prosecuted for war crimes; all the prosecutors and judges were nationals of the Allied powers and all the defendants' lawyers were German (Robertson 2000, p.214). Despite these failings, Robertson is convinced of the overall positive significance of Nuremberg:

> Nuremberg was a show trial, but one in which the victors' sense of fairness was as much on show as the vicissitudes of the vanquished ... Nuremberg stands as a colossus in the development of human rights law, precisely because its Charter defined crimes against humanity and its procedures proved by acceptable and credible evidence that such crimes had been instigated by some defendants. (Robertson 2000, p.215)

The charter of the Nuremberg Tribunal set a precedent, which later calls for an ICC and other tribunals would follow. It ruled that individuals were responsible for actions – they could not hide behind the sovereignty of states and claim that they were only obeying orders in the perpetration of heinous crimes. The Tokyo Tribunal also established the principle of criminal liability for permitting atrocities; in effect a concept of command responsibility that, later in the 1990s and thereafter, would be applied to the Serbian leaders Radovan Karadzic and General Mladic. From the outset, the nascent United Nations (UN) recognised the need for a body such as an ICC. Resolution 260 (9 December 1948) adopted the Convention on the Prevention and Punishment of the Crime of Genocide, and asked the International Law Commission (ILC) to investigate the desirability and possibility of setting up a body to try people for genocide. The General Assembly gave some attention to this theme in the 1950s, but no draft statute emerged for a long time, with – in particular – no acceptable definition of aggression being agreed upon. This was to prove a nagging definitional problem even when the Rome Statute for the ICC was agreed upon some 50 years later.

The Ex-Yugoslavia and Rwanda Tribunals[1]

In the 1990s, the call for international justice was revived to meet desperate situations in Rwanda and in ex-Yugoslavia. At the same time, in 1998 in the United Kingdom (UK), it was significant that the House of Lords recognised that the Chilean ex-dictator, General Augusto Pinochet, then temporarily resident in England, was individually responsible for terrible crimes committed under his stewardship as head of state. In short, in these contexts, arguments of national sovereignty were tried against principles

---

1. This section and the following draw heavily upon Amnesty International (2000), notably the series of ten fact sheets on the ICC: (1) 'Introduction to the International Criminal Court'; (2) 'The case for ratification'; (3) 'Prosecuting the crime of genocide'; (4) 'Prosecuting crimes against humanity'; (5) 'Prosecuting war crimes'; (6) 'Ensuring justice for victims'; (7) 'Ensuring justice for women'; (8) 'Ensuring justice for children'; (9) 'Fair trial guarantees' (10) 'State cooperation with the ICC' (Amnesty International 2000, London). See also Amnesty International, 'Concerns at the eighth session of the preparatory commission' [for the ICC], 24 September to 5 October 2001. Also drawn upon here is the United Nations' website 'International Criminal Court: Some Questions and Answers' (31 May 2001) (www.un.org/law/icc/statute/iccq&a.htm); and Geoffrey Robertson, *Crimes Against Humanity*, ch. 8, 'The Balkan Trials'; and ch. 9, 'The International Criminal Court', pp.285–367.

of international law and justice, and the former category was found to be wanting. Amidst widespread global attention, the case against Pinochet collapsed in the United Kingdom, on the grounds of the ex-dictator's unfitness to stand trial due to ill-health. Nonetheless, the spectacle of Pinochet being pursued for human rights abuses while residing abroad will surely impact on the thoughts and lifestyles of other individuals and human rights abusers seeking safety and security outside their own country.

The International Criminal Tribunal for the Former Yugoslavia (ICTFY), the Hague Tribunal, was set up by the United Nations Security Council (UNSC) – via Security Council Resolution 808 – on 27 May 1993. The mechanism for establishing this body was Chapter 7 of the UN Charter, which was specifically concerned with maintaining or restoring peace. In effect then, the ICTFY was an arm of the UNSC and, essentially, a response to the ethnic cleansing and human rights abuses that had bedevilled the territory in question. As such, it began work slowly – with not a single prosecution until 1997 – and only picked up momentum gradually. In August 2000, the Bosnian Serb leader Radislav Krstic was sentenced by the tribunal to 46 years in prison for his part in massacres at Srebrenica, perhaps the most shocking and sadistic act of mass killing in post-war Europe.

Subsequently, the ex-president of the former Yugoslavia, Slobodan Milosevic, was brought before the Hague Tribunal – although he refused to recognise its jurisdiction. It was, though, a significant occasion, since a head of state was being prosecuted for atrocities committed by troops under his overall command. Moreover, an important contribution to international law and justice was the Hague Tribunal's ruling that war crimes and crimes against humanity did not depend upon an international or internal armed conflict situation being classified as such. These crimes were now specifically and legally classified as so serious that they surpassed the restrictive interpretation of the 1949 Geneva Conventions.

In November 1994, another ad hoc body, the Rwanda Tribunal, was set up as an appendage to the Hague Tribunal, although it was based largely in Arusha and Kigali. Again, the new tribunal

– like its immediate predecessor – was a response to Chapter 7 of the UN Charter. In this context, the movement of armed refugees, as a result of the Rwanda crisis, was interpreted as a threat to the international peace and security of nearby states. Significantly, the Rwanda Tribunal recognised that crimes against humanity could be committed in peacetime. Both the Rwanda and ICTFY tribunals also recognised that serious human rights abuses could be committed not only by state actors – as Nuremberg ruled – but also by non-state actors that aspired or claimed to rule. A further important difference between Nuremberg and the two ad hoc bodies of the 1990s was that the latter tribunals did not exact the death penalty. This factor encouraged some perpetrators of serious crimes in Rwanda to opt for international justice rather than the potentially life-threatening rulings of their national courts. The Rwanda Tribunal has had some modest successes in bringing perpetrators of serious crimes to justice, including in 1998 the former Rwandan prime minister, Jean Kambanda, who pleaded guilty to the crime of genocide.

It is worth underlining the ad hoc nature of the ex-Yugoslavia and Rwanda Tribunals. They have been important steps towards implementing a system of international justice and, at the same time, they have provided full recognition of the rights of victims and the protection of witnesses. But a more comprehensive path to addressing questions of impunity, crimes against humanity, war crimes and the like, lay in the creation of a permanent international criminal court, with a wider, global remit. Indeed, those responsible for the operations of an ICC could learn from some of the lessons of its predecessors. For instance, human rights training for top personnel could be improved upon and it was important that prosecutors and judges were not housed together and serviced by the same support staff. In short, justice had to be impartially dispensed, and seen to be so.

The International Criminal Court

It was not until 1994 that the International Law Commission submitted to the UN General Assembly its draft statute for an

ICC. The General Assembly then proceeded to set up the Ad Hoc Committee on the Establishment of an International Criminal Court, whose report was then studied by the General Assembly before it set up the Preparatory Committee on the Establishment of an International Criminal Court. The last-named body, in 1996–98, prepared a draft for an international conference, which took place in Rome. The Rome Statute for an International Criminal Court was then adopted on 17 July 1998 by an overwhelming majority of 120 votes to 7. Among the minority against the statute were the world's most populous states: the USA, India and China. By December 2000, however, 139 states (including the USA) had signed up to the statute. The Rome Statute was scheduled to come into force when 60 countries had ratified it, and this culminated in the 1 July 2002 operational start. By November 2008, 108 states had become members of the ICC, with another 40 having signed but not yet ratified the Rome Statute.

The ICC was set up as a permanent body, which aimed to bring to justice individuals who commit the most serious violations of international humanitarian law: war crimes, crimes against humanity, genocide and (to be defined) aggression. War crimes are serious violations of the 1949 Geneva Conventions and other serious violations committed on a large scale in international armed conflicts. Crimes against humanity are prohibited actions perpetrated against civilian populations – such as murder, extermination, enslavement, deportation or forcible transfer of population, torture, rape, sexual slavery, enforced prostitution, forced pregnancy, enforced sterilisation, enforced disappearance and apartheid. Genocide covers specifically prohibited acts perpetrated with a view to destroying, wholly or partially, a national, ethnic, racial or religious group. The crime of aggression is still to be agreed upon and this definitional work has preoccupied the ICC Working Group on the Crime of Aggression.

Another key aspect of the ICC is its facilitation of witness participation in trials. The ICC is complementary to national jurisdictions and will only become active if national legal systems are unwilling or unable to pursue suspects. As such, the ICC can be seen as a court of last resort (Glasius 2006; HRW 2008;

Politi and Nesi 2004; Sands 2003; Schabas 2004, 2007). The Rome Statute was a compromise, since there was much discussion and dispute about the type of ICC to be set up. Robertson, for instance, divides the protagonists here into three groupings. First, there were those countries, including the United Kingdom, which wanted a powerful prosecutor, and an ICC genuinely independent of the UNSC and with a truly global remit. Second, there were those countries, including the USA, France and China that wanted an ICC beholden to the UNSC. Third, there were those countries, including Iran, Iraq and Indonesia, which did not want an ICC at all (Robertson 2000, pp.324–5). Of course, the discussions surrounding the ICC were not simply the preserve of states and IGOs (international governmental organisations). NGOs (non-governmental organisations) too – such as Amnesty International and Human Rights Watch – became closely involved in the campaign for an ICC. The main NGOs coalesced under the broad umbrella of the Coalition for an International Criminal Court (CICC), which was formed in 1995 and comprised about 1,000 organisations as well as international law experts from around the globe.

Amnesty International, the global human rights organisation, defined the ICC as 'an enormous step forward in the fight against impunity and those responsible for genocide, crimes against humanity and war crimes' (Amnesty International 2000). According to Mary Robinson, the former United Nations high commissioner for human rights (UNHCHR), the Rome Statute is 'a historic achievement, establishing for the first time a universal framework to end impunity for the most serious crimes under international law' (Robinson 2000). Robinson further contended that the ICC's statute enabled 'for the first time a major multilateral treaty, [and] codifies certain acts as war crimes when committed in an international armed conflict' (Robinson 2000). Another informed observer summed up these sentiments towards the ICC by stating that the statute 'is the product of years of negotiation between human rights organisations and governments worldwide for an effective international system of investigation, prosecution and trial to deal with the most heinous crimes by individuals'

(Feenan 2001). Welcoming the ICC as 'a giant step forward for mankind', British Foreign Office minister Peter Hain contended that tyrants and dictators across the world would sleep less soundly as a result of the ratification of the statute (Hain 2000).

For some observers, though, the ICC statute did not go far enough. For one thing, unlike Nuremberg, its remit is not retroactive. Hence, past violators of human rights have effectively been granted immunity from prosecution by the court. Once established, the ICC's progress has been steady rather than spectacular. For some critics, the activity of the ICC in its first decade of existence has been too modest. The first arrest warrants issued by the court were only forthcoming in July 2005. Other critics have pointed to the ICC's overwhelming preoccupation with several countries in the continent of Africa and serious crimes perpetrated therein. Significantly, to date, the ICC has not become involved in human rights violations in Iraq subsequent to that country's invasion by the so-called 'coalition of the willing'. The USA, we recall, is not a signatory to the Rome Statute; and also the ICC has not yet been able to define, and thus to exercise any jurisdiction over, the crime of aggression.

To date, the court has proceeded to investigate *and* take action in four specific situations: in northern Uganda, the Democratic Republic of the Congo (DRC), the Central African Republic (CAR) and Sudan/Darfur. In addition, the ICC's Office of the Prosecutor is investigating and assessing a number of situations for evidence of war crimes, genocide and crimes against humanity. In Uganda, the ICC's main concerns have been the activities of the Lord's Resistance Army (LRA), whose leaders have been accused of war crimes and crimes against humanity. A moving, informed and evidence-based account of the situation in northern Uganda has been provided by Tim Allen, who points to 'one of the worst humanitarian disasters in the world', with over a million people living in terrible conditions in displacement camps. According to Allen, 'until recently it has been largely ignored', but one of the key reasons for subsequent international attention 'is the role played by the recently created International Criminal Court' (Allen 2006, p.xiii).

In the DRC, in 2006, militia leader Thomas Lubanga Dyilo became the first person to be arrested by the ICC – for conscripting children under the age of 15 to participate in hostilities. Other suspects in the DRC were also charged and thereafter delivered up to the ICC for crimes including sexual slavery, murder and conscription of children under the age of 15. Lubanga's much-delayed trial in January 2009 was seen as something of a landmark in developing international law, since it constituted the first actual trial of the court. Even so, the ICC attracted criticism here, since the (laudable) focus on child soldiers did not include attention to other crimes committed, such as mass killings and torture (McGreal 2009).

As regards the Central African Republic (CAR), ICC investigations, prosecutions and arrests have focused on war crimes and crimes against humanity (including rape and other sexual crimes) perpetrated during fighting between rebel and government forces in 2002–03. The CAR ratified the Rome Statute in 2001 and, like the DRC, made a self-referral to the ICC. In 2008, Jean Pierre Bemba Gombo – leader of the Liberation Movement for the Congo and former vice-president of the DRC – was arrested for war crimes and crimes against humanity, including the widespread commission of rape in the CAR. According to one informed source: 'The case against Bemba has been heralded by CAR women's rights organisations, many of whom felt that the ICC belatedly addressed gender crimes' (*The Monitor*, 2008/9). In this context, it should be noted that the Rome Statute for the ICC was seen as the first international treaty to specify certain acts of sexual and gender-based violence as belonging to the category of the most serious crimes under international law (Glasius 2006, p.77).

In the case of Darfur, western Sudan, over several years, the human rights situation has given the indigenous peoples and the international community cause for concern. The situation in Darfur came before the ICC by way of a UNSC resolution. In 2007, ICC indictments for alleged crimes against humanity and war crimes – committed in 2003 and 2004 – focused upon a Sudanese government minister (Ahmad Muhammad Harun, ex-minister of the interior) and a Janjaweed militia leader, Ali Kushayb. The subsequent appointment of Harun as minister of humanitarian affairs and the Sudanese president's refusal to co-operate with the ICC indicate the lack of respect shown to the court by the Sudanese authorities. In June–July 2008, the ICC Prosecutor (Luis Moreno-Ocampo) declared the whole of Darfur to be a 'crime scene' and accused the Sudanese president (Omar al-Bashir) of being responsible for genocide, crimes against humanity and war crimes in the region. This was the first time that the ICC had invoked the crime of genocide. Moreover, it was the first time that a ruling head of state had been targeted by the ICC. There were fears that the step (notably the issuing by the ICC judges, in March 2009, of an arrest warrant for the Sudanese president) might lead to an increase in violence and the creation of an even more difficult operational environment for humanitarian organisations. Simultaneously, the ICC was fulfilling its mandate by addressing the perceived, ongoing practice of genocide. At the time of writing, the above cases are still in progress (Burniat and Apple 2008/9; Hagan and Rymond-Richmond 2009).

As the above narrative suggests, the establishing of an ICC was a protracted process. Since its establishment, the nascent ICC has not been able to yield tangible results (in the form of successful prosecutions) as quickly as some supporters and advocates would have liked. In this respect, one seasoned observer warned against expecting too much in the form of producing 'a scorecard of successful prosecutions': 'The success of the ICC should be evaluated not just to the extent that it punishes past atrocity, but also in terms of the effects its investigations have on reducing abysmal conduct in the present and future' (Sachs 2008, p.6).

Undoubtedly, though, the institution has undergone teething problems and it will be instructive to highlight some of these. For instance, the ICC has come up against the problem of seeking justice in the context and climate of ongoing violence. Indeed, the court has been accused of risking the prolongation of violence of conflict by seeking justice above all and thereby jeopardising peace deals. As Waddell and Clark explain:

> Seeking to dispense criminal justice *during* conflict and even in parallel with peace processes represents an ambitious vision for international justice – one that endeavours to reverse the historical trend of justice being postponed or bartered away as part of peace deals. (Waddell and Clark 2008b, p.17)

Also, the overwhelming focus on Africa has raised the question of why some places and not others. For some observers here, there is a post-colonial echo of outsiders perennially dispensing 'Western'-inspired forms of justice (see Simpson 2008). At the same time, there are concerns – especially prevalent prior to the ICC's investigations and action over Darfur – over the court's focus primarily upon *non-state* actors. Arguably here the ICC, at the risk of upsetting local populations, may not have wanted to jeopardise its relations with states on which to a large extent it depends operationally (see Clark 2008).

One useful assessment of the ICC has come in a recent report by Human Rights Watch (HRW 2008). In *Courting History: The International Criminal Court's First Years*, HRW recognises the progress that the ICC has made with its investigations. At the same time, some constructive observations are in order. The recommendations here include the call for more effective communication in the field between the ICC and affected communities, better protection for witnesses, enhanced resources to support investigations, and a more forthcoming engagement by the international community. As regards the latter point, HRW provides sobering words of warning: 'The biggest challenge facing the court is primarily outside of its control: apprehending suspects. The ICC must rely on the international community's cooperation to enforce its orders' (HRW 2008, p.4).

Not-so-splendid Isolation: The USA and the ICC

The ICC has not been universally welcomed. Some of the stiffest opposition has come from the USA. For one thing, the USA under President Clinton was reluctant to vote for the Rome Statute. Only in December 2000, at the 'eleventh hour', and arguably more with resignation than with enthusiasm, did the Clinton administration put its pen to signing up for the ICC. Full ratification was, however, another matter, and in 2001, the new Bush administration not only shied away from ratification, but even reneged on the USA's December 2000 signature. According to the former USA ambassador to the UN, Bill Richardson, speaking in August 2001:

> The Bush administration is discussing 'unsigning' the treaty. The administration has already rejected, or expressed reservations about, some half-dozen international agreements; the court appears to be next in line. But to pack up and leave now would send the wrong signal to the world and be a serious mistake. (*New York Times*, 21 August 2001)

Nevertheless, in May 2002, the Bush administration took the momentous step of officially distancing the USA from the statute and refusing to be bound by it.

The concerns of some USA opponents to the ICC centred upon fears of loss of sovereignty and the prospect of seeing USA military personnel or decision makers being prosecuted, albeit for heinous crimes, by a foreign court. Opponents of the ICC claimed that, if adopted and ratified, it would contravene the guaranteed constitutional rights of American citizens and open up the possibility of 'politically motivated' rulings against the USA. There were fears too concerning the competence of ICC judges and prosecutors, as well as (we recall) the definition of the crime of aggression. In addition, opponents of the ICC maintained that the USA, if it ratified the body, would forfeit the right to protect its national security. For example, it was feared that the USA would need prior approval before any military action took place, or it would run the risk of ICC prosecution. Adam Roberts, professor of international relations at Oxford University, vocalised strong and critical disappointment over the USA's attitudes towards the ICC: 'The biggest worry is that the US, with almost paranoid concerns about the prosecution of its soldiers, will not ratify the statute. For the ICC to work, US support is vital' (Roberts 2001).

In the vanguard of American hostility towards the ICC was the veteran right-wing Republican politician and influential chair of the Senate Foreign Relations Committee, Jesse Helms (North Carolina), who claimed to be unalterably opposed. Helms also co-sponsored a measure aimed at circumventing the ICC. The 2002 American Service Members' Protection Act (ASPA) aimed to restrict the USA from co-operating with the ICC and in UN peacekeeping operations unless the UNSC exempted Americans from the ICC's jurisdiction. ASPA would even jeopardise the USA's aid to states co-operating with the ICC, even if the ultimate goal here was to fight against international terrorism (see below). In fact, in 2002 the Bush administration went even further in its opposition to the ICC by pressurising states to sign up for bilateral agreements with the USA. These so-called 'Article 98 Agreements' or bilateral immunity agreements (BIAs) declared that signatories would not turn over USA personnel to the ICC if asked to do so by the international community. In return, the signatories could expect continuing support and goodwill from the USA. Unsurprisingly, supporters of the ICC – including the European Union (EU) as a bloc – opposed these agreements as dilutions of the spirit of the ICC statute. Moreover, eastern and central European states protested that they were now being squeezed unfairly by Washington and Brussels. These states aspired to join *both* the North Atlantic Treaty Organisation (NATO) *and* the EU, but the issue of the bilateral agreements was now seen as an unwanted factor of division between the USA and Europe.

The opposition to the ICC certainly went wider than the Pentagon – concerned about the thousands of American soldiers based across many parts of the globe – and the right wing of the Republican Party. Some of the USA's elected representatives even advocated non-payment of Washington's financial dues to the UN. This bizarre position seemed to be based on the erroneous belief that the ICC was an arm of the UN, instead of an international body in its own right. In effect, the issue of payments to the UN got caught up in the sentiments of hostility towards the ICC; and the debate even overlapped with the reaching of an agreement to alter the system of UN payments that, in fact, reduced the USA's financial contribution. Significantly, this obstructionist and go-it-alone stance was somewhat less conspicuous immediately after

11 September 2001, when the Bush administration, understandably, was keen to build bridges – on a military level.

However, by early 2002 the administration seemed to be hardening its attitude towards the ICC, as illustrated by the distancing of the USA from the Rome Statute in May and the subsequent pressure to achieve Article 98 Agreements. According to one view: 'The US has been getting nastier for the past six months and subverting the court with far greater energy and determination' (*Observer*, 20 September 2002). In response to the USA's approach to the ICC, Amnesty International launched an online petition and campaign for individuals to call upon governments not to enter the impunity (or immunity) agreements being proposed by Washington (Amnesty International 2002). The previous month, as the ASPA legislation made its way through the Senate and the House of Representatives, the European Parliament had passed a resolution accusing the USA of undermining the ICC's authority and jeopardising peacekeeping operations. Similar criticisms were heard against the USA in a heated debate at the United Nations Security Council. Nonetheless, in subsequent years the USA passed legislation designed at reducing the impact of the ICC. These developments included in 2004 the so-called Nethercutt Amendment, which cut aid to countries who had ratified the ICC and not signed bilateral agreements with the USA. Interestingly, one of the leading authorities on the ICC describes the above developments as 'little more than squalls, and the court has weathered them without major mishap' (Schabas 2007, p.30).

The same author points usefully to some of the deeper and fuller reasoning behind the USA's opposition to the Rome Statute. First, Schabas explains that the policy community in Washington was somewhat divided on how to deal with the ICC. Initially, the Clinton administration was not unfavourably disposed towards the idea of an ICC, but went cold on it when the Rome negotiations produced an institution that was distanced from the UNSC. However, the ICC's de facto challenge to the flawed mechanisms of the UNSC attracted many states to the Rome Statute. Indeed, it has been suggested that the USA's hostility to the ICC has been counterproductive: 'At times, it seemed as if opposition from the United States only enhanced the enthusiasm of other countries for the court' (Schabas 2004, p.23). Again, as Schabas later suggests: 'When the history books are written, United States opposition to the International Criminal Court will go down as one of its great diplomatic defeats' (Schabas 2007, p.32).

Arguably, the early American hostility to the Rome Statute has waned somewhat with the ratification and establishment of the ICC. For one thing, the policy of bilaterals (i.e. BIAs) was opposed by parts of the American military, notably in 2005–06, when it became apparent that in the absence of USA input other states might step in to provide the necessary support, solidarity and influence. Also, the Democratic majority in Congress has included powerful and prominent legislators who have opposed the BIAs and the ASPA. Again, Secretary of State Condoleezza Rice and her legal adviser, John Bellinger, were more co-operative with and complimentary about the ICC in the latter years of the Bush administration. As John Washburn, convenor of the American NGO Coalition for the ICC (AMICC), pointed out:

> Unless the Court has a spectacular failure in one of its current cases, it is likely that the USA will continue its discrete but open cooperation with the Court on Darfur and publicly express cautious optimism for the Court's work when it serves US national interests. (Washburn 2007, p.24)

Prior to the 2008 American presidential election, leading candidates, including Barack Obama, John McCain and prospective vice-president Joe Biden, expressed support for the ICC. At the time of writing it remains to be seen how the nascent Obama presidency will deal with the court in practice.

11 September 2001

On 11 September 2001, suicide bombers hijacked planes and piloted them into the twin towers of the World Trade Centre in New York, as well as into the Pentagon, in Washington. As is well known, several thousand individuals are estimated to have perished in the attacks. What did these dramatic and terrible events mean for the ICC debate? This section looks back at the time just before the inauguration of the ICC in 2002 and focuses on attitudes towards the court in the USA and beyond in the light of 9/11.

In theory, at least, the case for an international criminal court was stronger after 11 September. As Robert G. Patman argued, an ICC would be able to prosecute terrorists, such as those who masterminded the 11 September atrocities, and make it difficult for them to evade justice (Patman 2001). The ICC would also provide indisputable legitimacy and neutrality to the efforts to bring perpetrators of heinous crimes to justice. Again, Diane Marie Amann, professor of law at the University of California, Davis, School of Law – clearly writing as a concerned American – contended that:

> The attacks of September 11 changed everything. In an instant, we learned that, like it or not, superpower or no, we are part of the rest of the world ... In these last weeks, we have ... learned that international cooperation can be a good thing. That lesson ought to apply to the International Criminal Court ... The court will have jurisdiction over acts that are crimes against humanity, like the attacks of September 11. It could be the key to the fight against terrorism. (Amann 2001)

A near-immediate response by President Bush and the USA authorities to 11 September was to try to build up a coalition to help track down the perpetrators of the crimes. Countries, notably Afghanistan, accused of hiding suspected terrorists – essentially the prime suspect, Osama bin Laden – were also warned not to obstruct the cause of the coalition. What was striking then about the USA's attitude over this period was that the Bush administration moved from a position of increasing isolationism or unilateralism to one of suddenly seeking to build up global alliances – 'you're either with us, or against us' – against terrorism (see also Hainsworth 2003). For, as indicated above, right from the start the Bush administration had not only shown signs of retreating from the, at best lukewarm, support that the previous administration had demonstrated towards the Rome Statute – with President Clinton 'a reluctant and tardy signatory'

(Grayling 2001), but, in addition, Bush had turned his back on the Kyoto Treaty and the Anti-Ballistic Missile (ABM) Treaty, at the same time unilaterally pushing ahead with a new missile defence plan (dubbed Star Wars 2 or 'son of Star Wars'). All in all, this was interpreted widely as a 'go-it-alone' strategy from Washington. For instance, according to Andrew Stephen, writing in the *New Statesman*, Bush 'spent the first six months of his presidency insulting most other nations of the world. He tore up the Kyoto Protocol, unilaterally abandoned the ABM treaty, told the rest of the world he wasn't interested in the proposed international ban on biological weapons and so on' (Stephen 2001).

At home, the Democrats' leader in the Senate, Thomas Daschle, accused Bush of a failure of leadership in relation to international agreements: 'Instead of asserting our leadership, we are abdicating it. Instead of shaping international agreements to serve our interests, we have removed ourselves from a position to shape them at all' (Daschle 2001). Again, Heather Hamilton of AMICC linked the negative USA attitude towards the ICC (and ASPA) to the question of coalition-building against terrorism: 'The administration should realize that supporting legislation penalizing countries that join an international law enforcement mechanism is not the way to strengthen international efforts to bring terrorists to justice' (Hamilton 2001). Across the Atlantic, strong criticism of the Bush line came also from the well-known campaigning activist and performer Mark Thomas, who accused the USA of operating double standards in urging the world to unite against lawlessness whilst at the same time endeavouring to destroy attempts to create an international rule of law. As regards the ICC, Thomas explained: 'Nearly every major ally of the US and every member of the European Union supports its creation. If it existed today now, it would be the only internationally recognised, purpose-built court in which Osama bin Laden could be prosecuted' (Thomas 2001).

Mary Robinson, the former UNHCHR, defined the fatal attacks in the USA on 11 September 2001, as crimes against humanity. Tom Hadden, then a professor of law at Queen's University Belfast and a Northern Ireland human rights commissioner, suggested that this implied that the perpetrators could be tried before an ICC. But the same author also added a word of caution in this respect: 'It is ironic it was the United States which blocked the specific inclusion of terrorist acts in the statute for [the ICC]' (Hadden 2001, pp.11–12). There was still a strong argument, though, for pursuing justice by strengthening the international rule of law. Indeed, an international Hague-type tribunal or an ICC was seen increasingly as the best response to the question of bringing perpetrators to justice for crimes such as those committed on 11 September 2001. The inclusion of Islamic jurists in such courts would strengthen the legitimacy of such bodies.

At an international experts' conference on the ICC, held in the Philippines in October 2001, Chief Justice Hilario G. Davide called the ICC 'the missing link in international justice':

> The fears of terrorism which threaten world peace and stability demonstrate all too clearly the need for, among other things, a world constitution that can immediately respond to the demands of international justice without resorting to war, that is the opposite of peace. (Davide 2001)

While the Rome Statute did not specifically mention the word 'terrorism', there was a growing sentiment globally that terrorism of the type committed on 11 September might be classified nonetheless as a crime against humanity. With this in mind, Robertson and Wright, writing in *The Guardian*, suggested that a long-term effort to construct international machinery to fight international crimes was the best response to 11 September. A 'systematic attack deliberately directed against a civilian population involving acts of multiple murder' (Robertson and Wright 2001) could thus define – in the context of the Rome Statute – a new crime against humanity. Had the ICC been in existence on 11 September 2001, it would certainly have come into the equation of seeking global justice for the crimes committed in the suicide bombings and in the planning of these atrocities.

The period after 11 September was also notable for various European attempts to come to terms with the situation. For instance, in October 2001, EU governments and parliamentarians began to think more seriously about setting up an international terrorism tribunal, more or less along the same lines as the ICTFY. In the United Kingdom, for instance, 70 MPs signed a motion in favour of an international court, including provision for Islamic judges, and operating under the jurisdiction of the UNSC. Ideally, such a body would be more globally acceptable for trying 11 September suspects, even to Islamic countries, than a court in the USA (see Baldwin 2001). In addition, at the Conference of European Justice Ministers (Council of Europe) in Moscow, 4–5 October 2001, the ministers called for full support for the ICC as part of the struggle against international terrorism.

To sum up, the reality of the 11 September 2001 atrocities and the weighing up of their consequences became bound up with questions of global justice and international co-operation and, inevitably therefore, discussion about the role and remit of the ICC became a feature of the overall debate. This is a debate that is likely to run. Indeed, a related issue that we have been unable to explore here is the tension between calls for justice in the wake of September 11 and the potential for abrogating civil liberties through anti-terrorist initiatives in developed and developing countries.

Conclusion

The ICC is a relatively new institution, though the campaign to establish it goes back more than half a century. Robertson dates the first discussions back to 1937, when the League of Nations drew up a draft statute for a court to try international terrorists (Robertson 2000, pp.324–5). Thereafter, the Nuremberg and Tokyo tribunals were followed up by the passing of a UN reference to 'an international penal tribunal' as the 1948 Genocide Convention was drawn up. However, as the Cold War set in, various fledgling attempts to move the ICC debate along further came to nought. It was not until the 1990s – with the creation of the ex-Yugoslavia and Rwanda tribunals – that some practical substance was given to the ideas that eventually led to the signing of the 1998 Rome Statute.

Located in The Hague, the ICC builds upon Nuremberg and the ad hoc tribunals of the 1990s – with, for instance, full recognition given to the rights of victims and due regard for the protection of witnesses. At the same time, events in the USA – the Bush presidency, the New York and Washington suicide bombings – have impinged greatly on the discussion about and the progress of the ICC. Moreover, as Hadden suggests, any response to 9/11 should be kept within the general principles of international law and human rights standards:

> That is not just because there is an obligation on all states to adhere to international law and human rights. It is also because acting in line with those principles is the only way to ensure effective international co-operation, which in turn is the only way to ensure a lasting protection from international terrorism. (2001, p.11)

In this context and that of globalisation, the ICC has a lot to offer. After the ratification of the Rome Statute by the required 60 states, the ICC became the first permanent institution empowered to prosecute individuals for war crimes, crimes against humanity, genocide and (eventually) crimes of aggression. As a permanent court, the ICC diminishes the necessity of creating limited ad hoc tribunals and, at the same time, implies some important cost savings in moving away from a proliferation of one-off courts. Furthermore, problems and questions of delay and selectivity are more satisfactorily addressed and circumvented with the provision of an ICC with universal jurisdiction.

The International Criminal Court is not a panacea for resolving all the heinous crimes in the contemporary world. Moreover, as Bell contends, the ICC belongs to one of three dimensions of the relevant legal framework as regards punishment for past abuses. The framework here includes, firstly, international humanitarian law (notably the 1949 Geneva Conventions and their 1977 protocols); secondly, international human rights law that is treaty-based and customary law and; thirdly, 'crimes against humanity' (Nuremberg, ad hoc criminal tribunals and the ICC) (Bell 2003, p.260). Furthermore, the globalisation of justice cannot simply be equated with the ICC. To do so would be to raise expectations unwisely. As one commentator explains, 'the ICC represents one instrument in a panoply of judicial and non-judicial mechanisms' (Simpson 2008, p.74).

The ICC can be seen, therefore, as part and parcel of a broader fluorescence of human rights initiatives, including truth and reconciliation processes, the post-war attempts to prosecute human rights abusers (such as Nazi war criminals) via national jurisdictions, the creation of human rights instruments, such as national human rights courts, and the strengthening of national justice systems per se (Steiner and Alston 1996; Steiner, Alston and Goodman 2008; Waddell and Clark 2008a). In this context, Sachs makes the point that '[a]ppropriate forms of truth-telling and reparation can do as much as, or even more than, criminal justice to deal effectively with past abuses' (Sachs 2008, p.6). Indeed, where appropriate, this may include resort to traditional forms of justice, conflict resolution, and reconciliation.

Nevertheless, if properly resourced, supported, respected and mainstreamed, the ICC can make would-be perpetrators of serious crimes think twice, if the prospect of prosecution is a real one. As Robertson again suggests: 'Crimes against humanity will only be deterred when their would-be perpetrators – be they political leaders, field commanders or soldiers and policemen – are given pause by the prospect that they will henceforth have no hiding place' (Robertson 2000, pp.324–5). A leading article from the *Guardian* (21 August 2001) further summed up the potential value of the ICC: 'The principle behind the ICC is that the world community should have what any civilised national community has, namely a properly constituted means of dealing with right and wrong'.

A permanent and effective international criminal court is an important step forward in the globalisation of justice. The existence of international machinery to pursue perpetrators of serious crimes will hopefully serve as a warning to those states which refuse to do so – especially as prosecutions take place and persons in high places are called to account by the ICC, or indeed by other bodies. The arrests of prominent individuals such as Slobodan Milosevic (Yugoslavia), Radovan Karadzic (Bosnia–

Herzegovina), Charles Taylor (Liberia) and Jean-Pierre Bemba (DRC) send out the message that former national presidents or vice-presidents are not beyond the pale of international justice. Moreover, by establishing truth and justice, hopefully the ICC can enable societies and individuals to be better prepared to 'move on', knowing that criminals have been prosecuted and that impunity has not been allowed to prevail.

Therefore, it is worth re-emphasising that the provision of an effective and working ICC can constitute a deterrent – a warning to would-be perpetrators of serious crimes that they will be pursued and brought to justice. For these reasons, an ICC 'with teeth' is to be broadly welcomed and continually sought after. As discussed above, the court is still finding its feet after becoming operational in 2002. The ICC is very much at the crossroads as an institution.

References

Allen, T. (2006) *Trial Justice: The International Criminal Court and the Lord's Resistance Army*, Zed Books, London and New York.

Amann, D.M. (2001) 'A New International Spirit', *San Francisco Chronicles*, 12 October. www.stgate.com/cgi-bin/article.cgi?file=/c/a/2001/10/12/ED20619

Amnesty International (2000) *International Criminal Court: Checklist for Effective Implementation*, Amnesty International, London.

Amnesty International (2002) *International Criminal Court: US Efforts to Obtain Impunity for Genocide, Crimes Against Humanity and War Crimes*, Amnesty International, London, August, AI Index: IOR 40/025/2002.

Baldwin, T. (2001) 'EU Considers Tribunal for Terrorist Suspects', *The Times*, 30 October.

Bell, C. (2003) *Peace Agreements and Human Rights*, Oxford University Press, Oxford.

Burniat, N. and B. Apple (2008/9) 'Genocide in Darfur: Challenges and Opportunities for Action', *The Monitor: Journal of the Coalition for the International Criminal Court*, no.37, November 2008–April 2009, pp.1, 11.

Clark, P. (2008) 'Law, Politics and Pragmatism: The ICC and Case Selection in Uganda and the Democratic Republic of Congo', in Waddell and Clark (2008a).

Daschle, T. (2001) Remarks made at the Woodrow Wilson International Center for Scholars as part of a series called 'A New Century of American Leadership', 9 August. www.iccnow.org

Davide, H.G. (2001), quoted in *Business World* (Philippines) 17 October 2001, and reported on the website of the NGO Coalition for an International Criminal Court (CICC). www.iccnow.org

Feenan, D. (2001) Letter to the *Guardian*, 9 March.

George, S. (2001) 'Globalisation and the WTO', *NODE News*, September/October, NODE, Dublin.

Glasius, M. (2006) *The International Criminal Court*, Routledge, Abingdon.

Grayling, A.C. (2001) 'The World's Policeman Cannot be Above the Law', *Guardian*, 20 August.

Gunnell, B. and Timms, D. (2000) *After Seattle: Globalisation and its Discontents*, Catalyst, London.

Hadden, T. (2001) 'Human Rights v. Terrorism', *Fortnight*, no.399, October.

Hagan, J. and W. Rymond-Richard (2009) *Darfur and the Crime of Genocide*, Cambridge University Press, Cambridge.

Hain, P. (2000) 'Calling All Dictators', *Guardian*, 24 August.

Hainsworth, P. (2003) 'Towards the Globalisation of Justice: An International Criminal Court', in G. McCann and S. McCloskey (eds) *From the Local to the Global: Key Issues in Development Studies*, 1st edn, Pluto Press, London.

Hamilton, H. (2001) quoted in the *Coalition for an International Criminal Court (CICC) Newsletter*, 'UK Ratifies ICC Treaty as US Considers Anti-ICC Legislation', ICC Update, 23rd edn, October. www.ICCnow.org

Heater, D. (1999) *What is Citizenship?* Polity, Cambridge.

HRW (2008) *Courting History: The Landmark International Criminal Court's First Years*, Human Rights Watch, July.

McGreal, C. (2009) 'Warlord "press-ganged children" in Congo', *Guardian*, 27 January.

The Monitor (2008/9) 'Bemba Case Highlights Prosecutor's Resolve to Address Violence against Women and Ensure Effective State Cooperation', *The Monitor: Journal of the Coalition for the International Criminal* Court, no.37, November 2008–April 2009, p.10.

Patman, R.G. (2001) 'US Stance Reveals Double Standards: Bush Fears an International Criminal Court Would Limit US Military Action in Pursuit of National Interests', *Canberra Times*, 24 October.

Politi, M. and G. Nesi (eds) (2004) *The International Criminal Court and the Crime of Aggression*, Ashgate, Aldershot.

Roberts, A. (2001) 'War Law', *Guardian*, 4 April.

Robertson, G. (2000) *Crimes Against Humanity: The Struggle for Global Justice*, Penguin, Harmondsworth.

Robertson, G. and R. Wright (2001) 'Bush's Chance to Shape International Norms', *Guardian*, 14 October.

Robinson, M. (2000) 'Rights and Development Now Seen as Going Hand-in-Hand', *The Irish Times*, 11 December.

Sachs, A. (2008) 'Foreword', in Waddell and Clark (2008a).

Sands, P. (ed.) (2003) *From Nuremberg to The Hague: The Future of International Criminal Justice*, Cambridge University Press, Cambridge.

Schabas, W. (2004) *An Introduction to the International Criminal Court*, 2nd edn, Cambridge University Press, Cambridge.

Schabas, W. (2007) *An Introduction to the Criminal Court*, Cambridge University Press, Cambridge.

Simpson, G. (2008) 'One in Many: The ICC as a Tool of Justice during Transition', in Waddell and Clark (2008a).

Steiner, H. and P. Alston (eds) (1996) *International Human Rights in Context: Law, Politics and Morals*, Clarendon Press, Oxford.

Steiner, H., P. Alston and R. Goodman (2008) *International Rights in Context: Law, Politics, Morals,* Clarendon Press, Oxford.

Stephen, A. (2001) 'Gee Have you Heard? There's a World Out There', *New Statesman*, 8 October.

Thomas, M. (2001) 'One Rule for Americans, One Rule for the Rest', *New Statesman*, 15 October.

Waddell, N. and P. Clark (2008b) 'Introduction', in Waddell and Clark (2008a).

Waddell, N. and P. Clark (eds) (2008a) *Courting Conflict? Justice, Peace and the ICC in Africa*, Royal Africa Society, London.

Washburn, J. (2007) 'The United States' Slow March to Justice', *The Monitor: Journal of the Coalition for the International Criminal Court*, no.34, May–October.

Websites

Amnesty International	www.amnesty.org
Centre for International Human Rights Law	www.rightsinternational.org
Human Rights Library	http://heiwww.unige.ch/humanrts/
HURPEC human rights server	www.hurpec.net
International Commission of Jurists	www.icj.org
International Criminal Justice Resource Centre	www.internationaljustice.org

Justice Without Borders	www.justicewithoutborders.com
Lawyers Committee for Human Rights	www.lchr.org
United Nations Human Rights site	www.un.org/rights/
United Nations Index	www.unsystem.org

Part II

The Economics of Development

4

PERSPECTIVES ON AID: ANALYSING THE SYSTEM

Joanne McGarry

The foundations of the global financial architecture as we know it have been crumbling for some time. The current global economic crisis has rocked those foundations even further and over the coming years the framework for aid delivery will change from that which we know today. This chapter aims to address the following questions and is structured around these key issues. What is aid and what forms does it take? How and why do we have the aid system we have today? How do the public and governments in the global South perceive the system? Is the desire for increased *quality* of aid detrimental or complementary to the need for increases in the *quantity* of aid? Also what are the implications of this new aid effectiveness paradigm for non-governmental development actors? The chapter will also consider the direction in which the aid system might move over the coming years, taking into account the current global financial crisis. It will also examine what is needed to ensure that a future aid delivery system has poverty reduction as its primary goal. But first there is a need to consider some of the fundamentals of the aid system.

What is Aid?

According to the Development Assistance Committee (DAC) of the Organisation for Economic Co-operation and Development (OECD), foreign aid (or overseas development assistance, ODA) is the transfer abroad of public resources on concessional terms (with at least a 25 per cent grant element), a significant objective of which is to bring about an improvement in economic, political, or social conditions in developing countries (www.oecd.org/dataoecd/26/14/26415658.pdf). Expenditure which does not constitute aid and which is not included in the DAC's definition includes that on military or trade financing, public funding for cultural exchanges, funding for anti-drug or anti-terrorism activities abroad or for international peacekeeping operations. Including these areas of expenditure within aid budgets serves only to distort aid figures and to suggest that country donors are more generous than they actually are. Aid allocations should arguably only be counted when they are allocated towards improving the economic, political, or social conditions for people in developing countries.

Aid can be allocated in a number of ways. In the case of European Union (EU) countries, for example, aid may be given bilaterally or multilaterally. *Bilateral aid* is that donated from a donor government to the government of another country. This type of aid can take many forms: general budget support (GBS) is aid directly channelled into the central budget of another country or earmarked for a certain sector within the government's remit – like education or health (programme aid/sector support). General budget support can also involve donations to specific projects, like building a school in a district of the recipient country. *Multilateral aid* on the other hand is given from the government of a country to an international agency like the European Union (EU) or the United Nations (UN) and pooled with the other funds contributed to the multilateral agency for spending on development purposes. *Humanitarian* or *emergency aid* can be given by a country through multilateral channels or through the direct funding of national and international humanitarian organisations. Aid is also given by non-governmental organisations (NGOs) such as Trócaire, Oxfam and Save the Children, who are often funded by governments as well as receiving donations from the public. Aid from NGOs is often given to local civil society organisations in the recipient country. Later in the chapter the issue of aid effectiveness will be discussed; this is equally important for official bilateral donors – governments – and for NGOs.

The total global aid contribution from OECD countries for 2007 was US$103.7 billion. In absolute terms the United States of Amercia (USA), Germany, France, the United Kingdom (UK) and Japan contributed most in financial aid in 2007, with a combined total representing 63 per cent of total ODA. However, Norway, Sweden, Luxembourg, Denmark, and the Netherlands are the top donors relative to their countries' GNI (gross national income). To date these countries are the only states to meet the UN's ODA/GNI target of 0.7 per cent (www.results.org/website/article.asp?id=3558). Ireland, for example, is currently ranked as the sixth most generous donor amongst this group, spending €814 million on overseas development assistance (ODA) in 2007 (www.irishaid.gov.ie/latest_news.asp?article=1293). This represented 0.54 per cent of Ireland's GNI. Ireland is committed to the UN target of spending 0.7 per cent of its GNI on ODA by 2012. However, with the current economic downturn in the Irish and global economies, continued pressure on the government to reach this target remains a top priority for Irish civil society. While Ireland is currently on track to meet this commitment, most state donors are not and will need to make unprecedented strides to meet the 0.7 per cent target.

Reflections on Aid Delivery

In examining the aid system as we know it today, it is helpful to reflect upon how the present system evolved. When comparing the principles that guide the aid system of today with those of the 1990s, a significant difference has been in the progress made towards focusing on poverty reduction. However, the results of this poverty reduction focus have been slow to impact on human development figures and global poverty levels, with the United Nations' *Human Development Report* in 2007 stating that 22 countries in sub-Saharan Africa fell into the category of 'low human development', with almost half the world's population (3 billion people) (UN 2007) living on less than $2.50 a day (World Bank 2008).

The aid system of the 1990s consisted of a 'west knows best', top-down approach manifested in the relationships between Northern donors, international financial institutions (IFIs) and recipient governments in the global South. Structural adjustment programmes (SAPs), introduced in the late 1970s, created the paradigm that was to dominate global North–South financial relations until the 1990s, with the World Bank and the International Monetary Fund (IMF) implementing policy changes designed to reduce the fiscal imbalances of borrowing countries. Developing countries were asked to liberalise their markets and privatise their services in return for new or lower interest loans. Countries that failed to follow the advice of the IFIs were subjected to severe fiscal discipline. One of the many criticisms of SAPs was their lack of recipient-government participation and hence ownership of decisions made about their own development. Poverty reduction strategy papers (PRSPs) replaced SAPs to address this shortcoming, allowing governments to take more control of their economic development policies. This approach, while striving to be more participatory, was often seen to be flawed, with the development priorities of governments in some countries not being in line with priorities of civil society, often due to a lack of consultation (Trócaire 2006).

As well as moves away from structural adjustment, the aid architecture of the 1990s saw the introduction of the heavily indebted poor countries (HIPC) initiative, providing debt relief to least developed countries (LDCs). LDCs are those which, according to the United Nations, exhibit the lowest indicators of socioeconomic development, with the lowest Human Development Index (HDI) ratings of all countries in the world. To date, debt reduction packages have been approved for 33 countries, 27 of them in Africa, providing US$51 billion (in end-2007 net present value terms) in debt-service relief over time (IMF 2008). Strong social movements in the global South, e.g. Jubilee 2000, insisted that the aid architecture as it currently exists was no longer sustainable, with debt repayments in many countries amounting to more than expenditure on social services like health and education.

The current aid system often appears to be a contradiction in terms. On the one hand PRSPs and Joint Assistance Strategies (JASs) allow greater recipient-country participation in deciding how donors' support is used. On the other hand economic policy conditions which disregard the principle of ownership are also implemented. A report recently published by EURODAD, the European Network on Debt and Development, stated that more than two-thirds (71 per cent) of loans and grants advanced by the International Development Association (IDA), the World Bank's soft-lending arm, still have sensitive policy reforms attached to them as conditions. The majority of these are privatisation-related conditions. The report also found that as a share of overall conditionalities, economic policy conditions have at best remained unchanged and at worst gone up slightly – now constituting a quarter of World Bank conditionalities in poor countries (Eurodad 2007). While conditions relating to fiduciary responsibility are essential to ensure transparency for both donors and Southern governments, the imposition of economic policy conditions negates any other attempts by donors to respect recipient-country ownership.

A series of international conferences of the 1990s, and their broken promises, contributed to a general lack of confidence in the global-aid architecture and its institutions. In 2007 global overseas development assistance (ODA), excluding debt relief grants, amounted to US$103.7 billion. However, ODA has only risen at half the rate required to meet the Group of Eight (G8) and UN summit targets by 2010. The pledges made at these summits, combined with other commitments, implied that aid needed to be increased from US$80 billion in 2004 to US$130 billion in 2010 (at constant 2004 prices). If all current projections are taken into account there will be a donor aid deficit of US$34 billion by 2010 (Richelle 2008). Also, despite the agreements made by the G8 at Gleneagles, development aid for Africa has not increased by one dollar from 1995 (Bhattacharya 2007).

The millennium development goals (MDGs) are the overarching goals that defined the shifting aid architecture going into the twenty-first century. While flawed and highly ambitious, these goals represent a step towards a concrete, time-bound commitment to the implementation of economic, social and cultural rights and development goals, as set out in the UN conventions and summits of the 1990s. They were eventually agreed in September 2000. The multidimensional nature of the goals make them an important step beyond the use of economic growth as an indirect measure of poverty reduction. However, the goals are seen as being the 'ultimate solution' in international development and policymaking. This poverty eradication focus, while welcome, risks sidelining other already existing global standards, like human rights norms, in order to achieve the MDGs by 2015. The goals have removed the politics from development, focusing instead on a technical agenda of targets, facts and figures; a similar mistake was made by the 2005 Paris Declaration on Aid Effectiveness (Trócaire 2005).

Measuring the Impact of Aid

In developed countries, taxpayers are asking questions about the destination and impact of ODA. The public wants to be reassured that overseas aid is not being misspent or used for corrupt purposes. Donors and non-governmental organisations (NGOs) now have to show the impact of their work and how they are spending funds in developing countries. Assessing the impact of aid involves monitoring and evaluating the delivery of humanitarian objectives attached to aid delivery. Showing the impact of development assistance will be regarded as increasingly important by the public as well as government departments as they come under pressure during the increasingly challenging and uncertain economic climate.

The nature of measuring the impact of aid has changed from a decade ago, when donors focused their attention on whether the aid they provided succeeded in achieving their immediate goals, e.g. a school built, a teacher trained. The focus is now on how aid is affecting people's lives, and its contribution to poverty reduction. This is a far less tangible impact to measure and document, providing a significant challenge to donors and NGOs alike. With the lack of sufficient data from recipient countries and the difficulty of attributing development successes solely to aid as opposed to many other possible factors, it is difficult to measure the impact of aid within specific timescales in the recipient countries. For example, how could we measure the absence of aid in specific communities? These are just some of the factors which make assessing the impact of aid a challenging undertaking for donors and NGOs alike (Irish Aid 2008, pp.9–10). However great this challenge is, it is one that donors and NGOs must rise to. Donors and NGOs must also communicate the complexity and long-term nature of sustainable development and poverty reduction to their supporters.

The Aid Effectiveness Agenda

Questioning the efficacy of aid brings us to the aid effectiveness agenda, being deemed by some as the new paradigm for aid. Aid effectiveness refers to the process, led by the Organisation for Economic Co-operation and Development (OECD), to improve the effectiveness of the delivery of aid from OECD Development Assistance Committee (DAC) donors to recipient countries. The effective delivery of the MDGs is dependent on the requisite funds being available and the political will behind them. However, any increase in the quantity of aid must happen in tandem with an increase in its quality. Dissatisfaction with the inefficiencies of the old aid architecture has led to the aid effectiveness agenda, which strives to address some of the bottlenecks that have reduced the effectiveness of aid in the past and continue to do so.

From a civil society perspective the aid effectiveness agenda centres on addressing the power imbalance that exists within the current aid architecture. In the financial 'partnership' that exists between rich donor countries and recipient governments, power lies with the donor. Donors are in a position to demand certain policies and practices in return for aid, penalising recipients by withholding aid if these conditions are not met. Accountability in the current aid system flows upwards, with Southern governments accountable to donors, as opposed to being accountable to their own citizens on whose behalf aid is accepted.

The Paris Declaration, signed in 2005 by almost 100 signatories, including partner governments, bilateral and multilateral donor agencies, regional development banks and international agencies, aimed to redress the power imbalance and reverse the direction of accountability flows. In order to achieve this, the Paris Declaration aimed to put Southern governments in the driving seat, taking ownership of their own development and the aid provided to achieve it. An OECD-led process, the Paris Declaration was a significant step towards defining a common official agenda to improve the quality of aid. Many donors and Southern governments made a real commitment to improving how the aid system is implemented. Guided by five principles: ownership, harmonisation, alignment, mutual accountability and managing for results, the Declaration uses indicators, timetables and targets to measure donor and developing countries' progress in making aid more effective (Trócaire 2008).

A central problem however remains the architecture. As with the MDGs, the Paris Declaration is contributing to the depoliticisation of aid. The politics of aid have been removed in favour of a solely technical agenda. Donors are concentrating on the technical realities of development assistance, leading to an approach that tries to increase the *efficiency* of the delivery of aid, yet which will not necessarily lead to an increase in the *effectiveness* of aid. Delivering aid effectively and efficiently should be seen as only one part of a holistic vision of development and social justice, and one contributing element towards achieving development effectiveness. Indicators for development effectiveness should include the realisation of human rights, gender equality and environmental sustainability – which are 'the fundamental cornerstones for achieving good development results' (UNDP 2007).

The implementation of the Paris Declaration was reviewed for the second time in Accra, Ghana in September 2008, at the High Level Forum (HLF) on Aid Effectiveness. According to the monitoring report from 2005 to late 2007, progress against the targets of the declaration has been extremely slow (OECD 2008). The Accra Agenda for Action (AAA), the communiqué signed in Accra, sets out the roadmap for donors and partner governments between 2008 and 2010. While all such communiqués remain aspirational until they are implemented, some progressive language was agreed upon in the AAA. However, negotiators could not make progress on technical issues – such as tied aid, the use of technical assistance and the imposition of economic policy conditions by donors – during their deliberations. *Tied aid* refers to the tying of aid to the procurement of goods and services from donor countries, which can inflate the cost of aid by up to 30 per cent. This form of aid benefits firms and consultants from donor countries and reduces the freedom of partner governments to use aid for their own poverty reduction priorities. More powerful donors, such as the USA, Japan and the World Bank, held firm and blocked any attempt to make progress on more effective agreements on these issues. Progress made in implementing the Accra Agenda between 2008 and 2010 will be monitored, and a new declaration will be written. While civil society organisations were not consulted during the drafting of the first declaration, they have to date made their presence felt during the implementation and monitoring of the Paris Declaration, and are now well placed as recognised development actors in their own right, to ensure that the next declaration focuses on the achievement of development effectiveness rather than simply aid effectiveness.

Civil society has a hugely significant role to play in helping official donors and partner governments achieve the targets of the Paris Declaration. Indeed, without the proactive support and involvement of civil society it is unlikely that the aims of the declaration will be met. Globally, civil society's role in ensuring the accountability of governments to their citizens is a vital expression of democratic citizenship. This cannot be overlooked in the current debate and in the context of increasing aid flows. It is imperative that the space for civil society and parliaments to monitor the activities of governments and hold them to account is maintained and expanded. Without this, progress on good governance and anti-corruption will be limited (Trócaire 2008).

Implications for Civil Society

What are the implications of the aid effectiveness agenda for civil society? The aid effectiveness agenda involves moving to a shared-ownership approach, which strives to shift the balance of power from donors to Southern governments. General Budget Support is the modality of aid delivery which is deemed to best suit this approach, allowing Southern governments to plan for their own development with aid monies flowing into their central and sector budgets. However, with aid money being directed more towards governments, and donors attempting to be more harmonised – in line with the principles of the Paris Declaration – there is evidence to show that civil society organisations (CSOs) funding may be excluded from the process.

In some cases there is evidence that pooled donor funding is creating competition between local CSOs and international NGOs. It is also difficult for local CSOs to work through government systems to access funding. These systems are bureaucratic and laborious and may not favour certain thematic areas prioritised by local CSOs (CIDSE–Caritas 2007). The possible instrumentalisation of CSOs is another feature of GBS and donor harmonisation which must be considered and avoided. CSOs must be allowed to maintain their autonomy while sourcing funding from their governments. It is imperative that international NGOs should not occupy the space or funding opportunities available to local CSOs. Prior to the High-Level Forum on Aid Effectiveness in Accra, pressure was being placed on CSOs to align themselves to the principles of the Paris Declaration, due to the perceived fragmentation within the civil society community as well as that of official donors. At the end of June 2008 more than 70 civil society delegates, representing a rich diversity and large constituency of CSOs from both developed and developing countries, gathered in Paris to take up the challenges of CSO effectiveness in development. These CSOs decided that the Paris principles did not apply to them, due to their diversity and uniqueness, and also because the declaration was designed by governments for governments without any input from civil society. Subsequently, a global two-year Open Forum for CSO Development Effectiveness was launched, which will run from January 2009 to December 2010. This process aims to develop a set of 'development effectiveness' principles rather than 'aid effectiveness' principles to guide the work of CSOs. This process has been recognised in the AAA and governments have welcomed the invitation by civil society to engage with them in this process (see www.cso-effectiveness.org).

Too Many Cooks?

In the context of the worsening global financial crisis, the IFIs have lost much of their significance, credibility and reach. Many developing countries have repaid their loans to the International Monetary Fund (IMF) ahead of schedule, leaving the institution with a US$103 million budget shortfall in 2007. Due to the burdensome conditions imposed by that same institution these countries have stated that they will not be going back to the fund for future assistance (Halifax Initiative 2007). However, as the global financial crisis evolves and solutions are sought, these previously severed ties with the IFIs may be reconsidered by some countries. In the case of the World Bank, certain institutions have raised questions about the integrity of their research (Bretton Woods Project 2007), and there is evidence that many of the economic policy conditions imposed on recipient countries have had detrimental effects on the most marginalised populations (Eurodad 2007).

Some Latin American countries have turned their back on money offered by the Bretton Woods Institutions (the World Bank and the International Monetary Fund), favouring loans of capital raised from their own regions. The Banco del Sur (Bank of the South) was established in December 2007 by seven Latin American countries (Argentina, Bolivia, Brazil, Ecuador, Paraguay, Uruguay and Venezuela) as a response to a growing consensus in the region that the economic reforms demanded by the IFIs have not been positive for the region and that change is needed. However, those that have formed the Bank of the South face the challenge of what kind of institution they want it to be if it is to represent a credible alternative to the IFIs. Similarly in Asia, the Chiang Mai Initiative (CMI) came into being in 2000, following the currency crisis of 1998. The CMI was an alternative to what was deemed to be damaging advice given by the IMF to the region. It was seen to be a new mechanism that could quickly disburse short-term liquidity support to countries as a first line of defence against economic crises. The solution was to be found from within the region rather than from the IFIs.

The aid system has also become a lot more crowded in recent years, with new players such as private foundations, non-DAC bilateral donors, such as China, Brazil and India, and sector-specific vertical programmes emerging. All these new players have contributed to a much more fragmented aid system than previously experienced. For example, the contribution of vertical funds, such as the Global Fund to Fight AIDS, Tuberculosis and Malaria, the Global Alliance for Vaccines and Immunisation (GAVI), and the President's Emergency Plan for AIDs Relief (PEPFAR), accounted for approximately 10 per cent of Country Programmable Aid (CPA) for the period 2003–06 (Eurodad 2008).

China has committed to doubling its aid to Africa to US$1 billion per annum by 2009, and this aid is given with a 'no political strings attached' policy (www.worldpress.org/africa/2554.cfm). This policy has seen China giving aid to repressive regimes/elites not working in the interests of the poor or for development in countries with questionable human rights records, such as Sudan, Zimbabwe, and the Democratic Republic of the Congo. This makes China an attractive source of aid for many African countries, owing to its lack of conditionalities compared with aid from the IFIs. However, China has been criticised for its use of tied aid, in that the disbursement of its aid is dependent on the use of Chinese labour and resources, inhibiting local employment, incomes and capacity building. There is also a fear that the debt cancellations granted in the last couple of years through the heavily indebted poor countries (HIPC) initiative will be undermined by the substantial increase of loans from China, resulting in another debt crisis. However, China's approach to aid delivery and investment makes it a significant counterweight to the power blocs of the USA and Europe, and promises to alter the global structure of power, now and in the future.

Despite the proliferation of new players in the aid architecture and the fall from grace of some of the older players, loopholes in the system allow vast sums of money, which completely dwarf ODA, to flow from Southern to Northern countries. This is primarily facilitated by a lack of transparency in the financial system and the inability of today's financial architecture to regulate global financial flows effectively. Figures quoted by the World Bank estimate that illicit capital flows result in an outflow of US$500–800 billion a year from developing countries – that is, around $10 flowing out for every $1 of aid flowing in. It is also greater than the US$240 billion in foreign direct investment (FDI) and the remittances transferred to developing countries from migrants in the developed world (World Bank 2007).

With the aid system in flux, sustainable and predictable resources for development need to be generated which will grow independently of the whims of the next finance minister in any given country. The Financing for Development Conference (FfD) in Doha in December 2008 sought to review the implementation of the Monterrey Consensus, signed in 2002 to determine the new initiatives that would be necessary to meet the increasingly compromised MDGs. Follow-up international conferences on Financing for Development are expected to review the implementation of the Monterrey Consensus. The 2008 review conference addressed progress made, reaffirmed goals and commitments, and shared best practices and lessons learned. Innovative sources of financing development, which make up one element of the FfD conference agenda, may be more popular in the years to come if taxpayers' money is not as readily available for ODA. For example, the Leading Group on Solidarity Levies for Development, now comprising more than 50 countries, has developed a new levy on airline tickets and a new drug purchasing agency, UNITAID, to lower the costs of HIV/AIDs, tuberculosis and malaria drugs for citizens in the developing world.

The Leading Group has its origins in a joint declaration on hunger and poverty made by the former French president, Jacques Chirac, and President Lula da Silva of Brazil at the United Nations in September 2004. The levy has raised US$200–300 million dollars per year so far and its growth potential continues (Halifax Initiative 2007). The Currency Transaction Tax (CTT), if adopted, is predicted to yield $33.41 billion per annum additional to ODA targets (North–South Institute Briefing 2008). The FfD agenda also looks at mobilising domestic resources for development. There is huge potential for countries in mobilising domestic resources for development through national taxes, making them more accountable and more responsive to their own citizens.

There is no doubt that the financial crisis will have implications for all nations of the world. The IFIs have not coped well with the economic downturn and are now facing an overhaul not seen since their establishment in 1944. Civil society is in favour of this overhaul and indeed has been calling for it for decades. A new system must be able to deliver sustainable growth that will make the world more equal, eliminate extreme poverty and face up to the challenges of the coming decades. This system will require in turn a set of global-governance institutions and decision-making processes that are inclusive and participatory, and in which the voices of developing countries are given a far greater say.

Conclusion

Over the coming years, emerging economies like China, India and Brazil will be playing a prominent role in aid policy and practice, as will the vertical funds like the Global Fund and GAVI, and we may be seeing less of the Bretton Woods institutions. The key challenges facing development today and in the future include the need for fundamental structural change in order to reach the goals of poverty eradication and equality. Structural change is needed, not just in the global financial architecture, but also within governments in the global North and South. Change is needed in the structures that underpin and perpetuate social injustice, inequality and poverty. In the absence of full policy coherence by Northern governments, ensuring their policies do not undermine development efforts, progress will be too slow for those that need it most. Progress is also needed in trade reform, resolving sovereign debt problems, meeting the UN ODA targets and increasing the quality of aid. Also central to the effectiveness of aid is the operation of effective and transparent political and economic systems in recipient countries. These institutions need to ensure that public resources are used for poverty eradication and that democratic accountability and transparency are increased to enable citizens to hold their governments to account for the use of their own resources.

Many of the targets of the aid effectiveness agenda, if met, would go a long way towards improving the aid system for the benefit of its recipients in the global South and proving its effectiveness to tax payers in the global North. Change can be frustratingly slow and we often expect positive development results too fast from our partners in the South, having experienced development results in the North over decades. The people and politics must be brought back into the equation if we are to learn from our past mistakes and create a more positive future.

References

Bhattacharya, Amar (2007) 'Keynote Speech: The Changing Face of Global Development Finance', Intergovernmental Group of Twenty-Four, February, Ottawa.

Bretton Woods Project (2007) 'Briefing: Knowledge Bankrupted: Evaluation Says Key World Bank Research "Not Remotely Reliable"'. January.

CIDSE–Caritas (2007) 'Changing Dynamics and Strategies in Cooperation and Partnership for Sustainable Funding between Local Actors in the Field of Development', Europa Regional Seminar, November, Arusha, Tanzania.

Eurodad (2007) *Untying the Knots: How the World Bank is Failing to Deliver Real Change on Conditionality*, November, Eurodad, Brussels.

Eurodad (2008) *Reality Check: Global Vertical Programmes*, August, Eurodad, Brussels.

Halifax Initiative (2007) *Changing Face of Global Development Conference Report*, Halifax Initiative Conference, Ottawa. www.halifaxinitiative.org/index.php/past_events/Changing_face_of_GDF

IMF (2008) Factsheet, *Debt Relief under the Heavily Indebted Poor Countries (HIPC) Initiative*. www.imf.org/external/np/exr/facts/hipc.htm

North–South Institute Briefing (2008) *The Currency Transaction Tax: A Bold Idea for Financing Development*. www.nsi-ins.ca

OECD (2008) *2008 Survey On Monitoring the Paris Declaration: Effective Aid By 2010? What It Will Take*. http://siteresources.worldbank.org/ACCRAEXT/Resources/Full-2008-Survey-EN.pdf

Richelle, Koos (2008) 'Keynote Address: The Aid Effectiveness Puzzle', DG EuropeAid, October, European Commission, Maastricht.

Trócaire (2005) *More than a Numbers Game? Ensuring the Millennium Development Goals Address Structural Injustice*, Trócaire, Maynooth.

Trócaire (2006) Policy paper, *Strengthening Participation for Policy Influence*, September, Trócaire, Maynooth.

Trócaire (2008) *Briefing Paper: Ireland Using its Influence for Positive Change in Accra*, April, Trócaire, Maynooth.

UN (United Nations) (2007) 'Photo Finish between Iceland and Norway to Top Human Development Ranking', press release, 27 November. http://hdr.undp.org/en/media/LP1-HDR07-HDIPR-E_final.pdf

UNDP (2007) *Civil Society and the Aid Effectiveness Agenda, Linking the Paris and FfD Processes*, United Nations, New York.

World Bank (2007) *Global Development Finance*, World Bank, New York.

World Bank (2008) *Development Indicators*, World Bank, New York. www.globalissues.org/article/26/poverty-facts-and-stats

Websites

Bretton Woods Project	www.brettonwoodsproject.org
European Network on Debt and Development	www.eurodad.org
Halifax Initiative	www.halifaxinitiative.org
Human Development Report	www.hdr.undp.org/en/
Millennium Development Goals	www.un.org/millenniumgoals/
Open Forum for CSO Effectiveness	www.cso-effectiveness.org
Paris Declaration	www.oecd.org
Trócaire	www.trocaire.org
UN Doha Index	www.un.org/esa/ffd/doha/index.htm

5

IS TRADE AN AGENT OF DEVELOPMENT?

Denis O'Hearn

Mainstream economists have always proposed that trade is an important agent of development (defined as economic growth) as long as it is the 'right kind' of trade. Ironically, the 'right kind' of trade always seems to result in excluding the poorer regions from trading in goods that compete with the most profitable products from richer regions. Rather, they always seem to end up producing and trading commodities that the richer regions either need or desire in exchange for products that the richer regions produce and control. Yet, despite this apparent inequity, economic theory has always produced mechanisms whereby regions that follow them should expect to achieve economic development and modernity. They also produce analyses that explain the continuing poverty of certain regions by their failure to follow the right macroeconomic policies, primarily policies of *free trade* and fiscal restraint. This has been especially but not exclusively true of the most recent phase of globalisation, characterised by the so-called Washington Consensus.

Economic Theory, Trade and Development

The earliest arguments to this effect were the Ricardian models of *comparative advantage*. These were static models which simply proposed that each country or region should focus production on commodities it could produce most cheaply, and then traded with other regions for items its people needed or desired. The classic example was where two regions (say, Britain and Portugal) produced two goods (cloth and wine, representing clothing and nourishment). Both countries could produce both goods. But, since Portugal could produce wine more cheaply, while Britain was especially efficient in producing cloth, both countries would be better off if Portugal produced only wine and Britain only cloth, and then each traded for what they did not produce. Significantly, Ricardo argued that specialisation was advantageous even if Britain could produce *both* wine and cloth more cheaply, but the differential was greater in cloth.

There were three basic problems with this model of comparative advantage. The first was that it was static. There was no conception that in the long run regions might be advantaged by developing alternative skills or productive capabilities, even if they were presently at a comparative disadvantage in these areas of production. Thus, the conception of comparative advantage is ahistorical. Portugal could enhance its economy over the long term if it enhanced its production of cloth for trade instead of just concentrating on its current competitive advantage in wine. The more recent concept of *competitive* advantage suggests how a country or region might *develop* its abilities to compete in certain products, especially those that are most desired in the world economy, technologically advanced and, therefore, most profitable for those regions that dominate in their production (Porter 1990). Historically, we know that this was the basis of wealth generation and developed industries in West European countries (Senghaas 1985).

A second problem with comparative advantage was that, like most economic models, it had no conception of distribution. A region might trade for a basket of goods with a higher market value than it could produce domestically. But would this necessarily mean that its population is better off for having done so? To the contrary, the kind of political regime that is necessary to exploit a region's 'comparative advantage' may also be one that creates inequality and benefits a prosperous elite at the expense of the majority. Economics is not primarily concerned with this problem. When economists claim that a trading regime enhances a region's 'welfare' they are not referring to the social well-being of the majority in the region but to an abstract conception of overall 'welfare', with the prerequisite that resources must be allocated in an 'efficient' manner.

The third and perhaps most damaging problem with comparative advantage was that it failed to recognise the possibility of *unequal terms of trade*, in other words, certain regions might actually *exploit* other regions through trade. Specific products – for example, tropical resources and agricultural produce – might command prices that are far lower and, thus, disadvantageous compared to others (such as manufactured goods). Raul Prebisch and Hans Singer developed an analysis of international trade in 1950 that proclaimed a structural tendency for the terms of trade of developing countries to deteriorate in their dealings with industrial countries (Singer and Gray 1988, pp.395–403). In other words, countries of the South in trading with those of the North receive less than the full value for their primary goods, in exchange for overvalued manufactured products. Prebisch and Singer (and subsequent social scientists) empirically demonstrated that this was the model governing world trade during the twentieth century. And, analytically, they explained the basis of 'unequal terms of trade' by reference to differing conditions of demand for primary and manufactured products, the differential amounts of technology incorporated in the two sets of products, and the different conditions of labour (productive organisation and incomes) in the Northern and Southern hemispheres.

Accepting the thesis of unequal terms of trade leads one to conclude that the dynamic consequences of free-trade policies based on comparative advantage are (1) the accumulation of wealth in developed regions and (2) greater poverty in developing regions. Thus, trade would be an agent of development for the richer industrialised regions, but an agent of *underdevelopment* for the poorer, less industrialised regions of the world. Therefore, to reprise the earlier example, if Portugal continued to produce and trade only wine, while Britain *manufactured* and traded in cloth, unequal terms of trade would ensure that Portugal became poorer and Britain became richer. Moreover, if we bring global power into our analysis of trade, we can see that Britain or, later, the United States of America (USA), might use their global power to *ensure* that countries of the South continued to produce those products that commanded lower prices and lower profits. They might also use state power to assist transnational corporations (TNCs) to monopolise the most profitable products, which are, generally, the most high-tech industries (and, more recently, services).

The simple model of comparative advantage has, more recently, been developed by another model that replicates its outcomes – the maximum free movement of goods and money, and the regional production of local resources without government interference – but which has a more dynamic character. The Heckscher–Ohlin (H-O) model argues that each region's advantage arises from its relative factor endowments, that is, that a country should produce and trade in those products for which it is best endowed. Thus, countries with relatively abundant labour (countries of the South) should produce labour-intensive products while those with relatively more capital and technology (the North) should produce more technology-intensive products.

While H-O was superior to the Ricardian model, because it explained comparative advantage on the basis of differential endowments, it still suffered from a failure to recognise the historical pattern by which a country became 'endowed' with one factor of production or another. Mexico was not 'naturally' endowed with surplus labour, just as the USA was not 'endowed' with high technology. These conditions were developed over time through certain political and economic strategies. For now, it is sufficient to point out the apparent problem with H-O, which is that a country like Mexico is confronted with two different development paths. The first, preferred and prescribed by orthodox economists of the North, is to produce and trade labour-intensive products until such time as its relative factor endowments change and it moves into more capital-intensive lines of production. But if one accepted the possibility of unequal terms of trade, this path might lead Mexico into an underdevelopment trap, where it would perpetually trade undervalued labour-intensive goods for overvalued Northern products. Alternatively, Mexico could pursue a different development path (which, incidentally, was the historical path of the USA and Western Europe) by trying to *create* a different competitive advantage in higher-technology (thus, more profitable) modes of production.

For orthodox economists and economic policymakers, then, it was necessary to demonstrate that there was a dynamic process whereby *free trade could become an agent of development* by facilitating convergence between the richer and the poorer countries. It fell to Paul Samuelson to revive the connection between comparative advantage, free trade, and convergence between poorer and richer regions. Samuelson further developed the H-O model to 'demonstrate' (according to the orthodox parameters of his model) that specialisation and trade according to comparative advantage would naturally lead to convergence between the labour-intensive (poorer) and capital-intensive (richer) countries. *So long as there was free trade*, the North would export its relatively abundant capital to Mexico to mix with that country's cheap labour. Mexican labour would consequently become scarcer and the cost of labour would rise. In other words, free trade alone is an agent of convergence in incomes, factor prices and commodity prices between richer and poorer regions. One of the most important political aspects of Samuelson's analysis was the viewpoint that labour did not have to migrate in order for global incomes to equalise. It was sufficient for capital and goods to move freely. Maximum free trade would ensure global development and convergence without the need for large-scale movements of populations (a cynic might observe that this was quite convenient, since Southern people of colour were now replacing white Europeans as the major migrants into industrialised Northern countries) (Edwards 1985).

Policy Approaches

The orthodox economic approach is closely tied to the policy of free trade. Most current policy positions, from the USA right wing to European social democrats, clearly favour free trade and are vehemently opposed to protecting local markets against imports as an agent of development. The usual policy argument is that increased exports generate resources for developmental purposes, as well as the foreign exchange, to avoid foreign governmental debt. Thus, in theory it is not trade generally but *exports* that are the engine of growth and development. This model is often described as *export-led industrialisation* (ELI). It is argued that economic policymakers should strive to maximise export growth, and the best way to achieve this is through free trade.

There are, however, economists and social activists who, for developmental purposes, promote trade policies other than free trade. The traditional policy in this regard is *import-substitution industrialisation* (ISI). The argument here is that countries can upgrade their economic activities (in other words develop new *competitive advantages*) by protecting certain products, like basic manufactures and then machinery, until local producers are competitive enough to survive without protection. Another way to put it is that *infant industries* need protection from being competed out of business by mature firms from other countries, and trade policy (barriers to imports) is the most effective way to do this. A common argument against such protectionism is that there are no mechanisms to guarantee that protected infant industries will sufficiently mature to become competitive. Indeed, they are more likely to continue relying on protection for their profitability instead of innovating and becoming more efficient. For example, if there is political corruption in a country then local businessmen are likely to use their resources to ensure that politicians maintain trade protection for their industries.

Moreover, it may be possible to become competitive in a few lines of basic industry, during a period called *easy industrialisation*. But then it is much harder to *deepen* industrial development into more technically sophisticated lines such as machinery or high-tech products. If a country finds itself unable to deepen and produce resources that are necessary for basic manufacturing purposes – for example, to produce machinery to make cloth and not just to produce clothing – it will have to continue importing these necessary products and eventually incur trade deficits. This will, in turn, stop development dead in its tracks.

For some time, the arguments against ISI held sway within economics and in wider policy circles. More recently, however, the rapid growth of the East Asian economies has opened up a revived interest in some forms of trade protectionism for development. The refined protectionist argument is that countries should *strategically* or *selectively protect* certain key products, in a policy environment that encourages the producers of those products eventually to move into export. The Japanese car industry, for example, began by making cars for a tightly protected internal market. This market was not large enough for the car industry to become a major impetus toward sustained industrial growth, but the protective policies sustained the industry long enough for Japanese cars to become competitive. Then Japanese car makers entered the global market, with widely recognised successful consequences. Similar arguments have been made about the success of the South Korean electronics industry. The key point here is that protection is not sufficient to sustain industry in itself. A *developmental state* must also have a kitbag of economic incentives and sanctions that will guide local industries toward efficiency and export-orientation. Thus, the period since the 1970s saw the revival of interest in policies of *protection for export*.

Sociological Approaches

The sociology of development, as opposed to orthodox development economics, bases its analysis of trade and development largely on empirical observations of actual cases of 'successful developers' (like the recent East Asian states mentioned above or late-nineteenth-century European states) and less successful ones (too numerous to mention). Rather than basing its analysis on abstract models, this approach begins by observing and analysing actual political–economic institutions and actors. Thus, sociologists are more likely than economists to assume that capitalist markets are and will inevitably be controlled and distorted by states and corporations – the major agents of economic power.

Moreover, as corporations have enhanced their wealth and power, and attained global reach, their ability to influence and manipulate markets has become more profound. States, too, attained global reach and began to organise *inter-state institutions*, such as the World Bank and the International Monetary Fund (IMF). It was no accident that the British state sponsored its leading manufacturers by protecting trade in machinery during the so-called classical era of free trade in the nineteenth century. More recently, the ultimate institutional sponsor of free trade – the World Trade Organisation (WTO) – has made it a priority to protect *intellectual property*. In doing so, it protects the most profitable products of the world's large TNCs from the competitive environment of free trade, since their products are based on 'intellectual property'. Even if this were not the case, however, a strong argument could be made that 'free trade' is not really 'free' because such a high proportion of products that are traded across international borders are actually exported by one subsidiary of a TNC to another. As far back as the 1970s, a fifth of US exports and a third of imports comprised intra-firm trade, that is, exports of one subsidiary to another within a single company (Jenkins 1987, p.115). Intra-firm trade has undoubtedly risen during the 1990s and into the twenty-first century along with new forms of agglomerated investment that emerged during that time.

The importance of this manipulation of trade is the degree to which, as the *world-system approach* argues, international inequality is the product of a world-wide division of labour, in which certain (core) regions produce the most high-tech, high-profit products while other (peripheral) regions produce the most labour-intensive and lowest-profit products. This unequal division of labour expresses itself in two ways. First, certain poor regions largely specialise in primary products that command lower relative prices in international trade. Second, the world economy is made up of a series of *commodity chains*, in which the lower-profit stages of production (extraction, basic assembly) are concentrated in poorer peripheral regions, while the higher-profit stages of production (research, product development, high-tech production) are concentrated in richer industrialised regions. The increasing complexity of this division of labour causes the increased movement of goods between different modes of these commodity chains in international trade (Gereffi and Korzeniewicz 1994). Various parts of a car or computer may be produced in Malaysia, Mexico, South Africa, Britain or Ireland for final consumption in Germany or the USA, with each stage of production involving the importing of parts and resources, and exporting of semi-fabricates and final products.

The extent to which large corporations control this trade form hardly designates it as 'free' in the classical sense. It is more comparable to a cross-border version of central planning, although the planning board is a corporate board of directors rather than an arm of the state. The prices at which a computer or pharmaceutical TNC sells parts or chemicals from one subsidiary to another are not determined by 'the global market', but rather by corporate accountants whose business is not 'efficiency' but increasing profit margins in areas such as tax avoidance and the protection of technology.

Paths of Development

Students of imperialism have analysed the development of the worldwide division of labour through successive stages of colonialism (Magdoff 1969; also Wallerstein 1983). They have attempted to support the view that the interests of the core regions, whether in mercantilism or industrialism, have helped to mould, reproduce and reshape this division of labour and its constituent commodity chains. The extent to which regions are incorporated into this global regime of production and trade is crucial to their development possibilities and determines how trade impacts on their development. There are three broad regional developmental outcomes arising from commodity chains, although these may change over time or may be combined in a given region. For the most *peripheral* regions, the main outcome is marginalisation into the restricted production of primary goods, which are traded at terms that are insufficient to draw the region out of poverty. For the most advantaged *core* regions, a large proportion of local production is in products that incorporate large amounts of technology and 'intellectual property', so that exports are profitable and trade becomes an engine of (further) development. Regions at a stage of development between the core and the periphery have sufficiently profitable activities in intermediate modes of global commodity chains leading to export to enable them to maintain incomes substantially better than the marginalised primary exporters. Yet few of these regions ever catch up with the high-tech exporters in the core regions.

A region's location in the three broad productive and trading positions – which world-systems analysis has named the *core* (richest regions), the *periphery* (poorest regions), and the *semi-periphery* (intermediate) – is not a matter of chance or 'endowment', but one of historical development. Some critical analysts would go so far as to propose that regions can be 'locked in' to historical paths that either enable them to achieve further prosperity or make it more difficult for them to achieve upward mobility in the global divisions of labour (Arthur 1988; also Haydu 1998 and O'Hearn 2001). Empirical analysis has shown that there is relatively little movement between these regional positions, although mobility may appear fluid because of the attention given to upwardly mobile cases such as Western Europe, North America and, most recently, East Asia (Arrighi and Drangel 1986, pp.9–74).

The most marginal historical path to development is that of *export monoculture*, in which local farmers of a region become producers of a single crop for export. Some regions of west Africa, for example, are concentrated in the production of peanuts or cocoa for export. Central American regions are highly dependent on the production and trade in coffee beans. From the ahistorical point of view of orthodox economics, this is a 'natural' state of being: such regions are endowed with these products and have not yet developed their productive capabilities beyond a comparative advantage in such crops or extractive raw materials. Yet historical analysis shows that this is hardly a 'natural' state of affairs, but the result of how the region was incorporated into the world economy. McMichael, for example, in *Development and Social Change*, shows how a colonial division of labour was forced on such regions, breaking down their indigenous manufacturing industries and forcing the reduction of local production to export monoculture (McMichael 1996, pp.18–19; also Madeley 2000, pp.42–56). However, irrespective of how export monocultures were created, their salient feature remains the creation of a negative path dependency, in which overdependence on exports of a crop actually impedes the region's development. Farmers in a country like Guatemala can be offered reduced prices for their coffee beans even as the North American luxury coffee chains roast and sell them at record rates of profit. It becomes extremely difficult, if not impossible for the region to break out of its poverty trap and restricted pattern of trade, to the point that it may be plunged – as with the recent example of sub-Saharan Africa – further into poverty. Surely, this is an example of trade as an *agent of underdevelopment*.

The second historical path, that of the industrialised core, is in many ways the opposite of export monoculture. In this case, trade is almost certainly an agent of development (although these are the regions where it is least needed). In historical terms, perhaps the most interesting question about these regions is how they achieved such a position, in which trade became an engine of development. In other words, why are exports 'developing' rather than 'underdeveloping'? The transition of the major world powers to such a situation – e.g. the *hegemonic* states of Holland, Britain and the USA – may be generally explained by how they combined their overwhelming military power with new forms of economic organisation and means of sourcing raw materials to achieve global domination (See Arrighi 1994). But this is perhaps the least interesting historical path for other regions that simply want to achieve a higher degree of development. For such regions, more interesting cases include the small European states that achieved upward mobility during the latter half of the nineteenth century and the East Asian states (and possibly Ireland) which appeared to combine trade and development in the last decades of the twentieth.

The Scandinavian states provide some good case studies of upward growth within small regions (see Senghaas 1985). These small European countries, having been compelled to integrate into the world market, realised the gap that had opened up between them and the industrialised European core after the industrial revolution. But instead of continuing to adapt to an externally imposed division of labour, they developed the international competitiveness of their domestic infant industries. In particular, countries like Denmark encouraged broad-based agricultural revolutions and then used the gains from agricultural productivity to raise the average incomes of all of their economic sectors. This created a sufficiently robust internal market that was strong enough and, once protected against imports from the more powerful European countries, able to sustain domestic industrial products, especially with the specialised processing of local agricultural produce. While countries such as Denmark 'succeeded' in industrialising, through the use of strategic trade protectionism, other countries that accepted their narrow role of primary goods exporters to the rich European core (Ireland, Portugal, Spain, Romania) were further peripheralised and failed to industrialise.

Similarly, during the development of East Asian countries such as Japan, South Korea and Taiwan, according to analysts like So and Chiu these states did not follow neoliberal policies of free trade and free enterprise, but instead had 'a strategic role to play in taming international and domestic market forces and harnessing them to national ends' (So and Chiu 1995, p.12). For example, the South Korean state violated free-trade principles by extending subsidised credit and foreign exchange to its corporations, as long as they met targets for introducing new technologies and expanding exports. They also protected these companies against imports in local markets, with the proviso that they made satisfactory progress toward becoming strong exporters. Likewise, Taiwan violated free-trade prescriptions by protecting its key sectors from imports until its firms were able to compete in export markets. Despite neoliberal assertions that economic growth requires free enterprise and free trade, the experiences of East Asian economies appear to validate an alternative strategically protectionist approach.

The examples of Western Europe in the nineteenth century and East Asia in the twentieth appear to contradict the economic orthodoxy that favours free trade. They suggest that development is more likely to be achieved through strategic policies that include the protection of local economies. Free trade is an agent of further development only *after* a country or region has made the initial shift into competitive advantage in high-profit industrial products. Therefore, a country benefits from free trade after it has achieved upward mobility in the global division of labour from peripheral modes of production to core production and export.

But there is a recent third example that many experts believe to be a prototype of the benefits of free trade in the new globalised economy. Ireland is widely argued to illustrate the fact that free trade *is* an agent of development because it became one of the most liberalised countries in the world while developing one of the most rapidly expanding economies during the 1990s and into the twenty-first century. At the end of the 1980s, the (southern) Irish economy was stagnant, unemployment was at a record high not exceeded anywhere in the European Union except possibly Spain, and the state was one of the most indebted in the world. By 1994, however, the Irish economy began to boom, with GDP growth rates rising to 5.8 per cent and remaining at least as high to the end of the decade and into the new millennium. Irish per capita national income, which had been barely 60 per cent of the EU average in 1988, reached the EU average a decade later. Irish rates of growth were so high in the 1990s, at least by EU standards, that a 1994 article in Morgan Stanley's *Euroletter* asked, only partly in jest, whether Ireland was now a 'Celtic Tiger', aping the high-growth economies of East Asia (Gardiner 1994, pp.9–21). However, the sources of Irish growth are still debated. Most economists credit Irish economic success to neoliberal policies of free trade, fiscal controls, social partnership agreements that ensured pay restraint and flexible labour, the accumulation of highly educated human capital, exchange rate stability, and a generally favourable macroeconomic environment. In this liberal environment, some economists argued, trade (especially exports) clearly became an agent of economic growth.

There are, however, good reasons for disputing the neoliberal interpretation of Ireland's economic growth (and the model it produced), not least the very particular circumstances pertaining to the Irish experience. It grew rapidly during the 1990s for several unique reasons that enabled it to attract a historically high proportion of US-based TNC investments into Europe. Just as the single European market opened up in the early 1990s, the USA was going through a record period of economic expansion. After severe cutbacks in foreign investment during the 1980s, the USA began to reinvest in Europe, particularly with a view to getting its exports into the new EU 'big market'. Ireland was the ideal bridgehead from which to launch these new investments. It had an English-speaking workforce prepared to accept low wages and work flexibly, because unemployment rates were so high. The unemployed included engineers who were trained to work in the information technology (IT) companies that were the backbone of US investments. Moreover, the Irish government was not only committed to liberal policies like free trade and free enterprise, but also willing to offer huge incentives to any company that would locate in Ireland. These incentives included government grants and, most crucially, a corporate tax rate that was by far the lowest in the EU (10 per cent, compared to 30–40 per cent elsewhere). When the Irish state attracted the computer giant Intel to Ireland in 1991, several major IT firms followed it into Ireland over the next few years.

It was this inflow of foreign investments that shifted value-added profits into Ireland to exploit its low tax rates and underpinned its subsequent rapid growth. The dominant overseas perception of Ireland's economy was that free trade had encouraged rapid export growth and had thus become an agent of development. But this unique set of circumstances could hardly be repeated in developing countries. This argument is supported by the fact that Ireland's economic growth was so rapid in the 1990s because its population was very low (3 to 3.5 million), and capturing 20 per cent of US investments in Europe could therefore have a significant effect on economic growth. US investments alone directly accounted for 50 per cent of Irish growth in the 1990s and an even greater share in the early 2000s. Britain, by comparison, captured *twice as much* of the US investment in Europe, but had a population 20 times greater. Far from this resulting in rapid growth, Britain simply sank further down the European league table of economic prosperity.

Perhaps the most conclusive evidence against Ireland as an example of trade-led development is the short life of the Celtic Tiger. By 2001 transnational corporations were beginning to disinvest from Ireland and economic growth was concentrated not in the tradable sectors but in building and construction, including land speculation. By the time the global credit crunch hit in 2008, the once-vaunted Celtic Tiger was falling into deep recession. Other countries, most notably in Latin America, which had followed the free-trading prescriptions of the Washington Consensus during the 1980s and 1990s, were already following strategies of regulation and regional co-operation. These strategies promised to counteract many real or perceived social problems that had accompanied the USA/IMF/World Bank-induced neoliberal policies following the debt crisis of the 1970s.

The Washington Consensus and the Anti-Washington Consensus

The most recent push for free trade came in the form of the so-called 'Washington Consensus', a term coined by the economist John Williamson to describe a package of policy prescriptions that were pushed by the USA and other Western governments along with the international financial institutions (IFIs), including the IMF, the World Bank and the WTO. This policy package gained force after the tremendous rise in debts experienced by poor governments following the oil crises and irresponsible lending policies of banks during the 1970s. Thereafter, the IMF and the World Bank gave heavily indebted poor countries aid to service their debts, but in return required them to sign structural adjustment programmes (SAPs) that included such policies as privatisation of state-owned concerns, liberalisation of trade restrictions, and reductions in government spending on social welfare.

By the 1990s, these and other neoliberal policies escalated into the Washington Consensus, whereby poor nations throughout the world were induced or compelled to join free-trade agreements and to further privatise concerns – including basic services such as water and gas. Further impetus for such neoliberalisation came with the establishment of the World Trade Organisation in 1995 and regional trade agreements such as the North American Free Trade Agreement (NAFTA) in and after 1994. The WTO attempted to enforce agreements such as the General Agreement on Trade in Services (GATS) – which opens national markets in public utilities, transport and communications to takeover by giant transnational corporations – and Trade-Related Intellectual Property Rights (TRIPS) – which protects the rights of transnational corporations to avoid competition and maintain high prices on products such as drugs and software. At the same time, with the support of the EU and the USA, the WTO launched the so-called Doha Development Round of trade negotiations, which aimed to lower trade barriers around the world and to increase global trade.

The USA had further plans to expand NAFTA into a Free Trade Area of the Americas, which would encompass the entire Western hemisphere. These plans, however, met local resistance throughout Latin America and the other Southern continents. Social movements successfully opposed the privatisation of public utilities, and early in the new millennium an anti-Washington Consensus had emerged among countries of Latin America, led by progressive governments in Brazil, Argentina, Venezuela, and (later) Bolivia, Nicaragua, Ecuador and Uruguay.

Simultaneously, the Doha round met with chronic problems, both from resistance by people and governments of the global South, and from the refusal of the USA to remove its own high subsidies on agricultural produce, which remain a substantial barrier to trade. Successive WTO meetings were shut down by protests and internal resistance by the poorer countries, and policies such as GATS were successfully challenged by popular protest and governmental resistance. In Bolivia, for instance, popular protests in Cochabamba and El Alto reversed the privatisation of gas and water, while the Brazilian and South African governments successfully resisted attempts by the big drug companies to restrict programmes to make anti-retroviral drugs widely available to citizens with HIV. By 2008, the Doha round and the Washington Consensus were generally in disarray. Although the US government continued to directly resist the most vociferous members of the anti-Washington Consensus (Venezuela and Bolivia) and to try to gain support from the more moderate governments (Brazil, Chile) for a more restricted form of neoliberalism, it was clear that the grander plans for global free trade that had emerged in the 1990s would at best be put on hold for some years to come (Beeson and Islam 2005, pp.197–219).

Conclusion

Whether exports are an agent of development or growth is highly dependent on the specific circumstances of a country. Historically, it appears that free trade is *not* an agent of development; rather, trade is an economic instrument, like many others, that must be carefully managed if a country is to achieve economic growth. In most historical cases, the policies that led to development were the antithesis of the free-trade policies that are being prescribed today by the world's leading international economic institutions. In countries where aggressive free-trade policies were imposed, the result was often a diminution in the well-being of large segments of the population, who lost even the most meagre safety nets in housing or health policies, while paying greater proportions of their incomes for basic necessities such as water and energy.

References

Arrighi, G. and J. Drangel (1986) 'Stratification of the World-economy: An Explanation of the Semiperipheral Zone', *Review*, vol.10, no.1, pp.9–74.
Arrighi, G. (1994) *The Long Twentieth Century*, Verso, London.

Arthur, W.B. (1988) 'Self-reinforcing Mechanisms in Economics', in P. Anderson, K. Arrow and D. Pines (eds), *The Economy as an Evolving Complex System*, Santa Fe Institute, Santa Fe.

Beeson, M. and Islam, I. (2005) 'Neo-Liberalism and East Asia: Resisting the Washington Consensus', *Journal of Development Studies*, vol.41, pp.197–219.

Edwards, C. (1985) *The Fragmented World: Competing Perspectives on Trade, Money and Crisis*, Methuen, London.

Gardiner, K. (1994) 'The Irish Economy: A Celtic Tiger?', *Ireland: Challenging for Promotion*, Morgan Stanley *Euroletter*, 1 August, pp.9–21.

Gereffi, G. and M. Korzeniewicz (eds) (1994) *Commodity Chains and Global Capitalism*, Praeger, Westport, Conn.

Jenkins, R. (1987) *Transnational Corporations and Uneven Development*, Methuen, London.

Haydu, J. (1998) 'Making Use of the Past: Time Periods as Cases to Compare and as Sequences of Problem Solving', *American Journal of Sociology*, vol.104, no.2, pp.339–71.

Madeley, J. (2000) *Hungry for Trade: How the Poor Pay for Free Trade*, Zed Books, London.

Magdoff, H. (1969) *The Age of Imperialism*, Monthly Review, New York.

McMichael, P. (1996) *Development and Social Change: A Global Perspective*, Pine Forge Press, Thousand Oaks, Calif.

O'Hearn, D. (2001) *The Atlantic Economy: Britain, the US and Ireland*, Manchester University Press, Manchester.

Porter, M.E. (1990) *The Competitive Advantage of Nations*, Free Press, New York.

Senghaas, D. (1985) *The European Experience*, Berg, Leamington Spa.

Singer, Hans and Patricia Gray (1988) 'Trade Policy and Growth of Developing Countries', *World Development*, vol.16, no.3, pp.395–403.

So, A. and S. Chiu (1995) *East Asia and the World Economy*, Sage, Thousand Oaks, Calif.

Wallerstein, I. (1983) *Historical Capitalism*, Verso, London.

Websites

Centre for Global Development	www.cgdev.org
GATT	www.ciesin.org
History of Economic Thought	http://cepa.newschool.edu/het/
International Trade Centre	www.intracen.org

Magazine of the International Trade Centre	www.tradeforum.org
McMaster History of Economic Thought	www.mcmaster.ca/economics/
Third World Network	www.twnside.org.sg
UN Trade and Development	www.unctad.org
World Development Movement	www.wdm.org.uk
WTO	www.wto.org

6

ILLEGITIMATE DEBT: AN 'UNFASHIONABLE' FINANCIAL CRISIS

Nessa Ní Chasaide

When the banking crisis hit the headlines in September 2008, the problem of 'irresponsible finance' became a source of discussion and serious concern in households all over the industrialised world. The panic and anger felt by many was due to the realisation of how vulnerable societies are to the power of big finance. The greed, incompetence and irresponsibility exposed at the heart of the financial sector were not news, however, to people living in countries of the global South. The national debt that people in these countries have been paying for generations largely results from grossly unequal and opportunistic relationships between lenders and borrowers.

The negative impact of the debt burden in the global South has been of crisis proportions. It has denied the developing world urgently needed resources that have been diverted into debt repayment rather than social and economic development. Yet the debt crisis has not been acted on with the speedy freeing up of resources in the way that this latest financial crisis has been tackled. This chapter sets out the controversy surrounding the international lending system and the debts that have arisen from this system in recent decades. It concludes by analysing the disastrous impact these debts are having on the development of countries in the global South.

The Origins of the Debt Crisis

During the 1970s the price of oil rose dramatically, resulting in the oil-exporting countries depositing billions of dollars in oil profits in European and United States (USA) banks. There was a reckless rush by these banks to lend to governments and other institutions in the global South in order to capitalise on these profits. Southern countries, many of which were newly independent, were eager to borrow this easily accessible money. During the 1980s, however, borrowing countries faced declining income from exports and falling commodity prices, increases in interest rates, and a reduction in the foreign reserves needed to undertake international financial transactions. These economic factors placed indebted countries under massive pressure to meet their debt repayment deadlines. In 1982, several Latin American governments, led by Mexico, announced an inability to repay their loans, and the prospect of widespread defaults on repayments caused panic in lending institutions. The response of the leading international financial institutions (IFIs) in tackling the crisis, led by the World Bank, the International Monetary Fund (IMF) and the Paris Club (which handles government-to-government lending negotiations), was to agree debt 'work-outs' between borrowers and lenders.

The work-outs resulted in new loans to indebted countries and longer repayment time frames. Alongside work-outs were agreements by borrowing countries to implement policy conditions, known as structural adjustment programmes (SAPs), formulated by the World Bank and the IMF. However, this new policy regime resulted in a cycle of debt rescheduling, defaults on repayments, and the failure or refusal by borrowers to implement SAPs (Carrasco 2007). The response by lenders to the crisis was one of debt rescheduling and the restructuring of economies rather than providing debt relief. However, by the late 1980s the escalating problems arising from the debt crisis were impossible to ignore, with lenders forced to acknowledge that many of the loans they had extended could not be repaid.

The USA-initiated response to defaulting loans – called the 'Brady Initiative' after the then US treasury secretary Nicholas F. Brady – was a series of voluntary debt reductions through debt relief initiatives implemented by commercial banks. While some countries secured a reduction in their debt repayments through these initiatives, the debt burden remained a hugely significant drain on resources from Southern countries. Structural adjustment had a devastating impact, which most acutely impacted on the lives of the most impoverished and vulnerable people in borrowing countries (SAPRI 2004; Hertz 2004; Bond 2006). Importantly, the World Bank and the IMF, in their management of the crisis, embedded their role in national policymaking in borrowing countries.

The Emergence of the International Debt Cancellation Movement

Despite the problems of underdevelopment arising from the 1980s debt crisis, the debt problem remains unresolved. By 2008 the combined debt of borrowing countries stood at US$2.85 trillion, up from US$1.3 trillion in 1990 (Eurodad 2008). As a result, the protest movement against debt imposition has grown significantly and become increasingly well organised. In the global South, non-governmental organisations (NGOs), trade unions, community groups and other social movements began to demand outright cancellation by lenders of their debts and an end to the overreaching role of the World Bank and the IMF in policy decision making in their countries. Similarly, activists in the global North began demanding, on the back of high-profile campaigns such as Jubilee 2000 and Make Poverty History, that their governments take action to end the massive debt burden. The arguments in favour of debt cancellation include: the counterproductive role of the lending system in undermining the impact of development aid; the fact that the global South has already repaid its debts many times over; and the fact that much of the debt is illegitimate. Each of these points is considered below.

Debt is Counterproductive

The massive amount of debt repayments from borrowing countries to lenders far outweighs the resources that they receive in aid. This has given rise to a highly counterproductive system in international development finance. Put simply, there is a 'hole in the bucket' of resources. While aid is being distributed to countries in the South, more funds are flowing out through debt repayments, thus undermining the potentially positive impact of aid spending. This has resulted in an absurd situation in which rich governments and institutions are giving badly needed resources to Southern countries through one channel and taking them back through another.

The Debt has already been Paid Many Times Over

Given the enormous size of the debt burden, much of it is in fact unpayable and places a level of unacceptable suffering on people in Southern countries, especially on the economically most vulnerable. Moreover, there is the wider role of Northern countries to consider, owing to their historic contribution to poverty and economic underdevelopment in the global South through colonialism – which significantly contributed to the need of Southern countries to look for loans in the first instance. As the former Tanzanian president, Benjamin Mkapa, stated, in support of the debt cancellation movement in 2005: 'I encourage you in your advocacy for total debt cancellation for poor countries because, frankly, it is a scandal that we are forced to choose between basic health and education for our people and repaying historical debt' (JDC 2008).

Evidence of the continuing impact of debt was revealed recently when Kenya spent 20 per cent of its national budget on debt repayments; this amounted to the combined total allocated to six government ministries – health, water, agriculture, roads, transport and finance (ibid.). Moreover, the debts of the global South have been rescheduled innumerable times due to the incapacity of indebted countries to repay. This has resulted in much higher transfers of payments to lenders than was initially intended through the interest on loans. For example, in 2005 Nigeria owed US$34 billion on original loans of US$17 billion (Carrasco 2007).

The Debt is Fundamentally Unjust

The fact that many lenders have benefited economically from debt rescheduling points to vested interests in lender–borrower relationships. This is why debt cancellation campaigners view this problem as a matter of justice in global North–South relationships rather than a purely financial issue. Many repaid loans, and loans still awaiting payment, were irresponsibly extended for socially and environmentally damaging projects or initiatives that were never realised. Loans sometimes resulted in human rights abuses when used for purchasing armaments or were offered on unfair terms with damaging policy conditions attached. A particularly damaging loan was that extended to the Philippines in the 1970s to finance the building of a nuclear power plant on the Bataan peninsula. The project contract was awarded to a US company and was riddled with corruption, went wildly over budget and ultimately was never completed. The Bataan plant did not open owing to major safety concerns, since it had been built near an earthquake faultline (Christian Aid 2007, p.15).

The World Bank and other lenders have supported similarly disastrous projects, such as the Camisea Gas Project in Peru, which caused ecological devastation and the spread of infectious diseases among the people there (Amazon Watch 2007). Lending programmes were often devoid of considerations about human rights and the social and economic welfare of citizens in the borrowing countries – as in the case of the lending by the USA, the World Bank and the IMF to President Mobutu of Zaire (now called the Democratic Republic of the Congo – DRC) in the 1970s and 1980s. Loans amounting to billions of dollars were extended to Mobutu's corrupt administration and were sequestered for his own purposes rather than benefiting the people of his country.

The people of DRC continue to pay off a debt amounting to US$9 billion resulting from these bad loans (Watkins 2008).

Debt Audits

Is it the responsibility of the borrower or the lender in circumstances in which loans do not benefit their intended target group? In attempting to answer this question, Jubilee South (a network of Southern debt cancellation campaigns) has called for people in Southern countries to carry out national level 'debt audits' in order to establish the circumstances of loan giving and which loans their governments should repay and which they should not. Borrowing governments should clearly only accept loans that they can afford to repay and that will benefit their countries. But equally clear is the fact that lenders should not extend loans based on unfair terms that will overextend the borrower or that have political and economic conditions attached. Nor should lending practices support activities that will not benefit the people of the borrowing country. Lenders should not pressure impoverished countries in any way to accept unwanted loans or loans that they would clearly be unable to repay. In attempting to prevent damaging lending practices, social justice activists in impoverished countries are working to hold their own governments to account for bad loans accepted on their behalf. Similarly, activists in the global North are working to ensure that their governments support the cancellation of all illegitimate debts and prevent irresponsible lending to Southern countries. At present, debt cancellation coalitions are calling on Northern governments to support an inquiry into lending practices and the debts owed by Southern countries to lending institutions, particularly the World Bank and the IMF.

The Current Situation with Debt Cancellation

The debt cancellation movement has had some success in shifting political positions on the debt issue, with official debt relief initiatives established in 1996, 1999 and 2005, at least in part as a result of popular pressure. However, none of these measures has addressed the fundamental problem and in some cases they may have exacerbated the debt burden faced by poor countries. The most high-profile debt cancellation deal was that agreed by the Group of Eight leading industrialised countries (G8) in 2005, called the multilateral debt relief initiative (MDRI), which came at the height of the Make Poverty History campaign. This deal promised the cancellation of debts worth US$150 billion for up to 40 countries over 40 years; and, by the end of 2007, 22 countries had had debts cancelled to the value of US$42 billion. This sum was additional to the more than US$45 billion in debts cancelled through earlier agreements (JDC 2008). The developmental impact of these freed-up resources has yet to be fully evaluated, although real social benefits do appear to have resulted from these agreements. For example, since 2005, Malawi has secured 4,000 new teachers per year; Uganda has been able to abolish school fees, giving schooling opportunities to more that 5 million more children; in Tanzania the enrolments in primary school went up from 4.4 million in 2000 to 7.5 million in 2005; Mali has been able to pay for 5,000 new community teachers (JDC 2008). Notwithstanding global recession in 2009 and into 2010, debt relief must remain a focus for development. Jubilee Debt Campaign's report 'A New Debt Crisis?' states that '38 of the 43 countries that the World Bank calculates are most vulnerable to the economic crisis already required substantial debt cancellation before the current crisis, in order to meet the needs of their people'. Reforms of the global economy demanded by JDC include '[w]ider, deeper debt cancellation, amounting to at least $400 billion – a fraction of the bail-outs and stimulus packages recently proposed in the West' (JDC 2009, pp.4–5).

However, countries so far included in debt cancellation processes have also been subject to penalties through the implementation of World Bank and IMF policy conditions. These conditions were rooted in the debt cancellation decision-making process initiated by the World Bank and the IMF in 1996, the heavily indebted poor country initiative (HIPC). HIPC was a six-year process whereby national economies were analysed to determine their eligibility for debt cancellation based on their level of 'debt distress'. These countries then had to fulfil a set of economic policy changes in order to reach what was described as the 'HIPC completion point'. While there have been some amendments to how HIPC was implemented, many of the conditions attached to this process have had highly damaging consequences for indebted countries.

The World Bank and IMF practice of attaching mandatory policy conditions to debt relief initiatives is highly undemocratic, as it undermines the sovereign right of Southern countries to determine their own development paths. In addition, the policy prescriptions promoted by the IFIs have been highly controversial and have often been implemented with disastrous effects. In 2003, for example, the Tanzanian government privatised the water supply for Dar Es Salaam, the capital city, as part of a HIPC policy condition. This proved such a disaster that the government reversed the contract with the private company two years later (JDC 2006). It is important to note that while countries are implementing the economic restructuring required to fulfil these conditions they must continue paying their national debts regardless of the economic conditions prevailing there.

While the latest major debt initiative, the MDRI, provided outright debt cancellation for certain creditors, countries included in the deal have had to complete the full HIPC process before receiving debt relief. The MDRI targeted too few creditors and borrowing countries: the deal involved cancelling debts extended by three lenders – the World Bank, the IMF and the African Development Bank (ADB). However, the campaigning efforts of civil society groups resulted in the Inter-American Development Bank (IDB) agreeing in March 2007 to additional debt cancellation measures for some Latin American countries. A total of US$4.4 billion in debt cancellation was granted to Bolivia, Guyana, Haiti, Honduras and Nicaragua, but again, it is questionable as to how beneficial the deal actually will be to borrowing countries. The resources for this cancellation are to be drawn from the Fund for Special Operations (FSO) in the IDB, which means that the benefits derived from cancellation will be offset by cuts in cheap loans from the FSO to the same countries. This could mean losses of up to 25 per cent in concessional loans or aid designated for

Bolivia, Guyana, Honduras and Nicaragua (Eurodad 2007). There are similar concerns about potential reductions in aid to Southern countries, as the MDRI is funded by the International Development Association (IDA) of the World Bank. Borrowing countries may therefore not experience the financial windfall of debt cancellation, given the loss of much-needed aid. Moreover, the MDRI has excluded many low-income countries in desperate need of debt cancellation – such as Kenya, Bangladesh, Vietnam and Cambodia – from the debt relief facility.

There has been some progress on the issue of illegitimate debts, with greater recognition in official circles of the importance of illegitimate debt analysis. In 2006, for example, the government of Norway cancelled debts owed to it by five Southern countries, on the basis that it was 'co-responsible' as a lender in offering irresponsible loans (Abildsnes 2007). In a similar initiative in 2007, the government of Ecuador launched a national debt audit commission to examine the legitimacy, or otherwise, of its debts. The Ecuadorean commission is currently completing its report, with early indications suggesting that it will highlight massive irregularities in the loan contracts from international lenders. Both these cases represent major breakthroughs, which indicate that there are some governments willing to take courageous steps in questioning the prevailing orthodoxy of lender–borrower relationships.

However, even where limited victories are being secured on debt cancellation in the mutlilateral and bilateral arenas, new examples are emerging of exploitation of Southern countries in respect to debt. A particularly shocking practice that has arisen is that of opportunistic vulture funds that have launched legal actions against countries in the global South to recover debt. The recent example of Donegal International, the American commercial debt-collecting company – which sued the Zambian government in 2007 for an outrageous US$55 million to repay a loan of only US$3 million – demonstrates the unregulated and often immoral nature of the international lending arena (DDCI 2007).

The Other Side of the Coin: Responsible Financing

The practice of irresponsible lending raises the question of how to ensure responsible lending and borrowing in the future. Official bodies are far more comfortable discussing this issue than the issue of irresponsible lending in the past. This is partly due to the growing concern among traditional lenders of the impact of new lenders such as China or Venezuela, who have extended their own borrowing facilities to the Southern countries. Among these official initiatives is a G8 commitment made in 2007 to produce a responsible-lending charter in collaboration with the group of 20 Southern countries that emerged strongly at the WTO trade talks in Cancún in 2003. While civil society groups are concerned not to allow lenders to deflect attention from the historical irresponsibility in lending practices, they support the building of a set of standards that can underpin a responsible lending and borrowing relationship. Indeed, dialogue is needed both to resolve past injustices and to build a shared understanding on responsible financing standards. Efforts in this direction have already resulted in the formulation by the European Network on Debt and Development (Eurodad) of an important Responsible Finance Charter (Hurley 2008). Backed by the Commonwealth finance ministers from Cameroon, Ghana, Guyana, Malawi, Mozambique, Sierra Leone, Tanzania and Zambia at the Commonwealth HIPC finance ministers meeting held in Washington in April 2008, it outlines specific areas for action. The aim of the initiative is

> to provide guidance, fairness and certainties to borrower states and lenders as well as protect the citizens and environments of developing nations ... to ensure that terms and conditions are fair, that the loan contraction process is transparent, that human rights and environments of recipient nations are respected and repayment difficulties or disputes are resolved fairly and efficiently. (Hurley 2008, p.4)

Conclusion

Despite sustained protest from around the world, the crisis being lived through daily by people in the global South has largely been ignored by leaders of the developed world. Occasional piecemeal actions have not fully addressed the symptoms or the causes of the debt problem. The development non-governmental organisations (DNGOs) and coalitions campaigning on debt are calling on governments to take a proactive and principled role in promoting dialogue on the issue of illegitimate debts. Governments are encouraged to acknowledge creditor responsibilities in practising irresponsible lending and to urgently cancel illegitimate debts. Northern governments, with their international allies in multilateral bodies such as the EU, the World Bank and the IMF, should support the Responsible Finance Charter being promoted by Eurodad to ensure that *juster relationships* and *clearer standards* between lenders and borrowers can be agreed. The debt crisis in the global South demands urgent attention and action to remove the unfinished legacy of financial irresponsibility. Wealthy governments and financial institutions must take action and respond to the concerns of the debt cancellation movement. The alternative is to condemn another generation to bear the unacceptable burden of global inequality.

References

Abildsnes, K. (2007) 'Why Norway took Creditor Responsibility: The Case of the Ship Export Campaign', SLUG and the Norwegian Forum for Environment and Development.

Amazon Watch (2007). www.amazonwatch.org

Bond, P. (2006) *Looting Africa: The Economies of Exploitation*, Zed Books, London and New York.

Carrasco, E. (2007) *International Finance and Development*, University of Iowa, Iowa.

Christian Aid (2007) *Enough is Enough: The Debt Repudiation Option*, London.

DDCI (2007), 'Stop the Vultures Undermining Debt Cancellation in Zambia', Debt and Development Coalition Ireland, April. www.debtireland.org

Eurodad (2007) 'IDB now in MDRI but once again the Devil is in the Detail', March.

Eurodad (2008) '14 NGOs Write to UN Secretary General on Debt', February. www.eurodad.org

Hertz, N. (2004) *The Debt Threat and Why We Must Defuse It*, Fourth Estate, London and New York.

Hurley, G. (2008) *Eurodad 'Responsible Finance Charter'*, Eurodad, Brussels. www.eurodad.org

JDC (2006) 'Cut the Strings', Jubilee Debt Campaign UK, London.

JDC (2008) 'Unfinished Business', Jubilee Debt Campaign UK, London.

JDC (2009) 'A New Debt Crisis?', Jubilee Debt Campaign UK, London.

SAPRI (2004) *The SAPRI Report: Structural Adjustment*, Zed Books, London and New York.

Watkins, N. (2008), 'What Does Africa Owe?', Foreign Policy in Focus, February. www.fpif.org

Websites

African Forum and Network on Debt and Development — www.afrodad.org

Bretton Woods Project — www.brettonwoodsproject.org

Debt and Development Coalition Ireland — www.debtireland.org

European Network on Debt and Development — www.eurodad.org

Freedom form Debt Coalition — www.fdc.ph

Jubilee Australia — www.jubileeaustralia.org

Jubilee Debt Campaign — www.jubileedebtcampaign.org.uk

World Bank — www.worldbank.org

Part III

Development Policy

7

CLIMATE CHANGE AND DEVELOPMENT: WILL GROWTH END POVERTY, OR THE PLANET?

M. Satish Kumar

It has been observed that when the term environment is mentioned, the logical response is, 'Are you a scientist, or are you an activist?' Either way, the politicians in both the rich and the poor nations have become cautious of both these creatures. Even the most well-intentioned individual in the environmental discourse gets sidetracked into this either/or conundrum. However, this debate has become a convenient stick to berate both those who make sense scientifically and those who acknowledge the need to go beyond science into the realm of activism and behavioural change.

There is a 66 per cent probability that the global environment will be affected by global warming, with only a 34 per cent chance that it may not have any effect at all. Despite the growing body of scientific evidence, the debate on climate change has become far more rhetorical and value-laden as it has evolved. There appears to be an alarming gap between our knowledge of the problem and our willingness to act to address it. Thus, despite interest-rate rises and with world recession and inflation looming large, the production of luxury commodities has still not abated, which suggests that important lifestyle changes have yet to be made. Ultimately, political one-upmanship is blurring the boundary between myth and reality. This chapter looks at the vexed issue of climate change and places the debate into the geography of human development.

Consumption and Global Ecological Footprints:
The *Disposable Agenda*

One of the challenges of climate change is the extent to which we are willing to consider the ecological footprints arising from our consumption patterns. If we continue to consume and demand apples from Spain, guavas from Africa and a year-round supply of seasonal vegetables and tomatoes, can we pontificate on global climate change? This is the *disposable agenda* which always rears its head when there is seemingly no crisis in the international context. *New Scientist* stated that '[a] bowl of cereal has the same carbon footprint as a 7-kilometre journey in a 4×4. A steak is equivalent to driving 30 kilometres. But the way we eat doesn't have to cost the earth'. The logical corollary of this analysis is that perhaps the only way to reduce carbon footprints is to go vegetarian (Trivedi 2008, p.30).

One recent report states that China has overtaken the United States of America (USA) as the world's 'biggest polluter' (*Times of India*, 15 April 2008). The main reason for this, it suggests, is that China puts its economy before the environment. According to a Chinese government spokesperson, its overriding priority in tackling climate change is to maintain economic development. Bangladesh, by contrast, faces a climate-change-related refugee crisis resulting from its increasing vulnerability to flooding in low-lying areas (*Times of India*, 14 April 2008). Indeed, climate change means less water and food for the poor in many countries in the developing world. Consequently we have to discern the pace at which climate change is taking place, and the frequency of extreme climatic events is one clear indicator of how global warming is impacting on the environment. Moreover, the poorest communities in the developing world are those most vulnerable to climate change and least well equipped to address the consequences of extreme events such as floods, droughts and failed food harvests.

The whole paradigm of development is based on the concept of prosperity and is measured by consumerism and excess. The concept of prosperity is based on the imposition of costs in order to pursue narrow consumeristic values and tendencies. The per capita income of the richest individual is now 50 times that of the poorest. However, 200 years ago, this ratio was only 5 to 1. The Intergovernmental Panel on Climate Change (IPCC) in 2007 stated categorically that human activity was primarily responsible for climate change, and what the costs of inaction would be for the future. We can say with 90 per cent certainty that human emissions of greenhouse gases are responsible for warming the planet's surface. The IPCC's report states that climate change over the last 50 years has resulted in changes in frequency and/or intensity of extreme weather events:

- It is very likely that cold days, cold nights and frosts have become less frequent over most land areas, while hot days and hot nights have become more frequent.
- It is likely that heat waves have become more frequent over most land areas.
- It is likely that the frequency of heavy precipitation events (or proportion of total rainfall from heavy falls) has increased over most areas.
- It is likely that the incidence of extreme high sea levels has increased at a broad range of sites worldwide since 1975. (IPPC 2007)

The Maldives, for example, are only about 2 metres above sea level, making them especially vulnerable to rising water levels. Similar scenarios pertain to the Male or Solomon Islands and even Bangladesh. Much of the environmental damage is irreversible, but at this stage in the process of dealing with the problem we are still at the basic point of trying to educate citizens about the environment and global warming.

The Stern Review (2006) has placed into perspective the enormity of the challenges that face the future of the human race. The debate generated by this report has been fairly heated and the deliberations have thrown up key questions amidst a plethora of evidence on climate change. Reactions range from pure speculation on the ethics of risk aversion (Yohe and Tol 2008, p.231) to criticising the inadequate documentation of numerous scientific and social assumptions (Jensen and Webster 2007; Mendelsohn 2006; Nordhaus, Nyong and Kulindwa 2006; Pielke 2007; Tol 2006; and Yohe and Tol 2007). Some claim that perhaps Stern underestimated the impact of climate change (Neumayer 2007), while others firmly believe that human-induced climate change is a fabrication (Byatt et al. 2006; Carter et al. 2006). This latter idea seems to have resonated in specific conservative quarters in the debate on climate change, and both the sceptics and the pessimists seem prepared to disbelieve the overwhelming scientific evidence. The current consensus in the debate on climate change is that 'the Stern Review is right for the wrong reasons' (Yohe and Tol 2008, p.232). For his part, Stern (2006) argues that climate change could produce risks of major disruption to economic and social activity on a similar scale to those associated with wars and economic depressions. Therefore, critics of the Stern Report largely contend with the methods and assumptions of the review and not with its fundamental conclusions.

There is an overwhelming body of scientific evidence which suggests that climate change is a well-established phenomenon that requires specific, targeted attention and intervention. For example, one of the key factors associated with climate change is the increase in greenhouse gases caused by human activities. The established climate models have made it unequivocally clear that the current doubling of pre-industrial levels of greenhouse gases is likely to raise global mean temperatures between 2 and 5 degrees Celsius. Such a level of increases in greenhouse gases will be attained between 2030 and 2060. A warming of 5 degrees Celsius will be outside the current level of human experience, and the impact will adversely affect human activity in a manner not seen since the dark ages.

The key impact of climate change will be to accelerate warming by triggering the further release of greenhouse gases, leading to higher temperatures. The direct effect of this change will be that plants and soils will be incapable of soaking up carbon from the atmosphere – which will lead to the thawing of permafrost in the polar caps. This may cause a further 1–2 degrees of warming of the earth's atmosphere. Global warming will set in motion a chain reaction which could disrupt the water cycle and create unseasonal droughts and floods. While higher latitudes will witness higher rainfall, regions with Mediterranean climates will see major droughts. This is already visible in regions such as southern Spain, north Africa and Cyprus, which has not received rainfall for more than three years. Increasing desertification will be the order of the day, as well as increasing frequency of floods, cyclones and hurricanes. Changes in the distribution of heat around the world will disrupt the ocean currents and atmospheric circulation, leading to large-scale disruptions in regional, local and international weather patterns. The melting of the ice sheets will cause a catastrophic rise in sea levels around the world. While science dictates the nature of economics, scientific evidence does not necessarily carry over into the societal response to emerging threats and risk perceptions. Climate change has been regarded as one of the externalities associated with growth.

How Climate Change will Affect People around the World

According to the Stern Report climate change will threaten the basic elements of human life such as access to drinking water, food, health, the use of land – which has always been taken for granted – and the environment. A rise in average global temperatures of between 2 and 3 degrees Celsius would result in frequent droughts and floods. Melting glaciers would result in greater flood risks and interrupt the cycle of seasons that is critical for a biotic existence. This will have a drastic effect on the lives and livelihood of millions of people on the Asian continent who are dependent on agricultural production for their food. At the same time, declining crop yields will leave millions with food insecurity. Likewise, rising ocean acidification due to the higher concentration of carbon dioxide would decimate marine resources, which is part of our food chain cycle. A rise in sea temperatures of 3 to 4 degrees will increase the vulnerability of coastal zone populations from Bangladesh to small islands in the Pacific region, as well as major developed cities such as

Amsterdam, London, San Francisco and Venice. This would result in the permanent displacement of populations, with resulting pressures on governments. It is estimated that climate change will increase the probability of death due to malnutrition and will lead to an increase of vector-borne diseases such as cholera, malaria and dengue fever. At least 15–40 per cent of existing species will face imminent extinction due to global warming; and it will trigger abrupt shifts in the regional weather patterns of El Niño and the monsoons. There will be an increase in environmentally induced refugees, leading to greater geopolitical instability. Clarity over adaptation is critical for work on the impact of climate change, because large amounts of human adaptation could reduce the overall damage caused by climate change.

There are of course costs and implications of climate change for human development. The Stern Report recognises that climate change poses a real threat to the developing world, and without serious mitigation efforts this will become a major obstacle to any poverty reduction programme. Developing countries are most vulnerable to climate change, because the majority of these populations are dependent on the agricultural sector for survival. These countries have a lower adaptability capacity to climate change, with the recurrent cost of cyclones, hurricanes and floods amounting to 5 per cent of the GDP; and that factor is already present. Falling farm production will reduce the average income available to farmers, thus pushing them further below the poverty line. This will have a domino effect on their general security, including reduced access to health care and ultimately to a sustainable livelihood. Increasing poverty would result in 145–220 million more people in the developing world being made vulnerable to the effects of climate change and living below $2 a day. The increasing instability of the global climate will impact negatively on local climate regimes, resulting in mass migration and exacerbating the potential for conflict. Climate-driven changes are immediate, and we are already seeing evidence of this around the world: for example, in 'developed' New Orleans or 'developing' Bangladesh and China. Drought and desertification add further to climate-induced shocks to stable populations around the world.

These risks place even greater premium on fostering growth and development to reduce the vulnerability of developing nations to the well-established impacts of climate change.

The big question remains – can we reverse the dire effects of climate change? Here we need to evaluate carefully the deployment of policies that will assist in adaptation to increasing vulnerability to climate change. Responsible mitigation is crucial to avoiding the severity of climate-change impact. Indeed climate change threatens the sustainability of developmental programmes designed to ameliorate the continued sufferings of the poor in the developing world, where 'tropical geography has a substantial negative impact on output density and output per capita compared to temperate regions' (Nordhaus, Nyong and Kulindwa 2006, pp.3510–17). Strategies to manage the risks and impacts of adverse climate change can, if not managed correctly, lock people into long-term poverty traps.

The Impact of Climate Change

The impact of climate change on economic growth prospects and its implications for incomes and health are real. There is a real risk that climate change will have adverse implications for growth and development (Stern 2006, p.123). Income levels and economic growth will be adversely affected because of climate change, particularly with extreme climate variations across regions of the world. Lower levels of output and growth will result in higher levels of poverty. This will affect health and increase rates of mortality across poorer regions of the world. Moreover, extreme weather events can affect growth rates in developing countries. The adverse effect on factors of production will result in a catastrophic impact on the productivity of the agricultural sector, of the labour market, investments and available capital. Falling output and productivity in the agricultural sector will have major consequences across the global economy.

The current interdependence of agricultural products across the globe puts into perspective the consequences of climate change on both the developed and the developing worlds. Variability in climate regimes, particularly rainfall change, can severely restrict the options available across the rural community, limiting livelihood and trade potential. Studies show that hydrological variability reduces gross domestic product (GDP) growth by close to 38 per cent and increases poverty by 25 per cent. Thus, slower economic growth would increase the incidence of poverty and associated mortality rates among children below the age of five years. Stern's illustrative, integrated assessment model of how climate change affects output and economic growth suggests that the mean cost of climate change to India and South East Asia, Africa, and the Middle East will be between 1.9 per cent and 2.5 per cent loss in GDP by 2100. These figures may be higher, depending on the extreme climate change scenario. As with all models, it is unlikely that the full cost of climate change will ever be known. In all, lower per capita expenditure on health, sanitation and education will limit the capacity of poor countries to meet the United Nations millennium development goals (MDGs) and their specific targets.

Other likely effects of climate change relate to the scarcity of resources, increase in desertification, higher incidence of droughts and floods, and rising sea levels, resulting in the major displacement of population from traditional habitats around the world. Examples of this displacement include environmental refugees in Bangladesh, sub-Saharan Africa and the Pacific Islands. There are already instances of islanders from the Maldives and Tuvalu seeking migration rights and land in Australia and India as collateral security against climate change. The income for this initiative is being financed from the earnings of their tourism industry. It is estimated that at least 200 million people live in coastal regions of South Asia, and rising temperatures would lead to increasing numbers of these people being pushed into extreme hunger and poverty and ultimately seeking to migrate to more secure areas. To prevent such a catastrophe, there have been calls for major investment to protect areas susceptible to rising sea levels, floods, etc. Projected lower outputs resulting from the global financial crisis will provide little incentive to governments to provide investments on such a gigantic scale. For example, as Stern notes, 'a project to construct 8,000 kilometres (km) of river dykes in Bangladesh, a country with gross national income (GNI) of $61 billion, is costing $10 billion' (Stern 2006, p.129).

Furthermore, droughts, earthquakes and other forms of natural disasters could easily trigger conflicts and violence in the least expected parts of the world, let alone in those areas already susceptible to such violence. This could exacerbate religious, ethnic and political conflicts, which have been recognised as the breeding grounds for all forms of extremism in any given society. For example, adverse climatic conditions have fostered internal and international cross-border conflicts, especially in areas such as Darfur in Sudan. This is particularly problematic in areas which are not governed according to the principles of democracy and where resources are scarce. It is important to note that Stern does not attribute climate change as the single most contributory factor to increasing violence in nation states. Indeed, the risk of climate change affecting peace is far more probable in areas which are already poorly governed and suffering from political instability together with ethnic and religious tension. All developmental aspirations can be torn asunder by the challenges of mitigating and adapting to climate change.

Further research is needed to identify the links between climate change and conflict as well as other possible key implications such as gender inequalities, educational attainment and development, and health in poorer countries. It has been well established that increasing our dependence on biomass reduces the time available to study, both among children and adults. If we accept that endemic poverty makes developing countries more susceptible to climate change then it makes sense that facilitating an increase in economic growth and financial output will provide a bulwark in countering the threats posed. This is the only way to reduce vulnerability in developing countries to the inevitability of climate change. As Stern suggests, 'adaptation can only mute the effects and there are limits to what it can achieve' (Stern 2006, p.133).

Troika of Stablisation, Adaptation and Mitigation

Progressive responses to climate change call for dealing with the critical issues of stabilisation, adaptation and mitigation. The challenge of stabilisation relates to the fact that the higher the average global temperature, the higher the stable concentration of atmospheric carbon dioxide. Indeed, this still remains a black box in the IPCC prognosis, and the relationship between stabilisation levels and temperature remains conjectural and demands more empirical evidence. There is no doubting that carbon dioxide concentrations have risen by over one-third, from 280ppm (parts per million) in the pre-industrial era to 380ppm in 2005. The current concentration of carbon dioxide in the atmosphere accounts for around 70 per cent of the total warming effect on the planet. Stabilisation requires that annual emissions are brought down to the level that allows the earth's natural capacity to remove greenhouse gases from the atmosphere. Stabilisation calls for a concerted strategy, and action at a global level. Avoiding the risk of global warming also means reducing the costs of mitigation. However, a key question is how we reduce our dependence on high-carbon technologies. As the earth's natural capacity to absorb carbon weakens, this will make it far more difficult to achieve stabilisation. Delays in reducing emissions necessitate the implementation of increasingly more drastic measures for reducing global warming.

The important point to understand is that emissions can peak early and decline gradually and vice versa. Therefore delaying the peak in emissions from 2020 to 2030 would almost double the rate of reduction needed to stabilise at 550ppm of carbon dioxide. But paths requiring rapid cuts in emissions would not be economically viable in either the short or the long run. Historically one can identify major initiatives undertaken by countries to reduce emissions, including the adoption of nuclear power in France in the late 1970s; the Brazilian adoption of biofuels; the restoration of forest in China; the rush for gas in the United Kingdom; and the demise of the erstwhile Russian empire, which resulted in a reduction of emissions in the post-transition era.

Stabilisation of greenhouse gas concentration in the range of 450–550ppm CO_2e (emissions) will require substantial action from both the developed and the developing worlds in terms of reducing emissions. Indeed, stabilising greenhouse emissions requires a portfolio of options that are technologically oriented and delivered across diverse sectors of the economy.

The costs of mitigation are critical too. All efforts to reduce greenhouse gases are sure to be expensive, including the cost of introducing low-emission technologies and the provision of switching from high-emission-intensive to low-emission-intensive goods and services. Reducing fossil fuel emissions means further costs in alternative forms of energy use. The use of variant pricing mechanisms to cut demand for high carbon, emission-intensive goods and services are also part of the costs of mitigation. Here efficiency gains are a way forward, both to save money and to reduce emissions in the long run. The uptake of efficient technologies will go a long way towards reducing emissions, and a portfolio of technologies will be necessary. Mitigation costs will vary according to how and when the emissions take place. Low-carbon technologies will engage with on- and offshore wind capture technology; wave and tidal energy projects; solar energy technology; carbon capture and storage for electricity generation; production of hydrogen for heat and transport fuels; nuclear power; hydroelectric power; expansion of bioenergy from afforestation, crop and organic wastes; decentralised power generation; and hybrid and electric vehicle technology (with electricity generated using low-carbon technologies).

It can be stated with some confidence that the cost of mitigation will have differential impacts across regions of the world and across varying sectors. The structural adjustments required for climate change will be far more immediate, costly and painful than has been the case with economic adjustments to meet trade deficits. Thus regions which do not have specific policies and regulations in place to deal with climate change will see the migration of carbon-intensive activities into their territory, thereby placing enormous social, economic and political costs on the inhabitants in the region. The possibility of endorsing a quantitative global stabilisation target to reduce greenhouse gases is an effective risk-reduction policy. In the short term, the use of pricing instruments as a signal calls for tax options to keep a check on the cost of mitigation; tax policies, tradable quotas and regulations can play a more constructive role in the harnessing of markets for mitigation. Another way forward is to accelerate technological innovation to tackle climate change at a global, regional and local level.

Understanding the Economics of Adaptation

Adaptation to climate change is also critical to dealing with its unavoidable impact. This is particularly important for designing key policies in the developing world. However, it is important to recognise that adaptation in itself cannot resolve the climate change problem. It is possible to limit the negative impact of irrevocable change and, indeed, it is crucial to realise that without the establishment of strong and early mitigation, the costs of adaptation will rise exponentially. The speed of adaptation will likely vary across diverse species within the ecosystem. Strong public policy will go a long way in realising adaptation as well as mitigation targets. In fact adaptation will be *the* key response to reducing and managing vulnerability to climate change.

An understanding of the clear imperatives for adaptation in the developing world is critical in the context of climate change. In this respect, as the Stern report makes clear, 'development itself is key to adaptation'. Such adaptation should be an extension of good development practice and reduced vulnerability, by promoting growth and diversification of economic activity; by encouraging investment in health and education; by making greater efforts in enhancing resilience to disasters and improving disaster management practices; and, finally, by recognising the need for risk pooling and defining safety nets for the poorest. All of these measures require clearly defined policy frameworks to govern the task of effective adaptation by households, communities and firms. Focused and targeted developmental policies will help deal with issues of endemic and aggravated poverty. At any rate, adaptation actions need to be firmly embedded into development policy and planning principles.

One of the ways forward to deal with the impending consequences of climate change is to support the transition to a low-carbon economy. This calls for increased investment in energy efficiency to counter unchecked growth in demand. The transfer of technology to the poorer countries is possible with the assistance of greater international co-operation. Incentivisation to participate in efficient, low-carbon technologies will go a long way towards prioritising development options, thereby enhancing mitigation policies, which include energy security and improved air quality. There is no substitute for international support towards adaptation.

Conclusion

Climate change is irreversible and ignoring it is not a viable option. Indeed the cost of inaction would be far higher than the costs of adaptation. To mitigate the consequences of climate change, integrated global action is demanded. Given that the costs of adaptation will increase as the years go by, there is an imperative for greater co-operation between the rich and the poorer countries. Ultimately, there is no easy alternative to adaptation as a means of dealing with the impact of climate change. However, adaptation costs are hard to estimate, largely because of the uncertainties associated with the delineation of the precise impact of climate change. It is now essential to take measures to strengthen adaptation and develop a high-quality information base promoting the impacts of climate change – including vulnerability assessments at all levels and scales. Improving governance by actively involving civil society and strategically working to increase the resilience of livelihoods and infrastructure are critical in this regard. Success in dealing with climate change is possible only by integrating climate change policies at the national, sub-national and sectoral levels. This represents a considerable challenge, particularly when disposable resources are scarce in the developing world.

Mainstreaming adaptation principles to all policy agendas is going to be a major challenge for both the developing and the developed worlds. How do we protect the resilience of natural systems to support the livelihoods of millions of poor communities living in fragile ecological zones? Whereas mitigation is largely a short-term measure, adaptation encompasses a long-term approach in dealing with the impact of climate change. Lack of concerted mitigation efforts will jeopardise the possibilities of adaptation. We need to recognise that the poorer countries are the hardest hit in terms of the impact of climate change, though they have contributed the least to the problem in the first place. Communities in the developing regions of the world with the least draw on environmental capital are those which perform worst in developmental terms, with high proportions of their population lacking safe and sufficient water, sanitation, good quality housing, access to health care, secure livelihoods and basic civil and political rights. The priorities for development that is sustainable will vary depending on the use of resources.

Preventative measures are only effective if we understand the impact of our actions and our role in maintaining the ecological balance of the planet. This is where education for sustainable development (ESD) has a major role to play. Development education, environmental education and ESD have real potential to engage with the public on both environmental and sustainability issues as well as those concerning social welfare and development – such as food security and poverty alleviation. These agents of education can provide a starting point for engaging the general population on the question of climate change. Mahatma Gandhi was once asked by a British reporter: 'Mr. Gandhi, wouldn't you want India to reach the same level of prosperity that Britain has attained?' His answer then was very simple but at the same time very profound. He said: 'Well it took Britain conquering half this planet to reach its level of affluence. How many planets would India have to conquer to reach the same level of prosperity?' Ultimately, the starting point in addressing climate change is the action of taking responsibility for our plant and our vulnerable peoples.

References

Byatt, I. et al. (2006) 'The Stern Review: A Dual Critique – Economic Aspects', *World Economics*, vol.7, no.4, pp.199–229.

Carter, R.M. et al. (2006) 'The Stern Review: A Dual Critique – The Science', *World Economics*, vol.7, no.4, pp.167–198.

IPPC (2007) 'Climate Change: Synthesis Report'. www.ipcc.ch/pdf/assessment-report/ar4/syr/ar4_syr.pdf

Jensen, P.H. and E. Webster (2007) 'Is Stern Correct? Does Climate Change Require Policy Intervention?' *Australian Economic Review*, vol.40, no.4, pp.421–31.

Mendelsohn, R.O. (2006) 'A Critique of the Stern Report', *Regulation*, Winter, pp.42–6.

Neumayer, E. (2007) 'A Missed Opportunity: The Stern Review on Climate Change Fails to Tackle the Issue of Non-sustainable Loss of Natural Capital', *Global Environmental Change*, vol.17, pp.297–301.

Nordhaus, J.C., A. Nyong and K. Kulindwa (2006) 'Geography and Macroeconomics: New Data and New Findings', *PNAS*, vol.103, no.10, pp.3510–17.

Pielke, R.A. (2007) 'Mistreatment of the Economic Impacts of Extreme Events in the Stern Review Report on the Economics of Climate Change', *Global Environmental Change*, vol.17, pp.302–10.

Stern, N. (2006) *The Economics of Climate Change: The Stern Review*, Cambridge University Press, Cambridge.

Tol, R.S.J. (2006) 'The Stern Review of the Economics of Climate Change: A Comment', *Energy Environment*, vol.17, no.6, pp.977–81.

Trivedi, B. (2008) 'Dinner's Dirty Secret', *New Scientist*, 13 September, pp.28–32.

Yohe, G.W. and R.S.J. Tol (2007) 'The Stern Review: Implications for Climate change', *Environment*, vol.49, no.2, pp.36–42.

Yohe, G.W. and R.S.J. Tol (2008) 'The Stern Review and the Economics of Climate Change: An Editorial Essay', *Climate Change*, vol.89, pp.231–40.

Websites

Climate Neutral Network   www.climateneutral.unep.org
Europa   http://ec.europa.eu/environment/climat/home_en.htm

Friends of the Earth	www.foei.org
Greenpeace	www.greenpeace.org/international/
Grid-Adrenal	www.grida.no
Intergovernmental Panel on Climate Change	www.ipcc.ch
United Nations Environment Programme	www.unep.org
WWF, the global conservation organisation	www.panda.org

8

EUROPE, 'PARTNERSHIP' AND THE COLONIAL LEGACY

Gerard McCann

The 27 states of the European Union (EU) contribute significantly to the development of many of the world's most disadvantaged regions. The EU's collective economic and political power and its involvement with aid and trade initiatives across the globe have placed this supranational body in a unique position as both a long-standing partner to many developing regions and as a formidable actor in development policymaking. After China and India, the EU, with 493 million people, has the third-largest constituent population, representing 7 per cent of the world's population and accounting for approximately 20 per cent of global trade (EC 2007, p.50). As a powerful economic and trading union, the EU exerts influence over many developing regions in the form of favoured trading status, technical assistance or duty-free access to EU markets. Indeed, its system of preferential access to trade for external European states and developing countries has been evolving since the 1957 Treaty of Rome – the founding document of the European common market. By virtue of the roles played by the EU in the Group of Eight leading industrial powers (G8), the World Bank, the International Monetary Fund (IMF), the World Economic Forum and the World Trade Organisation (WTO), it has come to have an unprecedented influence over global economic trends. In effect, the EU's colonial history and its activities have come to shape international development policy, and, arguably, the ongoing process of globalisation. This chapter aims to survey the emergence of the EU's development policy, while assessing the key strategic interventions that the EU has made in its engagement with developing regions. It will also highlight the changes that have occurred more recently in the type of development that is being encouraged, and questions some of the ideological premises under which EU development policy has been shaped.[1]

Context

In 1963, when the first formal agreement between the European Community (EC) and its former colonies was signed, under the auspices of the Yaoundé Convention, the optimism of the post-colonial era carried with it an understanding that encouraged a reciprocation of interests. The convention was primarily the product of France's protection of its overseas interests, and it asserted that French involvement in the European common market system would have to be premised upon a role for former colonies of member states (their overseas countries and territories – OCTs). Indeed, the Treaty of Rome contained specific references to the connection between the European market and the former colonies. The relationship was explicitly stated in the Common Commercial Policy (CCP), which went so far as to stipulate rules regulating trade between the community and external countries (Flint 2008, pp.12–29). Defined as 'associationism', Article 110 of the treaty aimed to 'contribute, in the common interest, to the harmonious development of world trade, the progressive abolition of restrictions on international trade, and the lowering of customs barriers'. At this point the special relationship between the community and a number of former colonies was cordially integrated into the overall institutional and economic development of the common market itself. Moreover, the Treaty of Rome initiated one of the most enduring legacies of the optimism of the post-colonial era with the introduction of the European Development Fund (EDF). At this point in the history

1. The chronology of agreements made by the ACP Association and the European Community have been: Yaoundé I, 1964–70; Yaoundé II, 1969–75; Lomé I, 1975–80; Lomé II, 1980–85: Lomé III, 1985–90; Lomé IV, 1990–2000; and Cotonou, 2000–20.

of the community, the six original members allocated $581.25 million for the purposes of international development, $511.25 million of which was directed towards French dependencies (Swann 1995, p.359).

For the former colonies of EC members, Yaoundé represented an attempt to work through the complications of decolonisation. This developmental template provided a support mechanism and process which had immense potential for both political accommodation and a range of practical investment measures. For many regions it signalled a radical reconsideration of the European legacy in the developing world. The realignment was highlighted through the correspondence that was taking place around that time, notably, the first memorandum from the Commission of the EC to the Council of Ministers on 'Free Trade and its Conditions' (26 February 1959) – which was the first statement advocating international intervention by the EC. It noted that

> it would seem necessary that any large-scale elimination of customs barriers and quotas between highly developed countries on the one hand and developing countries on the other, should be accompanied by a concerted and active development policy. In point of fact, the experience shows that free trade of itself does not lead to the elimination of disparities in levels of development. (Weigall and Stick 1992, p.118)

The ideal of a reciprocation of interests – and ideological consensus – found form at this stage in the multilateral dialogue between the various states involved. The objective of the Yaoundé arrangement was for the association states (the former colonies) and the EC to contribute to a mutually beneficial trading mechanism with a spectrum of assistance measures. From 1964 until 1970 favourable international conditions helped to facilitate a process of co-operation whereby the 24 developing countries within the Associated African and Malagasy States (AASM) were given aid, preferential trading arrangements and political access. With the former colonies' enhanced capacity to lobby Brussels and to introduce more efficient production methods, they began to carve out a developmental advantage in their economic relationship with the EC (Dinan 2005, p.551). The evidence of the benefits of the mutual agreements between the AASM countries and the EC came with the growing demand for membership of the association by other developing countries.

The Lomé Agreement

By the late 1960s and early 1970s global geopolitical circumstances had changed somewhat, leading to consensus among all parties on the need for renewal. The Cold War was having a distinct and divisive influence on the developing world's economic outlook, as was the global oil crisis which took effect after the Six Day War in the Middle East in 1967. Moreover, progress in the European internal market system led to United Kingdom (UK) membership of the EC in 1973, and with it came the complications of its former colonies in the British Commonwealth and the needs of regions beyond francophone Africa and Malagasy. As a consequence the Yaoundé Convention was revived under the auspices of the Lomé Agreement. This was complemented with the establishment of the African, Caribbean and Pacific (ACP) association, which by 1975 comprised 46 former colonies of EC states. Lomé brought with it a sense of priority, with the EC and ACP members agreeing on the need for support and the principle of 'associational-ism', whereby development responsibilities were acknowledged by former colonial powers, and developing countries accepted their roles in managing indigenous development strategies. The first Lomé Convention (1975–80) contained a series of targeted development initiatives, including aid and technical assistance when requested; general measures to assist regional development; a system of preferences in trade, including free access to the EC for almost all produce from ACP countries; and the innovative system for the stabilisation of export earnings from products (STABEX). The latter initiative meant that ACP export prices were to be protected from the volatile fluctuations of the global market; in return the ACP countries were expected to formalise and prioritise their relations with EC states. The preferential and reciprocal aspects of the Lomé Agreements, which lasted until the

1990s, gave a framework to the ACP–EC partnership and for a significant period worked favourably for both parties.

The institutional arrangements that were established through the Lomé Convention – with a council that included a government minister from each of the ACP countries as well as EC officials, and the ACP–European Joint Parliamentary Assembly – provided a forum for the roll-out of initiatives and a management structure. While the optimism of the early years was realised through quantifiable progress on a number of fronts, the relationship grew more complex as EC membership began to expand, and it became more focused on economic integration and global competition. By the mid 1980s the ACP–EC countries had begun to alter their respective geoeconomic positions and were eventually to suffer a number of confrontations that were to place a strain on the whole Lomé process. This was most noticeable in the years after the Single European Act of 1986, when the EC realigned itself in terms of its global economic position, later to be compounded by the Maastricht Treaty (the EU treaty) in 1992. At this point the ideological consensus that had protected the more vulnerable regions from the rigours of the open market began to gravitate towards more laissez-faire conditioning.

In the 1990s new criteria were introduced into the complexity of initiatives that the Lomé agreement already contained. The right-ward and neoliberal turn of the European governments, and an increasing caution over working with governments in the developing world, brought about an EU-driven rethink, which meant that, while continuing to support ACP development, issues such as strategic regeneration, environmental protection, human rights, economic integration, and sustainable development in an economic sense were given greater precedence (Dinan 2005, p.551). The change in EU development policy became evident in the post-Maastricht period, most notably in Article 177 of Title 20 of the Maastricht Treaty (1992). Under the heading 'Development Cooperation', Article 177 states:

1. Community policy in the sphere of development cooperation, which shall be complementary to the policies pursued by the Member States, shall foster:
   - the sustainable economic and social development of the developing countries, and more particularly the most disadvantaged among them;
   - the smooth and gradual integration of the developing countries into the world economy;
   - the campaign against poverty in the developing countries.
2. Community policy in this area shall contribute to the general objective of developing and consolidating democracy and the rule of law, and to that of respecting human rights and fundamental freedoms. (Visit http://europa.eu.int/eur-lex for the treaty and attendant documents.)

For the first time in the course of relations between the EU and developing countries, trade and aid assistance were being questioned as effective means of development. With the realignment of the political economy of the EU came also the realignment of working relationships with external economic entities. The liberalisation of trading mechanisms was to become the rationale behind policy changes, coinciding with international shifts in the manner in which governments approached assistance and preferential trading agreements. It is worth noting that while the complexity of the Lomé Convention was causing problems for EU–ACP relations at a diplomatic level, the problems with trade complementarity were proving to be merely functional. Indeed, between 1986 and 1998, while total EU financial support to ACP states was €30 billion, the vast bulk (77 per cent) came through the Lomé structures (Jones 2001, p.416).

With the establishment of the World Trade Organisation (WTO) in 1995 and the EU's attempt to position itself as an active driver of the global economy in direct competition with the United States of America (USA), the Lomé system began to decline in influence and capacity. Irresponsible lending practices by the IMF and the World Bank resulted in a debt crisis for developing countries, which, taken together with the divergence in key development indicators (such as gross domestic product (GDP), life expectancy, health, educational attainment, etc.) between the EU and the ACP regions, the erratic fluctuation of commodity prices, diplomatic strains, pressures to liberalise, and in some regions dependency on aid, meant that there was an argument for root-and-branch reform of the ACP–EU relationship. Even the European Development Fund (EDF), which was a lifeline for many communities in the ACP states, came under question and was only saved through a timely intervention by the French during the review of the agreement in 1995.

Lomé, with all its constraints, offered precedents for intercontinental development policy and set out a sequence of actions that could provide evidence of progress. Specific precedents included the comprehensive nature of the involvement and its mutuality; the agreed institutional and logistical mechanisms for action; the principle of negotiation on activities and joint decision making; steady funding support; a bureaucracy that was transparent though cumbersome; and the fact that the ACP beneficiaries – with some reservations – found Lomé developmental. Conversely, the problems that the EU located in Lomé were to swing the balance against this style of development intervention and towards a more globalising focus. ACP powers had become politically weaker over the intervening years and the EU did not have the structures in place to deal efficiently with almost 80 participating developing countries. Also, the high level of dependency created by Lomé arguably had come to stifle development, with the evidence being that ACP trade with the EU had gone down year after year. As a result of reduced trade revenues, debt was economically crippling the ACP states and consequently undermining development (Jones 2001, p.420).

After the 1995 review it was accepted by the various interested parties, including the ACP bloc, that Lomé was in need of reform. It had served its purpose, but macroeconomic circumstances had altered significantly in the post-Cold War era and there was general consensus that change was needed. Indeed, some aspects of the Lomé system were obviously frustrating development.

For example, the fact that ten products dominated 60 per cent of ACP exports meant that between the key years 1976 and 1999, spanning the tenure of Lomé, the ACP's share of the EU market decreased from 6.7 per cent to 2.8 per cent (Jones 2001, p.420). In practice, the ACP states were finding it difficult to adapt to global market changes and, consequently, the value of ACP produce (the preferential goods) declined. This was compounded by the establishment of the WTO, which aimed to reduce protectionism and open markets that had been based on preference and co-operative bias. In addition, the member states of the EU were becoming more attentive to the fluctuations of globalisation, focusing more on the protection of their own markets – increasingly at the expense of ACP markets. The highly protectionist EU Common Agricultural Policy (CAP) and the 2000 Lisbon Agenda, with its primacy of 'competition', typified this EU realignment.

Cotonou

The upshot of the new post-Lomé market-oriented system was a demand, principally from the EU, for a new compact with the ACP states. The Cotonou Agreement (2000) was a product of two years of debate and negotiation and, as a follow-on from the Lomé system, was an awkward compromise that embedded some of the difficulties that had affected development policy since the 1980s. Basically, the EU wanted to disengage from the ACP bloc and bring together bespoke and flexible economic partnership agreements. There would also be prerequisites that would satisfy the political interests of the EU states in an uncertain environment after the Cold War. Cotonou was to be a longer-term but more adaptable commitment, intended to provide a framework for development policy until 2020. Different economies would be dealt with in different ways; it would include annual reviews, a more fluid approach to finance, and the facility to create free-trade mechanisms with one region while formulating aid intervention with another. The liberalisation of trade, particularly imports under the Generalised System of Preferences (GSP), would drive developing regions towards WTO criteria and compatibility, while the ACP would be given a level of flexibility until preferential produce could be worked out of the system. Also, private-sector activity was to be encouraged throughout the ACP in order to enhance market activity.

Signed in the capital of Benin on 23 June 2000, Cotonou was to be a wide-ranging partnership which aimed to bring the economic, humanitarian and political links between the EU states and the 79 countries of the ACP into a working system that would not only focus on the development of the regions involved, but also tighten the previous arrangements for engagement with the global economy. The European Commission was succinct in its rationale for the agreement, although its views often contrasted with the opinions presented by the ACP representatives:

> The Cotonou Agreement is a global and exemplary Agreement, introducing radical changes and ambitious objectives while preserving the 'acquis' [legal history] of 25 years of ACP–EU cooperation. It is based on five interdependent pillars with the underlying objective of the fight against poverty: an enhanced political dimension, increased participation, a more strategic approach to cooperation focusing on poverty reduction, new economic and trade partnerships and improved financial cooperation. (http://europa. eu.int/comm/development/body/cotonou/agreement/agr17_en.htm)

Ultimately, what Cotonou served to do was to advance the liberalisation of economic relations between ACP states and the more globally sensitive EU. It also came to highlight political conditionality within the agreement, by setting standards which the partners should put in place before being permitted to participate in effective programmes. This included respect for human rights, the operation of democratic principles, and respect for the rule of law. The ideal of 'good governance' was to become a catchphrase of the Cotonou discussions, and any partner who did not comply with the conventions was to be subjected to sanctions, political censure, or suspended from the agreement altogether (Dinan 2005, p.553).

The overarching aims of Cotonou were to become strategic differentiation and competitive engagement. As stated in the

Commission's 'Main Objectives and Principles': 'The *central objective* of the Partnership Agreement is to reduce and eventually eradicate poverty while contributing to sustainable development and to the gradual integration of ACP countries into the world economy' (EC 2001, p.1). Article 43, Objective 1 of the agreement is more targeted: 'Economic and trade cooperation shall aim at fostering the smooth and gradual integration of the ACP states into the world economy'. The main method of attaining this integration was to come through the network of regional economic partnership agreements (EPAs), each of which would interact with the EU agencies and tailor any development intervention that may take place. The regions that were designated within the ACP were central Africa, western Africa, eastern and southern Africa and the Indian Ocean, the Southern African Development Community, the Caribbean Region, and the Pacific Region. Since 2007 east Africa has become a point of contention and debate by providing a possible designated seventh region. Within each region there would be a system of preferential access to markets – conditional upon progressive liberalisation; a waiver on certain economic activities, working towards compliance with WTO rules; debt reduction; structural investment; the stabilising of export earnings with a view to liberalisation; the reform of political systems; and direct aid where necessary. The strategy was based upon the notion that production standards, competitiveness and political adherence would effectively manage ACP regions into development.

Aside from Cotonou, which at the time specifically targeted the ACP states for partnership, the EU also managed development arrangements with other least developed countries (LDCs), such as India, Bangladesh and Egypt. The targeting of the north African states of the Mahgreb and Mashreq groups (Algeria, Libya, Mauritania, Morocco and Tunisia in the former, and Egypt, Jordan, Lebanon and Syria in the latter) was particularly notable because it looked as if the EU was shoring up its own frontiers. The engagement with these states was an assurance of sorts that favoured regions, often on the periphery of the EU itself, would be provided with support and stability in an increasingly volatile geopolitical environment. This became particularly evident during the US-led 'War on Terror' from 2003 onwards. Intervention by the EU included financial support for development projects, support for EU private-sector investment, aid, loans and the so-called 'Everything but Arms' initiative (EBA). Named after the EU's council regulation on the initiative, the EBA granted 'duty-free access to imports of all products from the LDCs without any quantitative restrictions except for arms and munitions' (Dinan 2005, p.554; Flint 2008, pp.69–79). In doing this the EU moved for the first time from giving priority to former colonies to looking at development policy in terms of general LDC engagement and geopolitical security.

The partnership agreements with the various regions began causing difficulty shortly after the Cotonou process began. The historic trading relationships, those prior to the renegotiation of Lomé or the WTO protocol, gave ACP produce access to the EU markets, while protecting the ACP from imports. With the EPAs being based upon WTO criteria, ACP states found that they were obliged for the first time to progressively open their markets to EU imports. ACP producers were being eased into a competitive relationship with the EU itself. Indeed, the EU had been voicing concerns through the WTO, demanding that up to 90 per cent of trade barriers with all ACP countries should be removed within ten years. This was in full recognition that many developing countries depended on tariff revenue for public services. The changing patterns of EU development policy – the demands for a reciprocation of trade – were reflected in disputes between the ACP and EU representatives at a series of WTO and intercontinental meetings. This antagonism culminated in the September 2003 Cancún lockout, in which the 650-strong EU delegates to the WTO refused to admit ACP representatives to discussions on trade liberalisation that would invariably affect the development of ACP regions. The Cancún intergovernmental forum on global trade rules was to prove a turning point for ACP–EU dialogue. At this stage the relationship between the former colonies and the EU powers, and the mechanism that had sustained a flawed but agreeable communication of interests since the 1970s, had effectively come to an end.

Many of the ACP states believed that their economies could not cope with such aggressive market intervention in development strategies (Oxfam 2004). Eveline Herfkens, the United Nations Secretary General's co-ordinator for the campaign to promote the millennium development goals (MDGs), commented that 'EPAs are a real problem for poor countries ... LDCs that include many ACP countries have neither the time nor the capacity to negotiate strong agreements with the EU' (quoted in Oxfam 2004). Mukhisa Kituyi, Kenya's trade minister, voiced strong objections:

> The premise on which we started negotiations on EPAs was that when the Cotonou Agreement expired no country would be worse off than under Cotonou. But that was the beginning of the problem because the very notion of reciprocity, which is baked into this negotiation, goes way beyond what was provided for under Cotonou. (Quoted in T. Sharman 2005, p.11)

Festus Mogae, the president of Botswana, defined the problem starkly:

> We fear that our economies will not be able to withstand the pressures associated with liberalisation. This therefore challenges us all as partners to ensure that the outcome of the ongoing EPA negotiations does not leave ACP countries more vulnerable to the vagaries of globalisation and liberalisation, thus further marginalising their economies. (Quoted in Ochieng and Sharman 2004, p.10)

Conversely, EU trade policy with developing countries, which insisted on the opening up of markets to EU imports, was at odds with the internal regulation of the Union's own market. This was particularly evident with respect to agricultural produce. EU agricultural markets remain among the most highly regulated in the world and have been consistently protected from WTO intervention (although this is to be reviewed in 2013). Furthermore, given that most ACP regions and LDCs depend on revenue generated by tariffs placed on imports for public services, the reduction or wholesale removal of this revenue was bound to impact adversely on the services provided by governments in the least developed regions. The adverse effects of this European EPA strategy, combined with the WTO liberalisation strategy, can be witnessed across the globe, with wealth differentials and trade imbalances being greater than ever.

Cotonou and the EPAs in particular have brought forward problems for those developing regions that actively participate in the EU's development policy. Apart from the obvious implication of having left many regions at a competitive disadvantage in a rapidly liberalising economic environment, other complications for development policy have been emerging throughout the tenure of Cotonou. Multilateral and bilateral engagement between the EU and LDCs has been operating under different precedents and at different paces. The Scandinavian countries, for example, have been contributing significantly and imaginatively to global development, yet their efforts stand in stark contrast to the southern states of the EU. Contact and a sharing of experiences between member states, and indeed intra-community partnership, has not been a feature of the Cotonou process.

Scrutiny of operational engagements has highlighted differences of opinion on the EU's role in advancing development, and the manner in which development policy has been managed has come under attack. The Court of Auditors of the EU has repeatedly refused to endorse the development policy's accounts, monitoring of many initiatives is seen to be inadequate in view of the scale of operations, and the developing countries involved often find that their disadvantaged positions are compounded by arrogance from EU officials in Brussels. Ultimately, perhaps the most telling concern regarding the EU's development policy and its impact on many developing regions is inefficiency in delivery.

> Between 1995 and 2000, the average delay in the disbursement of committed funds increased from 3 to 4.5 years (much longer for some programmes). By 2000 the EU had about €20 billion in unpaid commitments and a backlog of 1200 uncompleted projects. (Jones 2001, p.426)

This problem has persisted into Cotonou.

In purely financial terms the scale of the EU's contribution to development continues to be influential. In 2006 four of the five countries to reach or exceed the United Nations' target of 0.7 per cent of gross national income (GNI) towards overseas development assistance (ODA) – Sweden, Luxembourg, the Netherlands and Denmark – were EU members (the other being Norway). In 2006 the EU provided an estimated €38.5 billion in ODA, making it the largest contributor of aid in the world. The combined ODA total of the 15 members of the Development Assistance Committee (DAC) that are EU members accounted for 57 per cent of total net ODA, and while the largest individual state donors in 2006 were the USA, followed by the United Kingdom, Japan, France and Germany, the EU's collective power places it in a unique position as a macroeconomic driver of global development. Unfortunately, as the Organisation for Economic Co-operation and Development (OECD) noted in 2007, aid contributions from the EU have in fact gone down, from 0.41 per cent to 0.38 per cent of GNI. With the EU agreeing to progress towards the millennium development goals, aiming to reach 0.56 per cent of GNI towards overseas development aid by 2010, evidence to date suggests that the community is struggling to match its own revised commitments to development aid, much less to achieve the long-standing target of 0.7 per cent (www.oecd.org). The global recession will invariably put greater pressure on development commitments as European states struggle to control their own budget deficits.

Conclusion

Co-operative assistance is the principal means by which the EU distributes support to developing regions – that is where a member state of the EU works with a favoured region for development and partnership purposes. This means that contributions to developing regions can be channelled either directly through the European Commission in Brussels, using the structures and budget of the EU, usually via the European Development Fund (EDF) or the Humanitarian Aid Office (ECHO), or through individual state mechanisms. With preference given on trade, financial support and humanitarian aid, there is a range of methods by which the EU and its member states effect development for upwards of 100 countries around the world. From the earliest statements on international development, the various NGO lobbies within the European Community have asserted the need for a proactive menu of policies to assist in the regeneration of regions that have been affected by economic underdevelopment, environmental circumstances or geopolitical factors.

The incentive to develop has been complicated by the legacy of colonialism and the fact that the majority of the LDCs are former colonial outposts of major European states. This has been evident from the establishment of the ACP and its work to influence EU development policy. The association represents some of the world's poorest communities and was formed to facilitate a 'partnership' with the EU states, with benefits intended to be 'reciprocal'. The attendant agreements of Yaoundé, Lomé and Cotonou have meant that there have been long-standing generational connections between the peoples and economies of the LDCs and the EU, connections that have shaped the manner in which the two blocs deal with each other. Consequently, there has arisen a situation in which the vast majority of developing countries are, through history, organically integrated with the destiny and fortunes of their former colonial powers in Europe.

The radical changes and adaptation of the EU–ACP relationship since 2000, after over 50 years of engagement, marks not only a shift in the approach taken by the EU to the developing world, but also, significantly, a change in the way in which the states of the EU have come to view partners and former colonies in the developing world. The enlargement of the EU to 27 states has ensured that the system of dealing with developing countries – with all its preferences and flexibility – has had to be renegotiated towards a more competitive global market in which the EU is a leading player. The results of this shift in strategy are already taking effect. As the global recession impacts outward from the developed economies, it has caused developing regions to question the authority and strategy that is being driven through the international financial institutions (IFIs) and ultimately to cast doubt on the leading economic nations' capacity to manage the faltering process of globalisation.

Since its inception the EU has had immense potential and influence in the developing world. The global prominence of the EU's major economic drivers – the former colonial powers – provided opportunities they could have used to orchestrate a development strategy similar to the recovery programme to rebuild Europe in the post-Second World War period. The EU has the capacity, wealth, and technological expertise to intervene in the developing world as an agent of progressive development. However, over 50 years after the Treaty of Rome and the EU's first intervention in the development arena, and a similar period of time since the former colonies fought to gain independence, the weakness and lack of coherence and commitment of the EU and its member states towards meaningful and effective development policies has resulted in the continued economic, social and political marginalisation of its partners in the developing world. Arguably, the EU has prioritised the strategic and economic interests of its members when designing development policy initiatives, and in this there is a systemic fault in EU development policy. Since the comparatively progressive Lomé Agreement has been superseded by the more neoliberal Cotonou Agreement and compounded by the global recession, the EU can be seen to have gradually reneged on its responsibilities, at the expense of the poorest and most vulnerable communities in the developing world.

References

EC (2001) *Cotonou Infokit*, European Commission, Brussels.

EC (2007) *Key Facts and Figures about Europe and Europeans*, European Commission, Brussels.

Dinan, Desmond (2005) *Ever Closer Union*, Palgrave, London.

Flint, Adrian (2008) *Trade, Poverty and the Environment*, Palgrave, Basingstoke.

Jones, Robert (2001) *The Politics and Economics of the European Union*, Edward Elgar, Cheltenham.

Ochieng, C. and T. Sharman (2004) *Trade Traps: Why EU–ACP Economic Partnership Agreements Pose a Threat to Africa's Development*, ActionAid International, London.

Oxfam (2004) *Six Reasons to Oppose EPAs in Their Current Form*, Oxfam, Oxford.

Sharman, T. (2005) *The Trade Escape: WTO Rules and Alternatives to Free Trade Economic Partnership Agreements*, ActionAid International, London.

Swann, Denis (1995) *The Economics of the Common Market*, Penguin, Harmondsworth.

Weigall, David and Peter Stick (eds) (1992) *The Origins and Development of the European Community*, Leicester University Press, Leicester.

Websites

ACP secretariat	www.acpsec.org
Bond UK NGO	www.bond.org.uk
Cotonou Agreement	www.acpsec.org/en/conventions/cotonou/accord1.htm
EU Development Site	www.eudevdays.eu/Public/Homepage.php
EU Directorate	http://europa.eu.int/comm/external_relations/
European Centre for Development Policy Management	www.ecdpm.org
European Network on Debt and Development	www.eurodad.org
European Parliament	www.europarl.eu.int
European Voice	www.european-voice.com
OECD aid statistics	www.oecd.org/dac/stats/
Third World Network	www.twnside.org.sg
UNDP	www.undp.org.pl/pliki/hdr2005_oda.doc

9
ACHIEVING THE MILLENNIUM DEVELOPMENT GOALS IN SUB-SAHARAN AFRICA: A GOAL TOO FAR?

Chrispin R. Matenga

Sub-Saharan African countries, as with other countries of the developing world, have been characterised by a number of development strategies since the genesis of United Nations (UN) development initiatives in the 1960s. The current development strategy of the global overseas development assistance (ODA) community focuses on the millennium development goals (MDGs) proposed by the United Nations in 2000, which feature poverty reduction and the attainment of seven other goals by 2015. However, the idea surrounding the formulation of the MDGs dates back as far as 1996.

In May 1996 a report titled *Shaping the 21st Century: The Contribution of Development Cooperation* was published by development ministers from the member countries of the Organisation for Economic Co-operation and Development (OECD) Development Assistance Committee (DAC), in which they presented their vision for development progress into the twenty-first century (Agenor et al. 2005, p.3). The ministers formulated a strategic framework aimed at achieving seven goals to promote social development and combat widespread poverty in low-income countries. In June 2000, a report titled *A Better World for All: Progress Towards the International Goals* was published, to monitor and report on progress towards the goals.

This resulted in the establishment of quantified targets for the seven goals and indicators for measuring the achievement of the targets that became known as the millennium development goals (ibid.). In September 2000, the international community adopted the Millennium Declaration and eight MDGs during the United Nations (UN) Millennium Summit held at the UN headquarters in New York.

The aim of this chapter is to assess the level of achievement of the MDGs' targets in sub-Saharan Africa, having passed the halfway point towards 2015. The paper draws upon reports and commentaries on the MDGs and Africa's development experience. It underlines the significance of the MDGs to sub-Saharan Africa, given the region's dismal economic performance and poor human development record. The chapter also discusses the level of commitment to MDGs by governments in sub-Saharan countries and considers examples of where the MDGs are delivering positive changes on the ground, where goals are not being met, and what that implies for development in the subcontinent.

MDGs and Sub-Saharan Africa: An Overview

The leaders of the 189 United Nations member states at the 2000 UN Millennium Summit committed themselves to eradicating poverty, promoting human dignity and equality, and achieving peace, democracy and environmental sustainability, and adopted the MDGs to meet these objectives (Khoo 2005, p.45). The goals are linked to 18 targets and 48 indicators. While these goals were launched in 2000, the baseline or point of reference to the progress made is 1990.

This section outlines the MDGs and targets as originally developed and adopted at the Millennium Summit. Goal 1 is to *eradicate extreme poverty and hunger*, and has two targets – to halve the proportion of people whose income is less than one dollar a day and to halve the proportion of people who suffer from hunger, between 1990 and 2015. Goal 2 is to *achieve universal primary education*, with the target of children everywhere, boys and girls alike, completing a full course of primary schooling by 2015. Goal 3 is to *promote gender equality and empower women*. This is to eliminate gender disparity in primary and secondary education, preferably by 2005, and in all levels of education no later than 2015. Goal 4 is to *reduce child mortality*, targeting the reduction of the under-five mortality rate by two-thirds by 2015. Goal 5 is to *improve maternal health*, reducing the maternal mortality ratio by three-quarters by 2015. Goal 6 is to combat HIV/AIDS, malaria and other diseases, with a target of halting, and beginning to reverse, the spread and incidence of HIV/AIDS, malaria and other major diseases by 2015. Goal 7 is to *ensure environmental sustainability*. This goal has three targets: the integration of the principles of sustainable development into country policies and programmes, halving the proportion of people without sustainable access to safe drinking water and basic sanitation by 2015, and achieving a significant improvement in the lives of at least 100 million slum dwellers by 2020.

Goal 8 is to *develop a global partnership for development*, and has seven targets. The first target is to further develop an open, rule-based, predictable, non-discriminatory trading and financial system. This includes a commitment to good governance, development and poverty reduction – both nationally and inter-nationally. The second target seeks to address the special needs of the least developed countries (LDCs), including tariff- and quota-free access for their exports; an enhanced programme of debt relief for heavily indebted poor countries (HIPCs) and cancellation of official bilateral debt; and more generous ODA for countries committed to poverty reduction. The third target is to address the special needs of landlocked developing countries and small island developing states – through the Programme of Action for the Sustainable Development of Small Island Developing States and the outcome of the 22nd special session of the General Assembly. Target 4 of Goal 8 is to deal comprehensively with the debt problems of developing countries through national and international measures, in order to make debt sustainable in the long term. Target 5 is to develop and implement, in co-operation with developing countries, strategies for decent and productive work for youths. Target 6 is to provide access to affordable essential drugs in developing countries, in co-operation with pharmaceutical companies. Target 7 is, in co-operation with the private sector, to make available the benefits of new technologies, especially information and communications technologies. In essence, MDG 8 is a means to achieving the other seven goals (UNDP 2005, pp.xii–xiii; Khoo 2005, p.47).

The Millennium Summit set out measurable targets for poverty reduction, hunger, diseases, literacy and environmental degradation, to be achieved by the year 2015. It is within this approach that developing countries pledged to work and design novel development strategies, initiatives and approaches tailored towards these goals. African leaders have adopted the MDGs as tools within their wider development planning frameworks, in order to alleviate the poor living conditions of the masses. Anchored within national development strategies that started with poverty reduction strategy papers (PRSPs) and national development plans (NDPs) in many African countries, the MDGs have also (theoretically) provided a vehicle for broad-based community participation in development.

While the MDGs were not designed specifically for Africa, but for all countries of the world, their achievement matters more for the subcontinent, where economic growth has been painfully slow and the majority live on less than $1 a day. It is also the only region in which poverty has risen in absolute and relative terms (ECA 2004, p.53), with 21 of the top-priority countries – where failed progress has combined with extremely low levels in human development – being located in sub-Saharan Africa. Therefore, the MDGs and their achievement in sub-Saharan Africa is a matter of urgent necessity if growth and human conditions are to improve. The value of the MDGs lies in the fact that they set clear, agreed and quantifiable targets that can be objectively verified; and since the targets are measurable, governments in both the developing and the developed worlds can be held accountable for their delivery (Gold 2005a, p.25).

A particularly important component of the MDGs for developing countries has been the establishment of global partnerships on development within their operating framework

(Gold 2005b, p.10). This concept of partnership has helped to erase previous North–South relationships based on domination and exploitation. Within the framework of MDG 8, developing countries are now supposed to work with developed countries on a new platform – as global partners in development efforts. It is important to underline the fact that the Millennium Declaration conferred clear obligations on all countries that ratified the MDGs to address development concerns and, eventually, their key human development challenges (UNDP 2007, p.1). The declaration also reaffirmed on many occasions that no country would go without the additional resources required to achieve the MDGs. Towards this goal, far-reaching international efforts were implemented to tackle external-debt problems in developing countries. These efforts included the HIPC initiative, in its initial and enhanced versions, and more recently the multilateral debt relief initiative (MDRI). These initiatives were intended to enable developing countries to reallocate freed resources towards more pressing sectors falling within the MDGs' framework.

It should be noted also that the MDGs offered a multifaceted approach to development that has helped reorient the way the international community perceives development itself. The goals represent a kind of consensus that development is more than economic growth, but is about people and their health, equality, gender, etc. In that respect, the MDGs are similar in nature to the 'basic human needs' concept that was prominent during the 1970s and 1980s.

Governmental Reaction and Engagement in MDGs

Achievement of the MDGs will depend, inter alia, on the political commitment of both sides of the MDG partnership agenda at the highest level of governance. A study by the United Nations Development Group (UNDG 2005) shows evidence of positive developments in sub-Saharan Africa on the endorsement of the MDGs initiative by governments. In almost two-thirds of countries, the MDGs have been mentioned explicitly as a priority in budget presentation by ministers of finance. In about one-third of countries, the goals have been debated formally in the legislature, the highest institution for any state. Regional reports for sub-Saharan Africa show it as having the highest proportion of countries (92 per cent) with some form of integration of the MDGs into development planning frameworks (UNDG 2005, pp.15, 23). Many of the strategies had been in the form of poverty reduction strategy papers (PRSPs) and for some countries, national development plans (NDPs) (ECA 2007).

Endorsement of the MDGs by governments in sub-Saharan Africa was also reflected in the efforts of regional bodies such as the Southern African Development Community (SADC) and the Economic Commission of West African States (ECOWAS). For instance, ECOWAS has adopted a regional poverty reduction strategy with the MDGs at its core, while SADC is in the process of developing a similar strategy (ECA 2008, p.2). Further, the Assembly of the Heads of State and Government of the African Union in Addis Ababa in January 2008 reaffirmed Africa's commitment to achieving the MDGs, by their adoption of a decision in support of the work of the MDG African Steering Group convened in September 2007 by the UN Secretary General (UN 2008a, p.3). However, the UNDG (2005) notes that although there is evidence of engagement, this does not yet constitute a breakthrough in the effort to achieve the MDGs in terms of significant shifts in priorities, policies, budgets, inclusion and development partnership.

Status of MDG Targets in Africa and Development Prospects

Since the beginning of the implementation process of the MDGs in 2000, most assessment reports on the progress of MDGs in developing countries have presented a bleak picture of sub-Saharan Africa, suggesting that the region would not meet the goals by the target date of 2015 (UN Millennium Project 2005; Commission for Africa 2005; United Nations 2005; and World Bank 2005). In 2007, the UN and the African Progress Panel appointed by the Blair Commission, all arrived at a similar conclusion – that Africa was well off track in achieving the MDGs (Brookings Institution 2008, pp.5–6). However, a more recent report by the Economic Commission for Africa (ECA 2008) notes that there is evidence that Africa is making progress in meeting the MDGs by the year 2015. This debate about whether Africa is achieving the MDGs is likely to take a similar form to that surrounding the World Bank/ECA structural adjustment programmes controversy that occurred in 1989 (Parfitt 1990; www.uneca.org). However on this occasion the situation appears to be reversed, with most countries in the global North and the international financial institutions (IFIs), such as the World Bank and the International Monetary Fund (IMF), generally pessimistic about progress in achieving the MDGs, while African countries and their institutions such as the ECA are more positive and are 'seeing light at the end of a tunnel'.

Meeting the Targets

This section discusses goal-by-goal progress on the African continent's level of achievement of the MDG targets for 2015.

Goal 1: Eradicate Extreme Poverty and Hunger

Goal 1 has two targets – by 2015 to halve the proportion of people whose income is less than one dollar a day, and to halve the proportion of people who suffer from hunger within the same time period. Due to lack of reliable and consistent data on income poverty on African countries, most reports have not reported on the target of halving those living on less than a dollar a day. Many African countries do not conduct regular household surveys which can be used to track progress towards the poverty targets (ECA 2008). In some cases, a country conducts these surveys over several years using different methodologies, thus presenting difficulties in comparing the results. However, the minimal data available on this score suggests that poverty reduction in sub-Saharan Africa has been slow. Between 1990 and 2004 the proportion of the population living on less than one dollar per day on the continent remained almost unchanged, i.e. 44.6 per cent in 1990 and 44 per cent in 2004 (ECA 2007, pp.53–4). In fact, sub-Saharan Africa is the only region in which poverty has risen in absolute and relative terms (ECA n.d., p.7).

On the goal of halving the proportion of people who suffer from hunger, evidence shows significant variations across sub-regions in Africa. North Africa (though not considered part of sub-Saharan Africa) has met the two targets on Goal 1, and many countries along the west coast of the continent are also on track (ECA 2008; ECA 2004, p.51). However, for the rest of sub-Saharan Africa the proportion of people suffering from hunger has not declined (ECA 2004, p.51). This lack of progress in eradicating extreme hunger and poverty can be attributed to a number of factors. First, the continent has had very modest rates of economic growth, having recovered from static or negative economic growth for most of the 1980s. The continent's current average annual growth rate is approximately 5.8 per cent (ECA 2008). This rate of growth is still considered significantly lower than the 7 per cent annual growth rate supposedly required to reduce poverty by half by 2015. If current trends in economic growth continue, halving poverty on the continent will only be achieved by year 2147 (ECA 2004, p.53). Secondly, and related to the above, the recent gains in economic growth in some sub-Saharan African countries have not translated into any meaningful employment creation, an important prerequisite for a reduction in income poverty (ECA 2007, p.53).

Furthermore, the continent's high population growth rate, which is in excess of 2 per cent per annum, is higher than the per capita food production, meaning that most African countries will for a long time continue to be net food importers. This problem is compounded by the current escalating global prices of staple foods, driven by rising incomes in China, India and other parts of the world, as well as the 'biofuel craze' that has seen an increasing use of large tracts of land for biofuel production. Similarly, climate change and increased weather variations, in view of the heavy dependence of Africa on rain-fed agriculture, pose a significant risk to the acceleration of growth and progress towards Goal 1 and other MDGs in the region (ECA 2008).

Goal 2: Achieve Universal Primary Education

The target for Goal 2 is to ensure that, by 2015, children everywhere, boys and girls alike, will be able to complete a full course of primary schooling. Sub-Saharan African countries lag behind other developing countries in attaining universal primary education. While earlier assessments had shown that sub-Saharan Africa was unlikely to achieve universal primary education (ECA 2004, p.51), current data shows a marked improvement in net primary enrolment in a number of African countries. Overall, the net primary enrolment rate for sub-Saharan countries increased from 53 per cent in 1990 to 64.2 in 2004 (ECA 2007, p.55). If this trend continues, many African countries will meet the target of achieving universal primary enrolment by 2015 (ECA 2008; ECA 2007, p.55).

Progress in achieving universal primary education is driven by large-scale enrolments in countries such as Zambia, Ethiopia, Mozambique, Mauritius and Kenya. Progress has been broad, occurring both in countries with very high initial net primary enrolment rates relative to 1990, and in those that had very low initial net primary enrolment rates, when the MDGs were adopted. For example, Zambia had a high initial net enrolment rate of 80 per cent in 1990, which rose to 97 per cent in 2006 (GRZ 2008, p.5), while Ethiopia had a low initial enrolment rate of 22 per cent in 1990, rising to 47 per cent in 2004 (ECA 2007, p.55). In most countries, data fails to indicate whether these children complete their primary education or not. There is also a problem with the quality of education being offered, and it seems that there is an overriding rush to finishing the race way in advance of 2015 at the expense of quality. Therefore, while many countries in Africa have almost attained universal primary education, this has not been matched with the quality of education being provided. For example, while enrolment rates have reached above 90 per cent in countries such as Uganda, Namibia, and

Malawi, the children's basic literacy rates for sixth-grade reading are 50, 48 and 32 per cent respectively (Brookings Institution 2008, p.34). In Zambia, the marked progress in enrolment rates must be set against low quality education, poor achievement levels, poor learning environment and teaching materials, and a huge pupil to teacher ratio. The average national ratio for grades 1–9 is 57:1 (GRZ 2008).

Evidence of progress in literacy rates for women and men in the age range 15 to 24 years is again mixed. While children's basic literacy rates remain low in parts of the subcontinent, as we have seen, the ECA (2008) notes that there has been considerable improvement in literacy rates in both national and foreign languages among youths in some African countries. For example, the youth literacy rate in Niger improved by 36.5 per cent in 2005 (ibid.). This has been attributed, in part, to improved enrolment in primary education.

Goal 3: Promote Gender Equality and Empower Women

Most countries in sub-Saharan Africa are on track to achieve gender parity in primary education by 2015. By 2005, at least eleven countries had already achieved gender parity in primary education, while 17 others had a gender parity index of over 0.90 in the same year (ECA 2008, p.7). However, there are significant variations in the rate of progress at the sub-regional level, with the highest levels of parity in southern and west Africa and lowest in north and central Africa. As regards achieving gender parity in secondary education, the picture remains mixed. Despite progress being made in gender parity in primary education, there is still a significant under-representation of girls in secondary education in most countries in sub-Saharan Africa. Thus far, eight countries have achieved gender parity in secondary education, while six others have achieved a gender parity index of over 0.90. Over the same period, however, 14 countries recorded reversals. At this rate of progress, it is unlikely that gender parity in secondary education will be achieved by 2015. The pattern in secondary education is also mirrored in the universities and tertiary institutions.

At the political level, women's representation in national parliament has improved in the majority of African countries. Sub-Saharan Africa has recorded the highest rate of progress in the world with respect to this target (10 per cent) over the period 1990 to 2007. However, at a decision-making level women are still grossly under-represented, except in a few countries, such as Rwanda, Mozambique, South Africa, Tanzania, Burundi, Uganda, Seychelles, Namibia, Tunisia, Eritrea and Ethiopia, where representation ranges between 21 and 48.8 per cent.

Goal 4: Reduce Child Mortality

The target for this goal is to reduce by two-thirds, between 1990 and 2015, the under-five mortality rate. In 1990, under-five mortality in sub-Saharan Africa stood at 185 deaths per 1,000 births (ECA 2007, p.54). This region has made the least progress (1.8 per cent) in reducing under-five mortality rates over the period 1990–2005, which translates into an annual improvement of 0.1 percent. However, the picture is again mixed. While in some countries under-five mortality has been increasing, in other countries – such as Eritrea, Ethiopia, Madagascar, Malawi, Niger and Tanzania – significant progress has been made in recent years. Recent data has shown that under-five mortality in Africa dropped from 166 per 1000 live births in 2005 to 160 per 1000 live births in 2006 (ECA 2008, p.11). As regards the infant mortality rate, only some marginal improvement from 110 to 95 deaths per 1,000 live births in the period 1990 to 2006 has been registered in central, east, south and west Africa as a whole (ibid. p.12). This rate of progress for reducing both under-five and infant mortality rate is, nonetheless, below the rate required to meet Goal 4 by 2015. Most progress has been made in immunising one-year-olds against measles. In most sub-regions, the proportion of one-year-olds immunised has increased to 64 per cent in 2005 from the 56 per cent recorded in 1990. Some countries within the sub-regions, however, recorded coverage rates greater than 90 per cent, while others had less than 40 per cent (ibid. p.12). HIV/AIDS and conflict have been important factors contributing to the high rate of under-five mortality. Progress in achieving the health-related MDGs has been limited by inadequate human and financial resources, and inefficiencies in the delivery of international support.

Goal 5: Improve Maternal Health

Monitoring progress on the target to reduce the maternal mortality ratio (MMR) by three-quarters between 1990 and 2015 is very difficult, due to the non-availability of updated data for all countries. However, the latest data on the maternal mortality ratio indicates that the vast majority of African countries experienced a very dismal improvement in the MMR of 1.8 per cent between 1990 and 2005, which, as with under-five mortality rates, amounts to an annual average improvement of 0.1 per cent (ECA 2008, p.13). More than 50 per cent of births in most sub-Saharan countries are still not attended by health personnel.

Goal 6: Combat HIV/AIDS, Malaria and Other Diseases

Sub-Saharan Africa remains the region of the world worst affected by HIV/AIDS and is far from achieving the target to slow down, let alone reverse, the spread of HIV/AIDS by 2015. An estimated two-thirds of the 33.2 million people living with HIV/AIDS globally are in central, eastern, southern and western Africa. In fact, in 2007, 76 per cent of the global total of 2.1 million adult and child deaths due to AIDS occurred in these four sub-regions. Women, especially, are disproportionately affected by HIV/AIDS. In 2007, women constituted 61 per cent of infected people in the four sub-regions. Southern Africa, however, continues to have the highest adult HIV prevalence rate, more than 15 per cent (ECA 2008, p.14).

The target of halting and reversing the incidence of malaria and other major diseases, such as tuberculosis (TB), by 2015 is equally off track in most of sub-Saharan Africa. Malaria accounts for a high percentage of child mortality and is endemic in 46 countries. Although progress has been made in the use of insecticide-treated bed nets by children under five in malaria-risk areas of central, east, south and west Africa (from 2.1 to 5 per cent between 2001 and 2005), this remains inadequate for achieving this target (ibid.). Rural areas especially are bypassed by some of these efforts.

With regard to TB, north Africa, where there has been an observed decline in its incidence, has been an exception. The other sub-regions in Africa show a rise in its prevalence and morbidity. The incidence of TB in sub-Saharan Africa has increased at the same rate as the HIV/AIDS epidemic, with the two being mutually self reinforcing. The sub-regions most ravaged under the burden of TB are southern Africa, followed by eastern and western Africa (ECA 2008, p.15). Innovative strategies such as the directly observed treatment strategy (DOTS) and the global Stop TB Strategy, which work to enhance effective approaches to combating TB, have been successfully implemented in many African countries. For instance, under the DOTS, the proportion of successfully treated patients increased from 72 per cent in 2000 to 74 per cent in 2004. However, the rate of progress at which countries are addressing the TB burden is too slow.

Goal 7: Ensure Environmental Sustainability

Environmental sustainability is too important a goal not to be met in sub-Saharan Africa. Yet evidence on the ground has shown that progress towards achieving the goal remains inadequate, and so it is unlikely to be achieved by the target date of 2015 (UN 2008, p.1). The proportion of land area covered by forest continues to decline at an overall rate of 3 per cent per annum (ECA 2008, p.17). Expansion of agricultural land and demand for wood fuel remain largely responsible for deforestation in most sub-Saharan African countries. Close to two-thirds of Africa's energy demand is met at the expense of forest.

Deforestation in Africa is an important factor in the loss of biodiversity; it is responsible for between 18 and 25 per cent of the greenhouse emissions that ultimately trigger climate change (ibid.). Climate change also stands as a critical factor that frustrates efforts to reduce poverty and hunger in a number of sub-Saharan African countries. Climate change triggers extreme weather conditions such as floods and droughts, and these are binding constraints on food production for the majority of the countries in Africa that depend on rain-fed agriculture.

As regards the target of providing safe drinking water and improved sanitation, recent data show some progress in a number of countries, although the changes are said to be too small for the target to be achieved of halving the population which lacks these services by 2015 (ECA 2008, p.18). For example, for sub-Saharan Africa as a whole, the proportion of the population with access to an improved water source increased from 49 per cent in 1990 to 56 per cent in 2004. Similarly, the proportion of the population with access to improved basic sanitation increased from 32 per cent in 1990 to 37 per cent in 2004 (ECA 2007, p.56). Provision of safe water and improved basic sanitation is marked by extreme inequalities, with the rural sector remaining marginalised relative to urban areas (ECA 2004, p.71; ECA 2007, p.56). The main obstacles to improving access to safe drinking water and improved sanitation in sub-Saharan Africa include the large resource outlay required, the difficulties of reaching geographically remote rural communities, and low investment in new water supply infrastructure.

Goal 8: Develop Global Partnership for Development

As already mentioned elsewhere, MDG 8 is a means to achieving the other seven goals. A recent report by the MDG Gap Task Force (UN 2008b, p.vii) observes that while the UN Millennium Declaration emphasised the need for a strengthened global partnership to achieve the MDGs, noticeable gaps still remain in delivering the global commitments in areas of aid, trade, debt relief, and access to new technologies and affordable essential medicines.

Thus far, the multilateral trading system has not adequately removed the inequities that disadvantage developing countries. For instance it is observed that developed countries have not yet reached any major agreement on the reduction or removal of agricultural subsidies, and no major breakthrough has yet been reached on non-agricultural market access (NAMA) negotiations (ECA 2008, p.18). Since its inception in 2001, the World Trade Organisation (WTO) Doha Development Round of multilateral trade negotiations has failed to produce an agreement on subsidies (UN 2008b, p.ix). Thus, most developing countries, and especially those from sub-Saharan Africa, have to date not enjoyed the benefits of market access.

Global commitments to meet the MDG target of addressing the special needs of the LDCs, as well as to provide more generous overseas development assistance (ODA) for countries committed to poverty reduction, have been characterised by a failure to deliver (UN 2008b, p.vii). Currently, only five out of the 22 OECD/DAC Countries, namely Luxembourg, Norway, Sweden, Denmark and the Netherlands, have met or surpassed the target of 0.7 per cent of GNI of donor countries set by the United Nations (ECA 2004, p.72; UN 2008b, p.vii). Moreover, efforts to improve aid co-ordination and alignment with the national priorities of developing countries, through the 2005 Paris Declaration on Aid Effectiveness, have been quite slow. The Accra High-Level Forum on Aid Effectiveness that took place in September 2008 was yet another effort towards accelerating and improving aid predictability and co-ordination (UN 2008b, p.viii). It is, however, not clear to what extent this latest commitment will yield tangible results within the allotted time frame, given the previous record of failure.

Servicing foreign debt has been one of the most vexing issues for most sub-Saharan African countries. Measures by the developed world to deal comprehensively with the debt problems of developing countries have included, inter alia, the heavily indebted poor countries (HIPC) initiative and the multilateral debt relief initiative (MDRI) – established at the 2005 Gleneagles Summit held in Scotland (ECA 2008, p.18). The HIPC initiative, a voluntary effort of all creditor countries, was introduced in 1996 and enhanced in 1999. It was intended to provide a fresh start to developing countries struggling to cope with their foreign debt. As of February 2008, at least 26 African countries had reached the decision point under the enhanced (HIPC) initiative (ECA

2008, p.18). Of these 26, 19 have so far reached completion point and are eligible for further debt relief under the MDRI – in which 100 per cent of the eligible outstanding debt owed to multilateral institutions by HIPC countries reaching completion point is 'forgiven' (ECA 2008, p.18; UN 2008b, p.x).

However, while progress has been made in dealing comprehensively with the debt problems of developing countries, especially African countries, there have been delays between the time of eligibility and reaching the decision point, as well as between the HIPC decision point and the completion point. These delays limit the number of African countries benefiting from both the HIPC and the MDRI schemes (ECA 2008, p.18). Even among those countries that have reached HIPC decision point, many continue to spend more resources on debt relief than on public education or health (UN 2008b, p.x). Overall, Goal 8 can best be described as spurious, in the sense that most developed countries have failed to meet their commitment in the MDG partnership framework. This in itself is a demonstration of a clear lack of political will on the side of the developed countries.

Conclusion

From the above discussion, it is clear that the record of performance in achieving the MDGs in sub-Saharan Africa is mixed. Within the countries of the region, there is evidence of progress in meeting some MDGs, but also of stagnation or reversals. And, as observed by the ECA (2008), a variation in performance is also evident when the sub-regions are used as the basis of analysis. North Africa, not considered part of sub-Saharan Africa, has posted significant progress on many of the MDGs when compared to sub-regions of the continent, while southern Africa – one of the richest regions – seems to have made the least progress on most of the MDGs. However, some African countries have made concerted efforts towards achieving the MDGs irrespective of the nature and pace of progress. Slow progress in sub-Saharan Africa should not be a cause for despair, because the countries implementing these goals started from contrasting social and economic positions.

Therefore progress should to some extent be assessed on the basis of starting conditions.

Achieving the MDGs demands an overall change in approach at both national and global levels. Deeper and more meaningful global partnerships will remain a necessary ingredient in the achievement of the MDGs. Developed countries need to scale up their efforts in aid provision, trade reforms, market accessibility and debt sustainability. On their part, sub-Saharan African countries need to continue to maintain the political will to implement the policies and programmes required to achieve the MDGs. The political leadership in Africa has exhibited political will by embracing civil society as partners in efforts to achieve the MDGs. However, players in the MDG game are not operating in a closed system. The cyclical nature of the global economy will continue to have a bearing on the economic well-being of both developed and developing countries. Commodity prices for African countries continue to experience swings on the international market that make financial planning and economic development difficult to deliver. While some commodities exported by African countries, such as copper, have enjoyed an all-time market high over the past four years, the reverse has taken effect since September 2008. In the absence of adequate and predictable foreign aid, countries experiencing low commodity prices may find it difficult to implement many of the programmes integral to the delivery of the MDGs.

References

Agenor, P.R., N. Bayractar, E.P. Moreira and K.E. Aynaoui (2005) *Achieving the Millennium Development Goals in Sub-Saharan Africa: A Macroeconomic Monitoring Framework*, World Bank Policy Paper 3750, New York.

Brookings Institution (2008) 'Are Millennium Development Goals Unfair to Africa?' Washington, D.C., 6 February. www.brookings.edu/~/media/Files/events/2008/0206_africa/20080206_africa.pdf

Commission for Africa (2005) *Our Common Interest: Report of Commission for Africa*, Department for International Development, London.

ECA (2004) *Economic and Social Conditions in Southern Africa: Implementation of the MDGs – Progress and Prospects*, Economic Commission for Africa Sub-regional Office for Southern Africa (ECA–SA), Addis Ababa, Ethiopia.

ECA (2007) *Accelerating Africa's Development to meet the MDGs: Challenges and the Way Forward for Southern Africa*, report on the 13th Experts' Meeting for Southern Africa (ICE), 14 March, Lusaka, Zambia.

ECA (2008) *Assessing Progress in Africa towards the Millennium Development Goals*, report presented at the Conference of African Ministers of Finance, Planning and Economic Development, Addis Ababa.

Gold, L. (2005a) 'Are MDGs Addressing the Underlying Causes of Injustice? Understanding the Risks of the MDGs', *Development Review*, Trócaire, pp.23–42.

Gold, L. (2005b) 'Editor's Introduction', *Development Review*, Trócaire, pp.9–13.

GRZ (2008) *Zambia Millennium Development Goals: Progress Report 2008*, Government of the Republic of Zambia, Lusaka, Zambia.

Khoo, S. (2005) 'The Millennium Development Goals: A Critical Discussion', *Development Review*, Trócaire, pp.43–56.

Parfitt, T.W. (1990) 'Lies, Damned Lies and Statistics: The World Bank/ECA Structural Adjustment Controversy', *Review of African Political Economy*, vol.47, pp.128–41.

UN (2005) *The Millennium Development Goals Report*, United Nations, New York.

UN (2008a) '*Achieving the Millennium Development Goals in Africa: Recommendations of the MDG African Steering Group*', June.

UN (2008b) '*Millennium Development Goal 8: Delivering on the Global Partnership for Achieving the Millennium Development Goals – MDG Gap Task Force Report 2008*'. www.un.org/esa/policy/mdggap/

UN Millennium Project (2005) *Investing in Development: A Practical Plan to Achieve the Millennium Development Goals: Report to the UN Secretary-General. An Overview*, Millennium Project, New York.

UNDG (United Nations Development Group) (2005) *Making the MDGs Matter*, 28 June.

UNDP (2005) '*Halving Hunger: It Can be Done. UN Millennium Project Task Force on Hunger*', summary version, Achieving Millennium Development Goals.

UNDP (2007) *Zambia: Debt Services to Meet the Millennium Development Goals*, Mission Press, Ndola, Zambia.

World Bank (2005) *Millennium Development Goals: From Consensus to Momentum*, Global Monitoring Report, World Bank, Washington.

Websites

African Development Forum	www.uneca.org/adfvi/
African Union	www.africa-union.org
Commission for Africa	www.commissionforafrica.org
Economic Commission for Africa	www.uneca.org
New Partnership for Africa's Development	www.nepad.org
United Nations MDG Tracker	www.mdgmonitor.org
United Nations MDGs	www.un.org/millenniumgoals/

10

GENDER AND DEVELOPMENT

Maeve Taylor

Gender inequality represents an enormous injustice and violation of the rights of half the world's population. The costs of such inequality in all societies – whether in the industrialised global North or the 'Third World' countries of the global South – are immense. Gender inequality is responsible for a huge loss of human potential, with costs for men as well as for women. An understanding of the structures that perpetuate gender inequality and the processes through which such inequality is manifested is critical for the formulation of development policies and programmes. This chapter discusses gender and development policymaking, and raises questions about the conceptual frameworks that influence such policymaking. It also examines the effectiveness of development and aid policy in reducing women's poverty, promoting women's empowerment and supporting women's human rights. The chapter is divided into three sections. The first of these, 'Gender Inequality: A Pervasive Injustice', describes the conditions in which women live and their position in contemporary society in the global North and South (usually referred to in development literature as 'the condition and position of women'). The second section, 'Economic Growth, Gender and Equality', discusses gender in relation to paid and unpaid work and macroeconomic policymaking. The third, 'Gender Policy and Development', outlines some principal trends in gender development policy approaches, including the policy frameworks of major development institutions, the international human rights framework and the role of non-governmental organisations.

The first two sections discuss the nature of gender power relations and the structures that reproduce inequality, thereby providing the conceptual underpinning for the critiques of development policy approaches described in the third section. Because much development policy assumes that economic growth leads to poverty reduction and greater equality, this section pays particular attention to the economic sphere. The field of gender and development inquiry includes the practices and discourses of development institutions, but also the research, analysis and theoretical discussion of diversely located academics and activists. While this chapter aims to highlight some key feminist critiques, it is beyond its scope to do justice to the wide and varied field of feminist contestation.

Gender Inequality: A Pervasive Injustice

Gender inequality is widely recognised as the most prevalent form of social disadvantage in all societies. Relative to men, women have lower status in the family, community and public spheres and have less political power, less economic autonomy, less earning power, and less access to the resources (e.g. money, education, credit, training) that bring status; they also carry a disproportionate burden of care work. Such disadvantage increases women's and girls' vulnerability to diverse forms of gender-based violence – to what has been termed a global epidemic of violence against women. Although the forms inequality takes and the degree to which it is manifested vary from society to society, women's and men's responsibilities, opportunities and influence are unequal in all societies.

The proportion of women in national parliaments has doubled since 1995, but the global average of women representatives in parliaments is still just 18 per cent. The European average is only slightly higher at 21 per cent, but this figure masks enormous variation. The average in Nordic countries is 41 per cent. The average for central Asia and eastern Europe is 13 per cent, half of what it was in 1987. The percentage of women representatives in the United Kingdom (UK) parliament is 19.5 per cent, with higher figures in the Scottish Parliament and the National Assembly for Wales – 33 per cent and 46.7 per cent respectively – and a lower figure of 16.6 per cent in the Northern Ireland Assembly. In the Republic of Ireland, the figure is considerably lower than the regional average, at 13.3 per cent. In 50 countries, less than 10 per cent of members of parliament are women; in 8 countries, there are no women in parliament (Interparliamentary Union website). The majority of the 1.5 billion people living on one dollar a day or less are women (UN Women Watch website). One in three women has been violently abused, often by an intimate partner. Of the world's 876 million illiterate people over the age of 15, two-thirds are women. Of the 150 million children from six to eleven years old who do not attend school, over 90 million are girls. Each year an estimated 500,000 women – the majority in poor countries – die as a result of pregnancy-related causes (Women's Environment and Development Organisation website).

Gender and HIV/AIDS:
An Example of Multiple Forms of Discrimination

Globally, the proportion of women and girls living with HIV continues to grow. In 1997, 41 per cent of those living with HIV were women and by the end of 2003 this figure rose to almost 48 per cent. In sub-Saharan Africa, 57 per cent of the 23 million infected adults are women (UNAIDS website). This trend, which is generally termed the 'feminisation of HIV/AIDS', illustrates some of the interconnections between multiple forms of discrimination (O'Kelly 2007). For example, millions of women around the world experience discrimination in, or are prevented from, going to or staying on at school, attaining health care or owning and inheriting land, or are subject to harmful traditional practices, such as female genital cutting, child marriage or forced marriage. The gender roles of men and women affect women's and girls' access to reproductive health information and services. Moreover, gendered power differentials often mean that women and girls are not in a position to make their own decisions about sexual relations, childbearing, contraceptive use and reproduction. The gendered impact of HIV/AIDS is acute, and the pandemic takes a brutal toll on women and girls.

The HIV statistics for women are closely interconnected to the economic inequalities between women and men. When women are economically dependent on men for their survival, a dependency compounded by their typically weaker position in terms of power in sexual relations, their ability to negotiate safe sex, within or outside marriage, is compromised. Thus, women's vulnerabilities – in terms of both greater physical susceptibility to infection, gendered power differentials, and societal tolerance of different mores for male and female sexual behaviour – are both drivers of the epidemic and obstacles to accessing HIV/AIDS prevention information, treatment and care. Of the estimated 10 million young people worldwide between the ages of 15 and 24 living with the virus in 2003, 6.2 million were young women and 3.8 million were young men (UNAIDS, International Centre for Research on Women).

Violence against Women: An Example of Power and Subordination

Gender-based violence is a global problem and one of the most widespread violations of human rights. UNIFEM, the women's fund at the United Nations, has described violence against women and girls as 'a problem of pandemic proportions that devastates lives, fractures communities and stalls development'. Violence against women takes many forms: domestic and intimate-partner violence, sexual violence, harmful traditional practices, trafficking in women and girls, and crimes against women in situations of armed conflict. It is a major cause of death and disability among women between the ages of 15 and 24 – higher than cancer, motor vehicle accidents, war and malaria. Violence against women is an issue throughout the world, and its relationship with gender inequality is complex: gender-based violence perpetuates relations of domination and subordination; discriminatory attitudes towards women allow many forms of violence to persist, in some contexts, virtually unchallenged. Where women lack decision-making power within the home, they and their daughters are particularly vulnerable to family violence. This vulnerability is compounded by limited options for preventing and responding to abuse, particularly where the social status of women within the community is low, and women are economically dependent on an abusive spouse. In many countries, discriminatory attitudes on the part of the police and judiciary mean that legal codes and government policies dealing with violence against women are not enforced.

Narrowing Gender Gaps: A Trend Towards Gender Equality?

Whether and to what degree the global picture of gender inequality is improving is highly contested. A broad consensus is that gender gaps – disproportionate differences or disparities between the sexes – have narrowed in some significant areas of women's social and economic lives. Over the previous three decades, girls' enrolment in primary and secondary school has increased throughout the world, female illiteracy has declined and women have had access to higher levels of education. Average female wages as a percentage of average male wages have increased. Women's life expectancy has increased, and their health continues to improve. Increased use of contraception has reduced levels of maternal mortality and reduced the burden of unpaid care on women and girls (Molyneux and Razavi 2005). However, great variation and great diversity can be seen in the indicators of progress for women, both between and within different regions, and the narrowing of the gender gap in some areas has failed to bring about equality in society more generally. Improvements in some areas must be viewed in the context of the extraordinary resilience of gender inequality in social, cultural, economic and political structures and systems.

> Gender inequality has proven to be much more intractable than anticipated. In several arenas women's capabilities and quality of life have worsened, not improved; legislative reform is not matched by changes in political and

social realities to enable women to use new laws; gains in one sphere have produced new, detrimental forms of gender inequality; women everywhere are having to fight to get their voices heard, despite new emphases on democracy, voice and participation. At the same time, arguments made by feminist researchers have become denatured and depoliticised when taken up by development institutions. (Cornwall, Harrison and Whitehead 2007, p.1)

Gender Inequality as a Human Rights Issue

Feminist analysts and academic theorists identify the pervasive and resilient inequality between women and men as patriarchy – the structures, systems and ideologies of male superiority and dominance and male values, interests and supremacy that have systematically and disproportionately denied women worldwide the conditions and possibilities for reaching their human potential. The inferior position of women has been reproduced through the norms of culture, tradition and custom; codified in laws and constitutions; and institutionalised in political, cultural and economic structures that create and perpetuate systematic discrimination resulting in deep patterns of inequality.

Women's subordination and the inequality between women and men have been recognised by the international community not only as priority issues of development policy but also as egregious violations of human rights. Systemic discrimination against women has been addressed in a series of legally binding treaties and action plans, the most significant of which is the Convention on the Elimination of All Forms of Discrimination against Women (CEDAW). Adopted in 1979, CEDAW was the first United Nations treaty to address women's rights comprehensively. CEDAW places obligations on states to take 'all appropriate measures' to eradicate the systemic discrimination disproportionately experienced by women in the civil, political, economic, social and cultural fields. The Cairo Declaration and Programme of Action (1994) established the right of women to decide the number and spacing of their children. In 1995, the Beijing Platform for Action was adopted as a global action plan for the implementation of CEDAW. One of the most wide-ranging articulations of governments' commitments to the human rights of women and girls, the Platform for Action proposed concrete measures to advance equality between women and men in 12 critical areas, including poverty, education and training, health, violence against women, the economy, and power and decision making. UN Security Council Resolution 1325 (2000) commits governments to incorporating a gender perspective in negotiating peace agreements, planning refugee camps and peacekeeping operations, and reconstructing war-torn societies, including representation of women at all decision-making levels in conflict prevention and management.

Such instruments are critically important, because they focus on gender equality as a matter of justice, and on women as citizens, rather than as mothers, wives and daughters. Enshrining such rights within international law places strong obligations on governments to take action to eradicate inequality between women and men in all fields. However, the intractability of gender inequality raises questions about the degree of political will within governments to implement human rights, and begs the question whether such top-down rights approaches are indeed capable of delivering gender justice. Furthermore, there is deepening concern that the policies of the prevailing economic model are acting as barriers to the enjoyment by women of substantive human rights. Women's organisations and feminist activists have consequently increased focus research and advocacy on economic and social human rights. The next section explores some intersections and contradictions between the discourses of human rights, gender equality and economy, and highlights the experiences of women – especially poor women – in the era of neoliberal macroeconomic policies that are aimed at the promotion of economic growth.

Economic Growth, Gender and Equality

One of the most contested assumptions in development policymaking is that economic growth brings equality. Critical to such an assumption is the belief that policy prescriptions that have generated growth in the industrialised North can be applied in the countries of the South. Compared with women in the North, women in the global South are in a very much weaker position to benefit from opportunities to enter the workforce; and, in the case of low-income, uneducated women, the implementation of such policy prescriptions can reinforce existing inequalities or create new forms of inequality. This section examines gendered conceptualisations of work, as well as the link between gender, development and the labour market. It then explores the experience of women in the workforce, concluding with an examination of gender and macroeconomic policies.

Gender, Work and the Paid Labour Market

A major trend in the world economy over the last 20 years has been the increased participation of women in the paid labour force in most countries. This trend has affected women in complex and sometimes contradictory ways. On the one hand, greater economic independence can have positive benefits for women's earning power that can enhance their status and social capital within the household and community and allow them to leave violent relationships. On the other hand, policies that aim to promote women's paid economic activity make the dangerous assumption that women who are not in the paid workforce are economically inactive.

Gender analysts draw on the work of feminist academics who challenge male-biased conceptualisations of work. They highlight the 'triple role of women', i.e. their involvement in three types of work: productive, reproductive and community work. Productive work refers to women's wage-paid or salaried work in the production of goods and services. Reproductive work is unpaid work connected with the family – for example, household tasks, housekeeping, child rearing and the provision of water and firewood fuel by carrying head loads. Community-related work includes taking care of community services, activities and needs. Although women and men within the household engage in all three types of activities, reproductive and community management work falls heavily on women because of their gender-ascribed roles. Even in more socially egalitarian countries, such as Sweden, women have the primary responsibility for family care and domestic work, whether or not they are in paid work, and although there is paid paternal leave, it is greatly underutilised (Molyneux and Razavi 2005). Women's community management and reproductive roles are not valued, because they are seen as 'natural' and non-productive, whereas work carried out by men is valued, either directly or indirectly, through paid remuneration, increased status, or political power.

Policies aimed at facilitating women's entry into the workforce tend to focus on women's productive role. Such policies make the assumptions that women's time is infinitely elastic and that work in the reproductive sphere will continue regardless of changes in the economy. Such assumptions ignore the implications for women's time, as well as the physical and mental health of women.

Micro-level: Women in the Workforce

Labour markets are highly gendered. Sex segregation of jobs, differential pay and gendered definitions of skills are among the pervasive, long-term and systemic discriminatory practices found in all parts of the world (Hassim and Razavi 2006; Molyneux and Razavi 2005). Although the entry of women into the workforce may have narrowed the gender gap in terms of economic activity, it has not resulted in the same pay and conditions for men and women. Women tend to earn less for the same number of hours of work and to work disproportionately in lower-paid, lower-status occupations. Moreover, the large-scale increase in numbers of women entering the paid workforce worldwide has occurred in parallel with two other trends: the growth worldwide of informal work and the increasing 'casualisation' of much work in the formal sector, whereby employers can sidestep social-security obligations and labour laws. These trends perpetuate the pattern in countries of the South where job security and work-related benefits remain privileges available to only a small sector of society, predominantly men. For example, women make up the vast majority of workers in export-processing zones, which are characterised by exploitative employment conditions and weak labour protection and where sexual harassment has been widely reported. Women are also in the majority of those working in the informal economy, where they carry out home-based piecework or work as market traders, domestic servants and street hawkers and are not covered by labour codes or social protection laws. In the non-formal sector, women tend to be over-represented in the more precarious and less well-paid occupations.

Gender and Macroeconomic Policy

Growing trends worldwide associated with World Bank and IMF conditionalities aim at promoting economic growth, and include the privatisation of public services such as water and electricity, reductions in social spending, and the introduction of user charges in the health and education sectors. Cuts in social spending reduce social safety nets and divert resources from public services, the impact of which is felt disproportionately by low-income households. Macroeconomic policies that aim to promote growth have specific gender effects, because they place additional care burdens on households headed by women, making the costs of welfare services prohibitive. Feminist economists argue that cuts in public spending are made on the assumption that the care deficit will be filled by families and, implicitly, by women. Cuts in health sector spending, in particular, shift the care of sick and convalescing members of the community onto women and also impose additional costs to women's own health, because women can less often afford to use such services.

Economic development has undoubtedly favoured some women, but it has tended to benefit the affluent over the less well-off and has been linked with deepening inequality between women of different classes and social groups rather than with equality between women and men (Molyneux and Razavi 2005). In many of the economies where growth has been achieved, e.g. China and Korea, women's wages are only 55 per cent of men's; the impressive levels of growth are not reflected in a narrowing of the gender pay gap. Indeed, it has been argued that growth has been achieved because production costs are kept low through the maintenance of the pay gap (Hassim and Razavi 2006).

Gender Policy and Development

Overview of Gender Policy Approaches

Critical to the development of gender policy is the understanding of gender adopted by development institutions and, in particular, the extent to which the relationship between gender and power is understood, at the personal, social, cultural, economic and political levels. Until the 1970s, the prevailing policy approach to women's needs was the welfare approach, which addressed women only in their roles as wives and mothers. The 'trickle-down' theory of modernisation holds that macroeconomic policies improve the economic position of poor men and therefore the position of their wives. Development programmes taking this approach focused on nutrition, mother and child health, and health care. In the 1970s there was a shift to women in development (WID) approaches, which were informed by feminist theory and the women's movement, and associated with the UN Women's Decade (1976–85) (Derbyshire 2002). This shift resulted in the appointment of women's officers and the establishment of women's units in development and aid agencies and institutions, as well as in government ministries. The conceptual underpinning of WID was an understanding of the subordinate position of women and the need to gain equity for women. This tended to be expressed in terms of the concern that women had been 'left out' of the processes of economic development. The aim of WID in practice, therefore, was the integration of women into development, and this approach resulted in a proliferation of women's projects – separate from mainstream development – and a focus on income-generating schemes.

WID's predominant analytical focus on gender roles has been widely criticised for failing to address how broader social relations, such as those relating to status and authority, are created and maintained, and for ignoring how gender inequality is perpetuated in some development agencies and government departments, as well as in the market (Razavi and Miller 1998). Moreover, in framing the problem as the lack of integration of women into development processes aimed at increasing economic growth, two problematic assumptions were made: that such development is an inherently benign and politically neutral process from which all can benefit, and that women are a homogenous category with shared interests. Feminist gender analysts within academia drew attention to the failure of WID approaches to improve either the conditions for women or the position of women – most income-generating projects failed to generate sufficient income or to change gender power relations within families and communities.

The key insight of the 'gender' approach, which emerged in the 1980s, is that gender equality requires attention to both the condition of women and the position of women, and necessitates the transformation of the social structures and institutions that systematically assign secondary or inferior roles to women (Madden and Dillon 2004). Gender and development (GAD) approaches originated in feminist academic thought and in feminist activism – women are seen as agents of change rather than as passive recipients of the benefits of development. In contrast with the WID approach, which is based on top-down processes of development, GAD critiques question prevailing assumptions about development, recognise the need for change across a broad range of development institutions and highlight the need for women to organise to bring about change.

The term 'gender' has been adopted both by grassroots women's organisations and by major development institutions, and two contrasting approaches emerged in the late 1980s. In the context of women's community development projects, a gender empowerment approach has been adopted at the grassroots level, focusing on developing the organisational skills, self-esteem and advocacy skills of women. This approach is associated with efforts to meet women's 'strategic gender needs' through bottom-up mobilisation. Within development institutions, understandings of gender inequality have broadened far beyond the WID approach.

This is particularly evident in the increasing recognition by planners of gender-based violence as a priority development issue. However, many critics have identified the tension between the need to change power structures as a central aim of the GAD approach, and the commitment to or potential for such transformative social change within national or international development agencies (Derbyshire 2002). In practice, the translation of feminist analysis into development policy has tended to ignore the broader structural analysis, and the shift from a women's development approach to a gender and development approach has involved little more than a name change.

During the late 1980s, a 'gender efficiency' approach emerged. Recognising that gender equality makes good economic sense and can help ensure that development interventions are more efficient, mainstream development programmes began to consider gender issues for the first time. However, this approach insufficiently recognised the patriarchal structures within which the social relations of women vis–à–vis men are entrenched. While poor women began to be seen as a sound political and economic investment, conveyed in development discourse as harder working, easier to mobilise and better credit risks, women's situation was presented as evidence of efficiency and not exploitation. Critics have emphasised that if development initiatives are truly to reflect a GAD approach, planners must look critically at broader economic, social and political structures within which women's exploitation is entrenched.

Gender Mainstreaming: A Strategy for Gender Equality

The current prevailing gender approach to development is gender mainstreaming – the idea that gender considerations should be mainstreamed across all policies and programmes as a cross-cutting priority issue. Gender mainstreaming as a strategy towards gender equality has its origins in the Beijing Platform for Action. As envisaged there, gender mainstreaming attempts to combine the strengths of the efficiency and empowerment approaches by focusing on a broader range of stakeholders and on the institutions, policies and programmes that affect the conditions in which communities, households and individuals function.

Two broad approaches to gender mainstreaming can be identified: the agenda-setting approach and the integrationist or instrumentalist approach (Madden and Dillon 2004). An agenda-setting approach views gender perspectives and the goal of gender equality as central to all activities – policy development, research, advocacy, dialogue, legislation, resource allocation, and planning, implementation and monitoring of programmes and projects. It seeks to ensure that institutions, policies and programmes respond to the needs and interests of women as well as men and distribute benefits equitably between women and men. Overall, it aims to reduce existing disparities between women and men in incomes, resources and opportunities, by transforming gender relations. An integrationist or instrumentalist approach, on the other hand, sees women as instruments of development policy and builds gender issues into existing development frameworks and interventions. In this case, the overall development agenda is not transformed, but each issue is adapted to take into account issues relating to women and gender. Women are integrated into as many sectors and programmes as possible, but sector and programme priorities do not change because of gender considerations. Development institutions tend to embrace agenda-setting language up to a point, but, in many cases, instrumentalist approaches predominate when policy is translated into practice.

The Millennium Development Goals: An Instrumentalist Approach?

The millennium development goals (MDGs) have become the overarching framework for development policy. However, many international networks and non-governmental organisations (NGOs) working for women's human rights and gender empowerment have serious concerns that the conceptualisation of gender by the MDGs facilitates the instrumentalist approach rather than transformatory approaches (see MacDonald 2003). The MDGs draw on research indicating that education for girls is the single most effective way of reducing poverty, and the only target for Goal 3 – to promote gender equality and empower women – is the elimination of gender-specific disparities in the field of education. Two other goals focus on maternal health and infant mortality. In the absence of other goals addressing structural discrimination against women in the political and economic spheres, the result is a narrow equation of girls' education and women's reproductive health with progress towards gender equality. Gender equality is a critical step to the achievement of women's empowerment, but empowerment requires more than equality of opportunity and equal access to resources. It means women having control over their own destinies.

The weakness of the MDGs in this respect is compounded by the widespread tendency to view gender equality as a strategy towards poverty reduction rather than as a development goal in itself. Thus, policy addresses women's needs within their caring and mothering roles in the traditional arenas of health, education and motherhood, and in the absence of strategies and resources aimed at women's empowerment, inequality goes unchallenged. This approach is doubly problematic, for not only does it instrumentalise women in areas where gender is given specific consideration, but, even where gender is positioned as a cross-cutting priority issue, there is a tendency to omit gender in the areas that deal most directly with foreign policy, macroeconomic policy and governance.

The New Aid Agenda

In spite of the broad acceptance of gender mainstreaming as a strategy to achieve gender equality and women's empowerment, the 'new aid agenda' embodied in the principles of the Paris Declaration 2005 is centred on mechanisms of aid delivery, with insufficient attention to support for human rights, democratic governance and gender equality (Craviotto, Alemany and Hopenhaym 2008). Fast-changing aid structures, such as direct budget support, pooled funding schemes for supporting civil society and other forms of donor alignment, could divert funding from grassroots women's organisations and advocacy organisations and thereby have potentially serious implications for work on gender equality and women's rights issues in the global North and South (GAD 2008).

The Women's Movement: Conceptualising Equality as a Human Right

The increasing prominence of gender inequality in development discourse over the past decades has been due in no small measure to analysis by feminist academics and to the advocacy of the women's movement. The UN World Conferences held in Mexico, Copenhagen, Nairobi, Cairo and Beijing in 1975, 1980, 1985, 1994 and 1995 respectively, offered key opportunities for mass lobbying to gain recognition of gender issues as human rights concerns. Although the main aim of the conferences was to provide intergovernmental decision-making spaces, they gave the impetus to activists in academia and non-governmental organisations, from both the industrialised North and the 'Third World' countries of the global South, to mobilise and demand action to promote gender equality. The Nairobi conference in November 2007 provided the stimulus for the creation of a number of international women's NGOs: for example, Development Alternatives for Women in a New Era (DAWN), the Women's Environment and Development Organisation (WEDO), and Women in Development Europe (WIDE). UN agencies – such as the Development Fund for Women (UNIFEM), the Research Institute for Social Development (UNRISD) and the Population Fund (UNFPA) – have also been central to the development of gender analysis, research and the implementation of programmes aimed at gender equality and women's empowerment.

Women's organisations highlight a wide range of issues, from sexual violence, reproductive rights and health, child mortality, sexual orientation, trafficking of women and the global sex industry, to concerns in relation to women and the economy in the context of globalisation. The linkages between the shifts in the global economy, the subordinate position of women in relation to sexual relations and the growth of the sex industry globally clearly overlap with many of the issues raised here. Women's organisations, North and South, play a crucial role in advancing gender equality and women's empowerment, through representing, supporting and defending vulnerable groups of women; providing community based education; ensuring that women's rights issues are on the agenda of policymakers; working for changes in legislation and in constitutions; and holding governments to account over their implementation of women's human rights. The advocacy of such organisations as DAWN, WEDO and WIDE has been influential in the conceptualisation of women's human rights – in particular, in relation to the recognition of violence against women as a human rights violation. The women's movement has consistently challenged the ways in which women's interests are depoliticised and marginalised through narrow understandings of gender that links women's roles with the private and domestic spheres and men's roles with the public spheres. NGOs in the women's movement globally have constantly reiterated the links between patriarchy and gender inequality, highlighting that approaches focusing only on basic or practical needs, without supporting societal change aimed at transforming unequal gender power relations, will not fundamentally alter gender inequality.

NGOs have challenged many of the assumptions underpinning most development policy. They have questioned the lack of coherence between policies aimed at economic growth and other development goals, such as human rights and gender equality. They have problematised the view of policymakers that economic development is an inherently benign and politically neutral process from which all can benefit. The same international feminist NGOs that participated in the UN world conferences of the 1990s continue to mobilise and engage in advocacy in relation to women's human rights in the context of the United Nations, but also in relation to trade policy in the context of the World Trade Organisation and, most recently, aid policy in the context of the Paris Declaration.

Conclusion

Gender is now recognised in the policies of most development institutions as a cross-cutting issue that must be mainstreamed across all policies and programmes (Taylor 2004, 2007). However, feminist development analysts have identified the tendency of development policies to depoliticise gender inequality and to instrumentalise women. Fundamentally, in order to be effective, development policy must not only address gender relations at the micro- and household levels, but must be part of a transformative process that aims to change gender power relations, eradicate discrimination and challenge patriarchal structures, at the personal, social, cultural, economic and political levels. Achieving gender equality requires action by governments and other development institutions, and must involve the participation of marginalised women, community organisations and non-governmental organisations. This is no more than what governments have recognised through their acceptance of the international human rights system and the ratification of CEDAW and their adoption of the Beijing Platform for Action. Gender equality is, fundamentally, a matter of justice and human rights, and a concern of all people, all states and all development institutions.

References

Cornwall, Andrea, Elizabeth Harrison and Ann Whitehead (2007) *Feminisms in Development: Contradictions, Contestations and Challenges*, ZED Books, London.

Craviotto, Nerea, Cecilia Alemany and Fernanda Hopenhaym (2008) *Making Women's Rights and Gender Equality a Priority in the Aid Effectiveness Agenda*, WIDE/AWID.

Derbyshire, Helen (2002) 'Gender Manual: A Practical Guide for Development Policy Makers and Practitioners', Social Development Division, DfID, London.

GAD (2008) *Gender Equality, the New Aid Environment and Civil Society Organizations*, Gender and Development Network, UK, January.

Hassam, Shireen and Shahra Razavi (2006) 'Gender and Social Policy in a Global Context: Uncovering the Gendered Structure of "the Social"', in S. Hassim and S. Razavi (eds) *Gender and Social Policy in a Global Context*, Palgrave, London.

MacDonald, Mandy (2003) *Gender Equality and Mainstreaming in the Policy and Practice of the UK Department for International Development*, GAD Network, London.

Madden, Siobhán and Eilish Dillon (2004) *Gender Mainstreaming: A Critical Overview*, unpublished, Banúlacht, Dublin.

Molyneux, Maxine and Shahra Razavi (2006) *Gender Equality: Striving for Justice in an Unequal World*, UNRISD, New York.

O'Kelly, Michael (2007) 'HIV/AIDS and Gender', *Development Review*, Trócaire, Maynooth.

Razavi, Shahra and Carol Miller (1998) *Gender Analysis: Alternative Paradigms*, UNDP, New York.

Taylor, Maeve (2004) *Looking at the Economy through Women's Eyes: A Facilitator's Guide for Economic Literacy*, Banúlacht, Dublin.

Taylor, Maeve (2007) 'Gender Mainstreaming and the White Paper on Irish Aid', *Trócaire Development Review*, Trócaire, Maynooth.

Websites

Association of Women's Rights in Development (AWID)	www.awid.org
Banúlacht	www.banulacht.ie
Development Alternatives With Women For A New Era (DAWN)	www.dawnnet.org
Gender at Work	www.genderatwork.org
International Gender and Trade Network (IGTN)	www.igtn.org
International Women's Rights Action Watch, Asia Pacific	www.iwraw-ap.org
Interparliamentary Union	www.ipu.org
Siyanda	www.siyanda.org
UN Women Watch	www.un.org/womenwatch/
UNFPA	www.unfpa.org
UNIFEM	www.unifem.org
Web portals developed by UNIFEM on specific themes:	
• Gender and HIV/AIDS	www.genderandaids.org
• Gender Equality and the MDGs	www.mdgender.net
• Gender Responsive Budget Initiatives	www.idrc.ca/gender-budgets/
• Women War and Peace	www.womenwarpeace.org

UNRISD	www.unrisd.org
WEDO (Women's Environment and Development Organisation)	www.wedo.org
WIDE (Women in Development Europe)	www.wide-network.org

Part IV

Human Development

11
VOICES OF POPULAR POWER IN LATIN AMERICA

Ronaldo Munck

There is no other region in the world where self-proclaimed progressive politicians have been democratically elected to power in country after country. In Latin America we have seen the first worker president (Lula in Brazil), the first indigenous president (Evo Morales in Bolivia) and one of the first women presidents (Michelle Bachelet in Chile) along with new- or old-left presidents in Argentina, Uruguay, Paraguay, Venezuela, Ecuador and Nicaragua – not to forget Cuba of course. What is most unique and therefore worthy of study is the combination of active grassroots movements for social change and a succession of elections bringing into political office self-proclaimed left or progressive governments. The mass media have referred to a 'red tide', but there is little analysis of why this turn has occurred and what its wider significance might be. This chapter thus seeks to examine the various facets of popular power in contemporary Latin America, to explain their roots and examine their prospects in the period ahead.

The new forms of social mobilisations and popular power emerging in Latin America challenge the dominant and faltering neoliberal model of how the market economy and representative democracy should work. Whether it is the Zapatista revolt of 1994 in Chiapas, Mexico, when we were being told such uprisings were now a thing of the past, or the participatory budgeting in many of Brazil's cities, there is a radicalising of democracy through citizens' participation. Some urban and rural mobilisations echo previous periods of mass movements, such as those of the 1960s and early 1970s. But others, such as the widespread mobilisation of indigenous people, particularly in the Andean countries, bring to the fore new demands for the right to cultural difference and self-determination. At the level of global governance, Latin American countries such as Brazil are playing a leading role in contesting the Washington Consensus, while Venezuela under Hugo Chávez continues to thwart the imperialistic plans of the United States of America (USA). Combined, these diverse forms of social, economic, political and cultural contestation are an explosive mix, and in global terms they represent the first systematic challenge to the uncontested rule of the Washington Consensus (see Sader 2008).

Context

Latin America has a long and continuous history of popular power mobilising and contesting the status quo. Mexico had its massive revolutionary upheaval in 1910, seven years before the Bolshevik revolution, transforming the land question and democracy across the continent. In 1952 the miners and other popular forces in Bolivia rocked the old regime. In 1959 Fidel Castro and his guerrilla army came to power in Cuba and inaugurated a long era of urban and rural guerilla warfare in many countries. In 1970 Salvador Allende was elected into office in Chile as an openly socialist candidate, only to be overthrown brutally by the military in 1973. As the cycle of revolutionary upheavals seemed to be coming to a close, the Sandinista Revolution in Nicaragua caused embarrassment to the United States of America throughout the 1980s. National revolutionary forces, peasant revolts, urban insurrections and even guerilla wars are an integral part of the political history of Latin America. Democratisation in Latin America has been shaped by popular mobilisations, and political culture is imbued with an understanding of the national popular imaginary.

National democratic development came to an abrupt halt across Latin America with a succession of ever more brutal military takeovers from the mid 1960s onwards. In 1964 Brazil's military put an end to a period of nationalist democratic rule under which mass mobilisations had flourished in both the rural and urban areas. In 1973 General Pinochet ended democratic rule in Chile and opened up the era of neoliberal pro-market, pro-globalisation strategies. Then in 1976 Argentina's armed forces ended the nationalist government's rule, ostensibly to put down the urban guerilla movement, but ultimately fostering pro-market, pro-globalisation strategies and instilling fear across a mobilised society. In Central America brutal dictatorships held the guerilla armies at bay but also kept civil society subjected through fear of the numerous death squads. Eventually, through a combination of changing international conditions and internal resistance, the forces of democracy prevailed and the rule of law returned to the continent. International conditions undoubtedly promoted this turn, assisted by the USA's not wishing to be seen to be supporting dictators in the mid 1990s. However, it is clear that democracy was also regained through the continuous willingness of many social groups to take action and promote positive social change in difficult circumstances.

The long night of the military dictatorships did, paradoxically, lead to the emergence of new and often more radical social movements. While trade unions could be closed down and guerrilla armies brutally pursued, not all avenues of social mobilisation could be closed. Under the prolonged Pinochet dictatorship in Chile from 1973 to 1990, there was a flourishing of what became known as 'new' social movements. Often under the protective wing of the Catholic Church, human rights movements began to protest arbitrary detention and disappearances. Women's organisations also began to organise openly in pursuit of basic needs. In later years there were mobilisations around environmental issues. All these mobilisations occurred around what could be called non-class or non-economic issues. They were often quite individualistic and particularistic, and they also tried to deny their 'political' character. Nevertheless they opened up a period of great cultural renewal and helped break the traditional left from the rather stale orthodoxies of people, party, nation and state.

The end of the Cold War and the collapse of the Berlin Wall in 1989 dramatically reduced the attraction of state socialism in Latin America. There was seemingly no alternative to the advance of economic globalisation and a limited democracy in which the only real choice was between different political parties espousing slight personalised variations of the same neoliberal message. However, by the mid 1990s social mobilisation was not only in the ascendant, but it was having a significant impact on the national political scene. In 2002, there was a major collapse of Argentina's economy (linked closely to that of the USA) and successive caretaker governments fell. This led to massive mobilisations, not only amongst the unemployed, but also by the middle classes, who saw their savings evaporate. Across the continent the new century began with local experiments in self-sufficiency, regional women's movement mobilisations, land takeovers and factory occupations. There was also the beginning of a continent-wide political movement against the free-trade policy of the USA and in favour of regionalism.

Rural Revolts

Mexico's revolution of 1910 was essentially a rural revolt led by the iconic figures of Emiliano Zapata and Pancho Villa and symbolising the importance of the land question. In the decades since, the rural populations have played a significant role in building popular power. The Cuban Revolution of 1959 was also primarily waged around land issues, even if set in the context of a national popular cause. Rural social movements cannot, however, be reduced to 'peasant revolutions'. That is because popular power emerges with quite different dynamics in the various sectors or strata of the rural population. If we examine smallholders, tenant-farmers, sharecroppers and landless rural workers we find they all have different grievances and are not motivated by a simple and abstract desire for land. Old and new forms of exploitation are combined, and so too, therefore, are the forms of popular power, which may combine economic demands, political freedom, social equity and cultural recognition.

Brazil is probably the Latin American country with the most active rural movement, going back at least to the 1950s. In the earlier period sharecroppers and tenants with insecure land tenure formed peasant leagues, while rural workers formed countryside-based trade unions. In the 1980s a major upsurge in rural mobilisation led to the creation of the Movimento dos Trabalhadores Rurais Sêm Terra (MST: Landless Rural Workers' Movement) which called for immediate distribution of land to the landless under the slogan 'occupy, resist and produce'. The MST has had a significant international impact and has been an active partner in the counter-globalisation movement with the slogan 'Another World is Possible'. Within Brazil, the MST has spearheaded over 1,000 land invasions or takeovers of large estates, demanding their expropriation and government support to settle landless rural families on these estates. While the MST has been criticised from within the left for some impetuous actions, it has undoubtedly shown the real potential for popular power in rural areas.

The Zapatista uprising in Chiapas (Mexico) – which began in 1994 – heralded a new form of popular movement, both within Latin America and globally. Significantly, this rural revolt began on the eve of the signing of the North American Free Trade Agreement (NAFTA). This agreement nullified the long-standing Mexican *ejido* system of communal land ownership and threatened local farmers and agricultural markets with the import of cheaper corn from the United States. The traditional way of life of the Maya peasant farmers who cultivated corn, predominantly in a communal way, was thus under threat. However, popular power emerged in Chiapas in ways which were anything but traditional. The transnational mobilisation of the Zapatistas and their supporters led to their being dubbed the first information age guerrillas (see Oelesen 2005), and they became a pole of attraction for the emerging counter-globalisation movement. This was at once a very traditional form of popular power – a rebellion for human dignity – and a very modern or postmodern call for a world beyond free-market dominance.

This short analysis of rural movements in Latin America is important because it counters the common urban-centric perspective. The dominant market conception of power assumes that global flows of capital are the only source of influence. Alternatively, if we accept that power is a class relation, as Petras and Veltmeyer do, then it is clear that while the dominant classes have financial and political resources, the 'peasants and rural workers have large numbers, a new form of (potential) organisation, and mass grassroots support' (Petras and Veltmeyer 2001, p.98). We have mentioned the Brazilian MST and the Mexican Zapatistas, but powerful peasant movements have also emerged in Ecuador and Colombia. The ongoing Colombian civil war has in fact pitted an overwhelmingly peasant and landless rural worker-based movement, the Fuerzas Armadas Revolucionarias Colombianas (FARC: Colombian Revolutionary Armed Forces), against a USA-backed political administration. The FARC, currently under siege by the authorities, still controls almost half of the national territory and is bound to play a major role in any political settlement. Consequently, the settlement will have agrarian reform at its centre.

In Ecuador, the new indigenous movement that emerged in the 1990s has undoubtedly been the most important national social movement in that country. It is particularly interesting because it highlights the tensions between class and ethnicity in the generation of popular power. While there is undoubtedly some continuity between this and other similar indigenous movements and the great indigenous revolts against the Spanish conquest during the colonial period, we clearly have a new situation today.

City Governance

Since the mid twentieth century Latin America has been rapidly industrialising, and this has led to urbanisation. This urban growth was much more rapid than that which accompanied Europe's industrialisation in the nineteenth century and its effects have been even more dramatic. The period from 1950 to 1970 saw a huge increase in rural–urban migration across Latin America.

Once in the cities the new arrivals faced a myriad of problems. Marginality was seen by sociologists as a psychological problem, in which migrants were unable to integrate. In reality their social marginality – in terms of living in slums outside the city and lack of stable jobs – reflected the dysfunctional development caused by external dependency. The crisis of urban management was exacerbated in the 1980s by the debt crisis which affected all developing countries. The future of the Latin American city will undoubtedly become conflictual, as some parts of the city are integrated into the new global order and others fall into decay and an alternative-survival economy.

The cities of Latin America have been the scene of some of the most dramatic popular uprisings over the years. In Argentina in October 1945 the popular General Juan Perón was arrested by the military regime, and this led to a huge march on the capital, Buenos Aires. The result of that momentous day – 17 October 1945 – was the release of Perón, the construction of a trade union or popular power alliance to support him and, ultimately, his election as president. In April 1949 in the Colombian capital Bogotá, the Liberal Party leader, Jorge Eliécer Gaitán, was assassinated, and massive urban riots ensued. Some 3,000 of his supporters were killed, beginning ten years of virtual civil war, known as *la violencia*. More recently there have been a number of massive urban protests against International Monetary Fund (IMF) austerity plans, in which popular power was constructed in the streets. The Caracazo, named after the capital of Venezuela, Caracas, was one such urban protest. In 1989, some 3,000 people were killed in the streets, protesting, rioting and seeking alternatives to neoliberal austerity policies. This event was part of the background which led to the rise to power of Hugo Chávez ten years later.

More recently, Brazilian cities have seen a most novel form of participatory governance, which has also fed into the construction of popular power. This move to contest the traditional top-down and patronage-based urban governance practices has had considerable impact, not only in Latin America but also internationally. The first participatory budgeting process was developed in the Brazilian city of Porto Alegre in 1989 (see Bruce 2004). A set of annual neighbourhood meetings saw residents elect budget delegates and debate and decide on future spending priorities. In this way citizens have had a real – if mediated – say on how city governments allocate their resources. Studies carried out on this process, including some by the World Bank (which has expressed considerable interest), show that they have had a real impact. Despite criticism that participation in this way is biased towards activist groups and not the popular masses, the democratic account-ability of urban governments has increased. Not only has public spending become more equitable in terms of meeting basic needs, but there are also clear signs of increased popular participation and, at the very least, greater levels of government accountability.

Democracy needs to be built through the political process, and that is where the weaknesses of the Latin American political system are most evident. It is also where popular power is beginning to construct alternatives, albeit usually in disjointed ways. Globalisation has tended to dissolve long-standing relations between the state, political parties and society, disrupting the synergies which could develop in an earlier era when national politics was a more cohesive domain. The transnational market has not only (re)shaped the socioeconomic structures of Latin America, but it has also utterly transformed the very notion of politics. Where the main driver of society and the development of popular power was once politics, now it is predominantly the market. Politics have become increasingly marketised, with the 'citizen' replaced by the 'consumer' as the central figure. New social movements may spring up and may represent new social demands, but there is a lack of coherent and cohesive political institutions to mediate between society and the state. For popular power to develop coherently in the future, new channels of political representation will need to be found.

Indigenous Stirrings

For many decades the indigenous peoples of Latin America have appeared divorced from the revolts and rebellions that have characterised Latin America. A poignant case is Ernesto 'Che' Guevara's failure to engage with the indigenous populations of Bolivia, something which contributed to his isolation and death in 1967. Likewise, Colombia's legendary radical priest, Camilo Torres, died in 1966 as a guerrilla group he joined found itself isolated from the rural and indigenous populations. However, various indigenous social movements have created change autonomously since around the mid 1990s, particularly, in Central America and the Andean countries.

Generally speaking, within the socialist tradition there has not been a great engagement with indigenous movements. That is because socialism is a device working towards modernity, and the indigenous movement smacks of traditionalism. When the new indigenous movements emerged in the 1990s, some Marxists were critical, dubbing them 'culturalist', and thus divorced from the class struggle. For their part, many indigenous movements were hostile to traditional socialist parties. However, it is possible to bridge that divide by starting from the premise that contemporary indigenous movements are essentially struggling against the social exclusion generated by globalisation and for a model of development which is sustainable, both socially and ecologically. The leaders of the indigenous movement expressed a dialectic of class and ethnicity very clearly when they stated: 'There were two visions: the indigenist cultural vision, focused on bilingual education, and the class vision, focused on land conflicts. The two merged when we realized that we could not have our culture without land' (cited in Selverston 1999, p.176).

In Latin America, citizenship has been a fairly meaningless concept for most of the continent's indigenous peoples. The myth of indigenous 'difference' is widespread. Official state pledges towards multiculturalism – even pious affirmations of 'our indigenous cultures' – have meant little for poor, marginalised and socially excluded populations. Even ostensibly revolutionary states, such as that of Sandinista Nicaragua, found it difficult to deal with the demands of indigenous populations. When race and ethnicity are the markers of social exclusion it is not surprising that cultural affirmation comes to the fore. However material conditions – land

and poverty in particular – are increasingly motivating indigenous mobilisations and shaping their demands. What has been occurring in the last decade is a consistent orientation towards powerful alliances between indigenous peoples, peasants and to a limited extent, the urban poor. The prospects of constructing an inclusive multifaceted form of popular power are real, even if dangers are always lurking.

From an international perspective it is clearly the Zapatistas who have had the most influence in bringing Latin America's indigenous struggles into the open. As one of the Zapatista leaders said in response to a question about the motives for the uprising: 'Indians have never lived like human beings ... but the moment came when those very same indigenous *pueblos* started to make themselves aware of their reality by means of reflection and analysis ... Thus they began to wake up' (cited in Gilly 1998, p.306). Not that Zapatismo was a purely indigenous revolt; there were land issues, democratic issues and national ones shaping the way popular power was built and the state contested. Yet it is significant that a key Zapatista slogan is *dignidad* (dignity), which links with the impetus for cultural affirmation mentioned above. Certainly there is an 'international Zapatismo' which forms part of the broad counter-globalisation movement, but on the ground in Chiapas this is still essentially an indigenous movement. Social inclusion, we might say, cannot be achieved without basic human dignity.

Challenges

The biggest political challenge facing Latin America today is undoubtedly the question of governability in the era of globalisation. How can a modicum of political stability and social cohesion be maintained when the economy is being buffeted by the increasing pressures of global free-market policies? While 'good governance' is lauded by the World Bank and the IMF, what they call for in practice is less government. What the new progressive governments in Latin America have in common is a bid to retain some state control over the national economy. They also understand that with social and economic inequality increasing as a result of globalisation, democratic governance becomes increasingly difficult. For their part, many voters are disenchanted with traditional party politics, which seem to have delivered a quite impoverished form of democracy. This all leads to a volatile political situation with a return, in some cases, of the type of populist politicians who prevailed in the 1940s and 1950s. Furthermore, new forms of violence are emerging that threaten not only the stability of the state but also the ability of the citizen to lead a peaceful existence (see Munck and Hume 2008).

The challenge from below is, for its part, constructing new forms of popular power in Latin America. There is less confidence in the benefits of tempering their demand to keep the so-called political centre on board. What is at stake here is actually the future of modernisation in Latin America. Modernity promised to bring industrialisation, urbanisation, universal education and social development. Today industries are collapsing, the cities are bloated, education is being privatised and upward social mobility has disappeared even as an aspiration. It was Mexico's path-breaking revolution of 1910 which inaugurated the dream of modernity in Latin America. It remains to be seen whether the Zapatista revolt of 1994 in Mexico will open up a similar renewal for the new period of postmodern, globalised Latin America now opening up. As John Peeler puts it, the continent 'has an opportunity to make a major contribution to the political theory and practice of democracy by pushing forward with a vision of radical democratic reform at a time when the stable democracies of the north seem unable to move' (Peeler 1998, p.201). With the global system severely shaken by financial scandals and collapses in 2008, Latin America may yet prove to be a pioneer in the building of a post-neoliberal order, much as General Pinochet served as an inspiration for Margaret Thatcher and Ronald Reagan back in the late 1970s when that order was being constructed.

References

Bruce, I. (ed.) (2004) *The Porto Alegre Alternative: Direct Democracy in Action*, Pluto Press, London.

Gilly, A. (1998) 'Chiapas and the Rebellion of the End of the World', in D. Nugent (ed.) *Rural Revolt in Mexico*, Duke University Press, Durham, N.C.

Munck, R. and M. Hume (eds) (2008) 'Violence: Power, Force and Social Transformation', *Latin American Perspectives*, vol.35, no.5.

Oelesen, T. (2005) *International Zapatismo: The Construction of Solidarity in the Age of Globalization*, Zed Books, London.

Peeler, J. (1998) *Building Democracy in Latin America*, Lynne Reiner, Boulder, Colorado.

Petras, J. and H. Veltmeyer (2001) *Globalization Unmasked*, Zed Books, London.

Sader, E. (2008) 'The Weakest Link? Neoliberalism in Latin America', *New Left Review*, no.52, July–August.

Selverston, M. (1999) 'The Politics of Identity Reconstruction: Indians and Democracy in Ecuador', in D. Chalmers et al. (eds) *The New Politics of Inequality in Latin America*, Oxford University Press, Oxford.

Websites

Andean Community	www.comunidadandina.org/endex.htm
Cuba Solidarity Campaign	www.cuba-solidarity.org
Database of the Americas	http://pdba.georgetown.edu/history.html
Democratic Platform	www.plataformademocratica.org/English/
Landless Workers' Movement	www.mstbrazil.org
Latin America Solidarity Centre	www.lasc.ie
Latin American Network	http://lanic.utexas.edu/las.html
Nicaragua Solidarity Campaign	www.nicaraguasc.org.uk
Terra de Direitos	www.terradedireitos.org.br
Venezuela Solidarity Campaign	www.venezuelasolidarity.org.uk
Zapatista Army of National Liberation	http://zeztainternazional.ezln.org.mx

12

REDEFINING REFUGE:
THE SHIFTING STATUS OF THE REFUGEE

Anna Morvern

This chapter contends that United Kingdom (UK) immigration control, in the broader context of European borders, has lost any moral grounding that it may once have claimed to have. In examining in some detail changes to the UK language and legislation around refugees, the central question asked in this chapter is: What is happening to our human relationships if both refugees and citizens are being redefined as 'border concepts'?

Shifting Definitions

The 'shady' figure of the 'asylum seeker' has displaced the figure of the 'refugee' both in policy circles and in popular understanding. Matthew Gibney has noted that the rise in the profile of the 'asylum seeker' in public discourse has come at the expense of the 'refugee' and has had negative political consequences (Gibney 2006). As the figure of the 'asylum seeker' displaced that of the 'refugee', so the 'claimant' has now displaced the 'asylum seeker'. While the media, particularly the popular press, played a crucial role in the first displacement, legislation is primarily responsible for the second. The corresponding metamorphosis of citizens in this new legal and political landscape has been investigated with insight by Giorgio Agamben, whose analysis demonstrates that the refugee has become 'nothing less than a border concept' (Agamben 1994).

What was a Refugee?

Changing laws have transformed the refugee from a figure who was perhaps perceived to have a moral claim to enter and to stay, into an unwelcome figure, whose exclusion and expulsion can now legitimately be effected by almost any means. The reasoning of Agamben in his thoughts on the building of the concentration camps offers a possible methodology to explore these changes:

> The correct question regarding the horrors committed in the camps, therefore, is not the question that asks hypocritically how it could have been possible to commit such atrocious horrors against other human beings; it would be more honest, and above all, more useful, to investigate carefully how – that is, thanks to what juridical procedures and political devices – human beings could have been so completely deprived of their rights and prerogatives to the point that committing any act toward them would no longer appear as a crime. (Agamben 1994)

This questioning approach is critical of any response that only consists of simple incredulity at atrocities; yet it allows for an investigation of the truth behind inhuman measures that strip people of their rights; and this in turn enables opportunities to emerge for seeing and doing things differently. The focus on close examination of juridical and political developments advocated by Agamben in his work on the growth of the death camps inspires the following examination of changes to our treatment of refugees.

The difference between the refugee and the general emigrant, or immigrant, is one devised by international law. The international definition of the refugee is contained in the 1951 Convention Relating to the Status of Refugees and the later 1967 protocol. One hundred and forty-four states are party to the convention and the protocol, with the United Kingdom having become a signatory in 1954 and Ireland in 1956. These treaties were created partly as a moral response to the plight of Jews who had failed to find protection when fleeing from the Nazis; but they also reflected the Cold War foreign-policy objectives of Western European states in the 1950s. States signed up to the convention to make political capital by suggesting that they would offer sanctuary to those seeking to flee the communist states after the Second World War – thereby manifesting a mix of moral and political ambitions. Despite the status of the Refugee Convention as a 'living instrument', and its evolving interpretation by lawyers who have constantly pushed the boundaries of the legal category of the refugee,[1] the international legal definition of the refugee is narrower than that which is commonly held, which Goodwin-Gill notes might include all those in flight from oppression, a threat to life or liberty, prosecution, deprivation, destitution, war or civil strife, and natural disasters including earthquakes, floods, drought and famine (Goodwin-Gill and McAdam 2007). The law distinguishes between types of migrants, and the Refugee Convention, tainted since its inception by the political objectives of states, continues to privilege those with civil and political reasons for fleeing, which is controversial. Notwithstanding its limitations, the international law which created the legal figure of the refugee arguably accorded those entering Western states a moral aura derived from the collective perception of European states that it was good to offer sanctuary to those forced to flee.

From 'Refugee' to 'Asylum Seeker'

Gibney contends that the 'rise of the asylum seeker and the fall of the refugee' have gone hand in hand. The only difference between the 'asylum seeker' and the 'refugee' in law is that an asylum seeker has applied for refugee status and is awaiting a decision, whereas a refugee is a person who has had a positive decision on an application for asylum and been granted full refugee status (in practice, in the UK, this currently allows the person five years' leave to remain in the country). However, in public discourse, and particularly in the mainstream press, the dubious figure of the immoral, undeserving 'asylum seeker' has displaced the moral, deserving figure of the 'refugee' in the United Kingdom

---

1. Baroness Hale of Richmond, *R. (on the application of Baiai and Others) v. SSHD* [2008] UKHL 53, paragraph 34.

and across Europe. Even purportedly liberal newspapers consider that refugees' right to remain is not a given, but that they should instead earn their right to be here. An article in the *Independent* newspaper, for example, commented:

> The bigots argue against themselves ... when they allege that those claiming political asylum are 'really' economic migrants seeking to make themselves better off, or that they will 'take our jobs'. If they are able to better themselves by working hard or creating jobs for others, we should find ways of letting them in. (*Independent*, 11 February 2000)

The message here is that it is not enough simply to be here seeking refuge; rather, the asylum seeker has to be ready to 'buy in' to the economic system, to 'better themselves', to 'work hard' and 'create jobs for others'. In this new discourse, 'asylum seekers' are commonly characterised as 'welfare cheats, competition for jobs, security threats, abusers of host state generosity, and even as the killer of swans' (Gibney 2006).

From 'Asylum Seeker' to 'Claimant'

An even more reductive and deleterious vision of the refugee has displaced that of the 'asylum seeker'. This is the figure of the 'claimant', which is a creation of legislation. One of the major pieces of domestic legislation in recent years to define the refugee in the United Kingdom was the Asylum and Immigration (Treatment of Claimants, etc.) Act 2004, which inscribed in law and thereby offered institutional credibility to many of the negative illusions about the 'asylum seeker'.[2] The Act formalised associations between seeking refuge and criminality, the first part creating a range of new offences, expanding crimes in relation to 'assisting unlawful immigration' and offences of entry into the UK without documentation. The Act also supported the notion of the 'asylum seeker' as 'other', with Section 19 circumscribing the freedom

2. For example, in the following cases seeking rights for women, which brought new groups into the ambit of Refugee Convention protection: *Shah* and *Islam* (women victims of domestic violence without the protection of their state) and *Fornah* (women who fear subjection to female genital mutilation). *R. v. IAT, ex parte Shah* [1999]; *Islam* v. *SSHD* [1999] 2 AC 629; *Fornah* v. *SSHD* [2006] UKHL 46.

of British citizens to marry immigrants and foreign nationals, requiring the would-be spouse or civil partner to make a costly application to the Home Office seeking permission to marry. The UK government claimed that these laws were to prevent sham marriages, an argument strongly dismissed by the country's first female Law Lord, who said:

> There are many happily married couples who do not live together and many more who do not have children together. Nor are all so-called 'sham' marriages entered into for 'a nefarious purpose'; as Lord Simon of Glaisdale has pointed out, 'Auden married the daughter of the great German novelist, Thomas Mann, in order to facilitate her escape from persecution in Nazi Germany'.[3]

Section 8 of the Act set down various forms of behaviour deemed to be damaging to an asylum seeker's credibility, such as 'failure without reasonable explanation to answer a question asked by a deciding authority'. These sections infused immigration legislation with a new level of cynicism, giving credence in law to the myth of the 'asylum seeker' as 'bogus' – as someone who should be treated, even by the courts, with automatic suspicion and disbelief instead of being greeted with an open mind. Under the auspices of immigration control, the minutiae of individual actions and behaviour are liable to scrutiny, and any behaviour deemed indicative of non-compliance with government procedures is criminalised. Section 35 of the 2004 Act, which concerns 'co-operation' with 'deportation', for example, specifies that the secretary of state can require an individual subject to immigration control to:

(a) provide information or documents to the Secretary of State or to any other person;

(b) obtain information or documents;

(c) provide fingerprints, submit to the taking of a photograph or provide information, or submit to a process for the

---

3. At the time of writing, the UK government is consulting on a new Immigration and Citizenship Bill, published July 2008, which sets out aims of 'strong borders, selective migration, ensuring newcomers earn their right to stay, playing by the rules, managing any local impact' (see UK Border Agency website).

recording of information, about external physical characteristics (including, in particular, features of the iris or any
other part of the eye);

(d) make, or consent to or co-operate with the making of, an
application to a person acting for the government of a State
other than the United Kingdom;

(e) co-operate with a process designed to enable determination
of an application;

(f) complete a form accurately and completely;

(g) attend an interview and answer questions accurately and
completely;

(h) make an appointment.

Failure to comply with any of the above is an offence punishable
by up to two years' imprisonment.

This repressive legislation exists alongside other measures to
deter people from claiming asylum in the United Kingdom. These
are outlined by Gibney and include sanctions against airlines, ships,
lorry drivers and others for carrying undocumented passengers,
new visa regimes and increasingly restrictive work permit systems,
all limiting the ability of refugees and other migrants to reach
the United Kingdom (Gibney 2006). If they manage to arrive in
the United Kingdom, many would-be refugees face destitution or
indefinite detention in immigration removal centres in Scotland and
England, in the context of increased imprisonment of immigrants
across Europe. An asylum seeker can be detained at any time on
the authority of an immigration officer under the Immigration
Acts, with no time limit and no automatic, independent review
of the detention. Immigration detainees are also held in police
stations, prisons and holding centres. There have been many recent
deaths in the detention centres, by those who took their own lives
rather than being subject to forcible deportation and return to
their country of origin (Medical Justice n.d.). In the face of evident
human desperation resulting from detention and deportation, the
UK and European governments remain openly committed to an
intensification of these inhuman measures. The UK Border Agency,
for example, has announced plans for a 'large-scale expansion

of Britain's detention estate', boasting that asylum figures are at their lowest in 14 years, with a person being deported every eight minutes (UK Border Agency 2008a).

The 'refugee' used to enter with legitimacy, fortified by the moral foundation of the convention, whereas the 'asylum seeker' was seen to break and enter, perceived and often labelled as criminal and quickly dismissed as inauthentic. The self-perception of what the UK immigration minister bizarrely calls 'the indigenous population' metamorphosed too as this displacement occurred; where before, citizens might have been encouraged to flatter themselves that they were moral guardians of civil and political rights, welcoming and open-hearted, they have been encouraged to view themselves as judgemental, cynical and unwelcoming – the gatekeepers of a fortress.

From 'Claimant' to 'Border Concept'

Confronted with the mythical figure of the 'asylum seeker' being variously described in the media as criminal, bogus and other, we could at least challenge these myths, citing our own experiences of advising or befriending refugees. But once these myths were given status in law and in practice through inscription in legislation, the 'claimant' displaced both the 'refugee' and the 'asylum seeker'. Any desire to welcome others is restricted by the increasingly bureaucratised, dehumanised, and sometimes militarised processes of the 'border control', which comes from visions of threat, security and exclusion instead of visions of humanity, morality and co-operation.

Examples from European countries show that defensive border-control processes are supported by the use of ever more intrusive, zealously violent, or automated and militarised measures to control refugee movement. In the United Kingdom, immigrants in transit from detention have been subject to 'handcuff injuries, including swelling and cuts to the wrist, sometimes leading to lasting nerve damage', bruising, head/neck/back pain, cuts, bleeding, fractures, dislocations, organ damage, psychiatric damage and self-harm (Wistrich, Arnold and Ginn 2008). In Switzerland, the parliament has recently approved the use of Taser stun guns during the forced deportation of immigrants (Statewatch 2008). Meanwhile, in Spain, the Guardia Civil, a joint military and police force, operates an 'Integrated System of External Vigilance' (SIVE), to police the maritime border between Europe and Africa that is the Strait of Gibraltar. State-of-the-art technology detects vessels so that they can be intercepted before they arrive in Spain, with the system now covering the entire Andalucian coast (Serraj 2008).

The immoral degradation of refugee law and policy could not have happened without a degradation of human and political relationships, and the response by governments to the refugee crisis is characterised by a lack of human or political engagement. For example, the former UK minister for nationality, citizenship and immigration noted of the detention of immigrant children in the United Kingdom:

> Nobody wants to detain children. So, why does it happen? As a parent myself of three small children, I have a simple motive. I insist that we keep families together and not split them up ... The sad fact is that children end up within our detention estate because their parents refuse to go home ... some parents physically disrupt their trip to the airport by behaving violently or even harming UKBA and airport staff in front of their children. (Byrne 2008)

The minister's claims to be identifying with detained immigrant parents facing deportation and to be following a humanitarian and moral approach sound completely hollow, given his failure to recognise the differences in their parental situations and his adherence to inhuman measures of border control and forcible deportations with disregard to the basic freedoms of ordinary people.

Conclusion: From 'Border Concept' to 'Human'?

In February 2007, an aeroplane manned by the airline XL Airways was used to remove around 40 people to the Democratic Republic of the Congo, as part of the UK Government's removal operation, 'Operation Castor'. In October 2007, XL Airways, following dialogue with protesters, issued a public statement that it would no longer assist the forcible removal of failed asylum seekers:

> We had a contract with the Government along with other carriers, for a range of flying. Under this contract we operated one flight in February to DR Congo as part of this contract, without full understanding of the political dimensions involved. Our chief executive [Phillip Wyatt] had made it quite clear to all concerned that we will not be operating any further flights of this nature ... We are not neutral on the issue and have sympathy for all dispossessed persons in the world, hence our stance. (Verkaik 2007)

By contrast to this recognition of solidarity, the removal of all the economy-class passengers from a British Airways flight to Lagos, when they objected to the forced deportation of a distressed man on board their flight, is a nightmarish premonition of the treatment of refugees and citizens if the state maintains this level of control, following the translation of all humans into 'border concepts' (Agamben). As Robert Fisk says, albeit euphemistically: the normal passengers were 'an inconvenience' to be controlled and contained in the all-important process of the ejection of the man without papers (Fisk 2008). What better illustration of the operation of Hannah Arendt's 'radical evil', whereby all people are rendered superfluous? Arendt wrote:

> Radical evil has emerged in connection with a system in which all men have become equally superfluous. The manipulators of this system believe in their own superfluousness as much as in that of all others ... Political, social and economic events everywhere are in a silent conspiracy with totalitarian instruments devised for making men superfluous. (Arendt 1973)

All the passengers were rendered superfluous to the journey when border control took over, except the one who was being eliminated from the territory, who was, by their definition, already superfluous as he was there only to be removed.

'The border', rather than people, has become ever more central to the language of the UK state. The Home Office department responsible for immigration in the United Kingdom has changed names over a very short space of time from 'UK Immigration and Nationality Directorate', to 'UK Border and

Immigration Agency' to 'UK Border Agency'. Likewise, the minister's title has changed, from 'minister of state for asylum and immigration', through 'minister of state for immigration, citizenship and counter-terrorism', to 'minister of state for borders and immigration'. These name changes seem to reflect a shift in focus away from immigration control with any pretension of a human face, through policy influenced by a security agenda, to the end result of pure policing of the border with no regard for the people there. Where 'border control', instead of human relationships, becomes paramount, citizens no less than refugees are increasingly the objects of suspicions that they are 'criminal', 'bogus' or 'other'. Citizens only possess rights on the basis of the contingency of citizenship identity, which has recently become the subject of classes, ceremonies and extensive government policies and legislation (UK Border Agency 2008b). The necessity for proving citizenship in order to claim even basic rights such as the right to liberty thus becomes a demand of the state, as the recent widespread mistaken imprisonment of British nationals without documentation in the immigrant detention centres revealed: 'The trawl [to detain foreign nationals to be deported from the United Kingdom] was so undiscriminating that it included some British citizens' (HMIP 2007). Our identification as citizens, here, relies on the collection and surveillance of biometric identity data, proving place of birth or inherited nationality. This is a project already clearly well under way, evidenced by the rapid growth in collection of travel data of all kinds. For example, radio frequency identification (RFID) tags were recently embedded in the boarding cards of 50,000 passengers travelling through Manchester airport in order to track them further (Privacy International 2007), while the new Border Agency language refers to people in the United Kingdom as 'the identity management landscape', where 'biometric capture' will ensure that 'individuals are locked in to a single identity' (UK Border Agency 2008b). The rejection of refugees by reference to a border between citizen and non-citizen – a border which no longer exists as a geographical land border of the country but has emerged in 'a range of new places ... the high seas, consular offices, and foreign airport' (Gibney), no less than in social security offices, job centres and civil registry offices within the United Kingdom – further strips refugees of all those legal rights that belong to citizens alone.

Agamben, who calls the present the time 'before the extermination camps are reopened in Europe', urges us 'to call into question the very principle of the inscription of nativity and the trinity of state–nation–territory which is based on it' (Agamben). Any vision of including refugees and other migrants into existing legal and political structures which subject us all to being reduced, singular or opposed identities does not offer a powerful alternative. As Agamben demonstrates, this sort of inclusion is not as humanist as it first looks, nor is it desirable, because the human being is irreducible to the identity of refugee or citizen and cannot be fully human in structures which are built to reinforce this opposition, however inclusive they pretend to be. Agamben draws an optimistic conclusion:

> In as much as the refugee, an apparently marginal figure, unhinges the old trinity of state–nation–territory, it deserves instead to be regarded as the central figure of our political history ... the refugee should be considered for what it is, namely nothing less than a limit-concept that at once brings a radical crisis to the principles of nation-state and clears the way for a renewal of categories that can no longer be delayed ... Human beings are *argos* – beings that cannot be defined by any proper operation, that is – beings of pure potentiality that no identity or vocation can possibly exhaust. (Agamben 1994)

The challenge, faced with the details of the current legal and political structures, is to reassert human relationships to manifest a territory without the borders, a place where we are not contained by the deathly logic of immigration control which carries the threat of rendering any of us superfluous as 'border concepts'. Our open minds are the first things we need to reclaim in order to inhabit a moral territory in which the imposition of limited identities is rejected in favour of the replacement of inhuman borders by human relationships.

References

Agamben, G. (1994) 'We Refugees', European Graduate School. www. egs.edu

Arendt, H. (1973) *The Origins of Totalitarianism*, Harvest Books, Florida.

Byrne, L. (2008) 'We are Trying to Find Alternatives', *New Statesman*, September.

Fisk, R. (2008) 'It's Easy to be Snotty with an Airline so Haughty that it Regards its own Customers as an Inconvenience', *Independent*, 26 April.

Gibney, M. (2006) '"A Thousand Little Guantanamos", Western States and Measures to Prevent the Arrival of Refugees', in K.E. Tunstall (ed.) *Displacement, Asylum, Migration*, Oxford University Press, Oxford.

Goodwin-Gill, G. and J. McAdam (2007) *The Refugee in International Law*, 3rd edn, Oxford University Press, Oxford.

HMIP (2007) 'Foreign National Prisoners: A Follow-up Report, January 2007', HM Inspectorate of Prisons, London.

Medical Justice (n.d.) 'Suicides in Immigration Detention'. www. medicaljustice.org.uk/content/view/257/75/

Privacy International (2007) 'Travel Surveillance', December. www. privacyinternational.org

Serraj, K. (2008) 'Au Coeur de la surveillance electronique européenne', in *Le Courrier de l'Atlas: Le Magazine du Maghreb en Europe*, September.

Statewatch (2008) 'Parliament Approves Use of Tasers in Deporations', September.

UK Border Agency (2008a) press releases, 26 February and 19 May 2008. www.ukba.homeoffice.gov.uk

UK Border Agency (2008b) 'Identity Cards for Foreign Nationals: Pilot Process, April 2008–November 2008'. www.ukba.homeoffice.gov. uk

Verkaik, R. (2007) 'Major Airline Refuses to Help with Forcible Removal of Immigrants', *Independent*, 5 October.

Wistrich, H., F. Arnold and E. Ginn (2008) 'Outsourcing Abuse'. www. medicaljustice.org.uk

Websites

Bail for Immigration Detainees (BID)   www.biduk.org
British Refugee Council   www.refugeecouncil.org.uk
Electronic Immigration Network   www.ein.org.uk

European Council on Refugees
  and Exiles   www.ecre.org
Medical Justice   www.medicaljustice.org.uk
Northern Ireland Community of
  Refugees and Asylum Seekers
  (NICRAS)   www.nicras.org.uk
Privacy International   www.privacyinternational.org
Refugee Action Group   www.refugeeactiongroup.com
Refworld   www.unhcr.org/cgi-bin/texis/
                                      vtx/refworld/rwmain/
Statewatch   www.statewatch.org
UK Border Agency   www.ukba.homeoffice.gov.uk
United Nations High Commissioner
  for Refugees   www.unhcr.ch

13

UNDERSTANDING AND DEALING WITH CHILD LABOUR: PROBLEMS AND PROSPECTS

Madeleine Leonard

In October 2007, the *Observer* newspaper published an exposé of children making clothes for The Gap, a United States-based (USA) transnational clothing retailer, in a Delhi sweatshop (McDougall 2007). The story made headline news throughout the world and served as a reminder that many children in developing countries (referred to in the remainder of the chapter as 'majority world countries') continue to work in highly exploitative circumstances with the fruits of their labour ending up as cheap products for consumers in some of the richest countries in the world. The exposé focused on Amitosh, a ten-year-old boy who had been working 16-hour days over four months for no pay. Along with 40 other children, he was brought to Delhi from his parents' village, in an impoverished rural area, by men who had toured the village seeking child workers. The men paid his parents a fee in return for the promise of his labour. His parents had been assured that it would not take long for Amitosh to pay off this debt, but after four months, he had yet to receive any pay and was working in almost slave-like conditions. This form of child work is referred to as 'bonded labour' and is considered by the United Nations as a modern form of slavery. Despite being prohibited by international law, Anti-Slavery International estimates that between 10 and 20 million people are subjected to debt bondage throughout the world. Apart from the bondage aspects of this story, the existence of child labourers in India illustrates the ongoing inability of the Indian government to monitor and deal effectively with the issue of child labour. India's Child Labour Prohibition and Regulation Act (1986) prohibits the employment of children under 14 years in hazardous jobs, which includes work in the garment industry. Moreover, the exposé came after The Gap had introduced a rigorous social audit system in 2004 to weed out child labour in its production processes. So how should we deal with this type of child labour? Often exposés such as the one outlined here cause moral outrage in developed societies (referred to in the rest of the chapter as 'minority world countries') and typically result in a boycott of products made by child workers or a boycott of the company accused of using child labourers to make their goods.

However, the issue of child labour is a complex, multifaceted phenomenon, and the strategy of boycott is not necessarily the best solution. Moreover, it needs to be stressed at the outset that children work in varying contexts in majority world countries, with only a minority being employed in the production of goods that end up in global retail chains. O'Donnell, van Doorslaer and Rosate (2002) estimate that over 70 per cent of working children in majority world societies are involved in family-based work. Hence, by focusing on children involved in the production of goods for export, there is a danger of reducing all child work in majority world societies to these forms and ignoring other mainstream and often more positive examples of children's economic activities. Bearing in mind this qualification, the purpose of this chapter is to explore in more detail the existence of this type of child labour, as it is often the most publicised form of children's economic activities and, as a result, tends to inform public opinion on the topic. Opening this activity to greater scrutiny reveals a number of myths regarding child labour and its solutions. The chapter begins with a brief overview of child labour. Understanding and dealing with child labour necessitates examining some of the supply-and-demand factors around the utilisation of child labour, and this forms the theme of the second section of the chapter. This is followed by a brief discussion of children involved in the production of goods for export, as this practice invokes the greatest moral condemnation of child labour and often leads to calls to ban all forms of child work. The chapter concludes with a discussion of solutions to the existence of this type of child labour and emphasises the importance of ensuring that child workers' views are incorporated into the analyses.

The Prevalence of Child Labour

It is difficult to obtain accurate statistics on child labour, for a variety of reasons. Some children do not have proper birth records and therefore may be invisible workers. Others work in the informal sector, where their work activities often go unrecorded. Even where records exist, since there is a lack of consensus about definitions of child labour, statistical measurements are open to all sorts of subjective judgements. The International Labour Organisation (ILO) is the most important international organisation that compiles statistics on working children. They estimate that around 218 million children are economically active throughout the world, with around 126 million involved in hazardous work (ILO 2006). Their statistics indicate that child labour is not simply a majority world phenomenon or a relic from a pre-capitalist era; rather, children are found working in all regions of the world. However, in terms of crude percentages, child labour is more prevalent in majority world societies compared to minority world societies, with 2 per cent of children in minority world societies working, compared to 29 per cent in sub-Saharan Africa. While the remainder of this chapter deals with child labour in majority world societies, it is not my intention to link this to cultural differences between minority and majority world societies, but rather to suggest that inequalities in the global system which often perpetuate poverty in majority world countries sometimes makes it necessary for adults in such societies to rely on the economic activities of their children.

The ILO defines child labour as 'work that deprives children of their childhood, their potential and their dignity and that is harmful to physical and mental development' (ILO 2006). This very broad definition makes it difficult to compile comparative statistics on the extent of child labour, as individual countries may determine what counts as child labour and their varying interpretations may be at odds with international understandings. The ILO organised a meeting of experts in Geneva in April 2008, to discuss the lack of a common understanding of child labour across various countries and debated whether an overarching definition was possible or even desirable. Their discussions highlighted how the terminology itself was open to dispute, with some countries using the term 'child labour' while others preferred terms such as 'working children' or 'economically active children'. These last two terms encourage more positive interpretations than the negative connotations associated with the first. The terminology used may also impact on how one country calculates the number of child workers compared to another, and may influence responses on how to deal with child workers. Hence, statistics on child labour always need to be treated with caution, and one should be aware that the language used to describe child work is never neutral and by itself encourages positive or negative associations at the outset. As Ennew, Myers and Plateau point out, 'the nature and scope of the work that children perform and its effects, cannot be grasped without understanding that the "term" [child labour] has various meanings, each of which produces different descriptions of its nature and measures of its scope' (2003, p.2). The ILO experts concluded that an unambiguous conceptual framework remains of critical importance to informing our understandings of the issue and how to deal with it (ILO 2008, p.5).

Supply-and-demand Factors

Why do children work and why do employers utilise children as workers? The answers to these questions suggest that child labour is a multifaceted issue necessitating multifaceted responses. One of the most common reasons children work is because of the poverty facing them and their families. At the same time, reducing all child work to poverty factors ignores the cultural significance of contributing economically to one's family and community in specific societies. The 'Western' notion of the dependent, innocent, helpless child may hold little sway in societies in which work is considered as an essential part of life – enhancing individual self-esteem, contributing to the economic viability of households and communities and teaching essential work-related skills that may be crucial to the child in his/her adult life. Hence it is inappropriate to consider child labour in terms of individual children devoid of family and community environments. Nonetheless, poverty may be a core explanation for some of the more exploitative types of child work found in majority world societies. For example, as outlined earlier, in extreme cases children may be drawn into the labour force as bonded labourers. Parents are paid a sum which the child is bonded to pay off; but the employer ensures that the debt is never repaid. Sometimes parents, themselves the victims of bonded labour, may have little option but to bond their children too into labour, to repay the debt. However, in the majority of cases, parents, families, households and communities may simply need the additional income generated by children working.

Supply-and-demand factors are ultimately influenced by processes of globalisation and the workings of the international system. For example, the International Monetary Fund (IMF) and the World Bank, through their structural adjustment programmes, created highly precarious conditions for many households in the majority world. These programmes often resulted in drastic cuts in government expenditure, particularly in social and education budgets, abolition of subsidies for basic goods, currency devaluation, increases in taxation, and trade liberalisation, encouraging a greater focus on the production of goods for export. To cope with their worsening economic situation, many households respond by bringing additional household members, including children, into the formal and informal economies. On the demand side, children are an attractive labour force because they are cheap. Many of the manufacturing sectors in which children are employed are ultimately related to the practices of multinational corporations based in minority world countries. These enterprises often contract out the labour-intensive aspects of the production process to majority world countries, where labour is cheaper, less organised and less regulated. These contractors in turn often rely on small-scale subcontractors, who try to undercut their competitors and secure contracts by employing child workers. Competition is often fierce. In relation to the garment industry, multinationals with their headquarters in minority world countries face stiff competition from China, where garments are produced in state-owned sectors in which the government may fix an artificially low price to capture the international market. The myriad of subcontracting arrangements that link minority and majority world countries together often draw child workers into the labour market, either formally or informally.

Children's Involvement in the Production of Goods for Export

Children involved in the production of goods for export receive disproportionate coverage in media accounts of the prevalence of child labour in majority world countries. Often there is an assumption that this is the most common form of child labour, despite a range of reports which estimate that the export sector may account for less than 5 per cent of working children (Noguchi 2002, p.360). At the same time, estimating the numbers employed in this sector is difficult, due to the fact that aspects of the production process often take place in the informal sector, rendering many workers invisible. Hence, while statistics on this aspect of child labour should be treated with caution, nonetheless there is qualitative evidence to suggest that children are involved in a vast array of manufacturing enterprises producing a wide range of goods that will eventually be sold in richer minority world countries. Bequele and Boyden (1988) present a number of case studies involving children working in leather tanning in Egypt; in quarries and shipyards in Colombia; at gold panning in Peru; in the garment industries in the Philippines; and in the carpet industry in India. Work conditions are often substandard, with many children working in crowded and unsanitary workplaces with poor ventilation and lighting. Often work processes are labour-intensive, with production being carried out by hand rather than by machine.

The garment industry is a case in point. Sancho-Liao (1994) estimates that around 4 million girls between the ages of 5 and 14 are employed in the garment industry in the Philippines alone. These children are often hired without a formal contract and paid wages below the minimum set by the law. The carpet industry in India is another core example of a production process that makes heavy use of child workers. This type of labour-intensive, low-technology industry actively seeks cheap workers, and children present an ideal, cheap and often unorganised labour force. Children often have to sit for long hours in crouched positions, which stunts their growth. The wool fluff is injurious to their lungs and the dyes and chemicals used in the production process often cause skin problems. In Gulrajani's (1994) research 97 per cent of children reported that their parents had been paid a lump sum for their labour power, for which they were expected to work for up to ten years, with no pay, to eradicate the debt; 84 per cent of child workers in this study typically worked a ten-hour day, seven days a week, 365 days a year. The majority were subjected to violence and other forms of punishment, including being deprived of sleep and food. Children may be drawn into export production as members of families. The family may be involved in work that has been subcontracted out to them on a piecework basis and, as a result, draws on the labour power of all family members to meet set targets. Children may also work on commercial agricultural plantations producing crops for export. They may be part of a family labour system in which the whole family are employed as hired hands. The move from subsistence agriculture towards cash-crop production encouraged by organisations such as the IMF and World Bank has resulted in the displacement of many small-scale peasant farmers, whose lands were appropriated for export production. These displaced families become cheap sources of labour for export agriculture. Working conditions are often hazardous, with children being exposed to harmful chemicals on a daily basis.

This brief overview suggests that subcontractors dominate the industries which make use of child workers. Lee-Wright (1990) points out how local employers are often compelled to rely on small-scale subcontractors because of the competitive nature of the global economy, which often enables multinational corporations in minority world countries to distance themselves from local practices involving child labour. Myrstad (1999) outlines a case study from Pakistan in which about 50,000 workers are employed in 325 factories producing surgical instruments. There are no child labourers in any of these factories. However, the semi-finished instruments are sent out to subcontracted workshops in the surrounding villages where the factories are located for polishing, filing and drilling of holes. Children as young as seven are employed in these workshops. After the finished instruments are returned to the factories, they are eventually shipped abroad to the USA, Germany and the United Kingdom. Myrstad concludes, 'buyers and importers often monitor the factories that they buy from, but this monitoring does not reach down to the subcontractors' (1999, p.77). Hence understanding and dealing with this type of child labour necessitates exposing the whole chain of commodity production to scrutiny.

While the supply-and-demand factors outlined in the previous section may shed some light on why children work, Boyden, Ling and Myers (1998) caution against utilising this traditional approach and suggest that it often detracts attention from the differential effects of work on children. While this section has focused, albeit briefly, on some of the negative factors associated with children working in the export sector, children's ability to deal with such work practices are far from uniform. For example, Boyden, Ling and Myers argue that resilience and vulnerability are not universally experienced, so that some children may be more resilient and less vulnerable than others working in the same occupation (ibid.). They also suggest that it is necessary to focus not only on the work itself, but also on the support systems children have, which might enable some children to cope with their working lives more effectively than others. If a child's work is valued by his/her family and community, it could contribute to his/her sense of esteem. Hence the child's vulnerability at work is often mediated by the wider social, economic and cultural context in which it takes place, suggesting that universal solutions aimed at all children may be an insufficient response to such a complex issue. It is to solutions to child labour that the chapter now turns.

Dealing with Child Labour: Short-term and Long-term Solutions

There are a number of international frameworks for dealing with the issue of child labour. The United Nations Convention on the Rights of the Child (1999) under Article 32 specifies the child's right to be protected against economic exploitation. The ILO, through its Worst Forms of Child Labour Convention no.182 (commonly referred to as C182) specifically highlights the need to eliminate the worst forms of child labour (such as those outlined in this chapter) as a priority. C182 came into force in November 2000 and by October 2002 it had been ratified by three out of every four member states of the ILO, making it the most rapid ratification process in the ILO's 80-year history (Noguchi 2002, p.355). The ILO distinguishes between worst form activities 'by definition' and worst form activities 'by condition'. The former refers to work practices that are so exploitative or unacceptable that they cannot be reformed. Bonded labour clearly falls into this category (Bales 2004).

Work practices that represent worst form 'by condition' include a wide range of activities which are carried out under conditions which are hazardous: for example, children being exposed to abuse at work, working excessive hours, being exposed to dangerous chemicals, working in unhealthy environments or under difficult circumstances. However, it is the working conditions that make the work hazardous rather than the occupation being hazardous per se. In other words, there is scope for reform. While the ILO rightly signals out worst forms for specific attention, its overall policy remains influenced by an abolitionist stance which ultimately aims, somewhat unrealistically, at ensuring the adoption of its earlier Convention 138 of 1973, which advocates nation states setting universal policies about the age at which children can legally work. C182 requires ratifying states to establish appropriate mechanisms to facilitate the removal of children from the worst forms of child labour.

As with Convention 138, this often results in nation states introducing or more effectively applying legal bans on working children. However, as Standing points out, 'if a phenomenon is not allowed to exist in law, little can be done to improve it ... By being made illegal, in effect their [child workers'] defencelessness is increased' (1982, p.617). Moreover, Woodhead's (1998) research with working children in Bangladesh, Ethiopia, the Philippines, El Salvador, Guatemala and Nicaragua, which asked them what they would do if the government introduced a legal ban preventing children aged under 15 from working, revealed that only 28 per cent felt that they or their families could comply with the law. By contrast, 65 per cent stated that they would have little option but to evade the law and if necessary move to working underground in the informal economy, where abuses would be even more difficult to detect. This suggests that legal remedies need to be treated with caution, as they may have unintended consequences.

As outlined earlier, subcontractors dominate export-oriented industries. Subcontracting firms are often informal and unregistered. They also tend to have a limited lifespan, setting up in one location and, within a short time frame, closing down or relocating elsewhere. Some children work as part of family units in both urban and rural settings, making detection even more difficult. In urban settings, if children work at home, they are often outside the reach of labour inspectors. In rural areas, whole families are often employed by subcontractors in agriculture producing crops for export. Often the adults in the family are utilised by subcontractors as casual labourers, and to meet quotas these families often enlist the help of their children. In such situations, the subcontractor can evade responsibility for child workers. Other subcontractors directly employ children in their own right rather than as members of families.

It is often competition rather than greed that drives subcontractors to employ child workers. Kolk and van Tulder point out that for small local subcontractors, employing children is a necessary component of a cost-reduction strategy and vital to increase very low profit margins. While the cost savings achieved in this way are a relatively small percentage of the final consumer price, the use of child labour can double the local entrepreneur's own small income. (2002, p.293)

The existence of this myriad of small-scale subcontractors makes it difficult for multinational corporations to implement codes of conduct ensuring that no child workers are involved in the production process. The Gap's policy is that if it discovers children being used by contractors, then the contractor must remove the child from the workplace, provide him/her with access to schooling and a wage, and guarantee the child the opportunity of work once the child reaches the legal working age. These penalties would clearly be expensive to implement and should deter contractors from engaging in this practice. However, the existence of a multitude of subcontractors makes such a policy difficult to put into practice. But even if contractors abided by these rules and did not employ children, what is the likely outcome? Quite obviously the problem of child labour does not simply disappear, as societal economic conditions have not changed. As Kolk and van Tulder put it:

at first sight, one is inclined to applaud strict measures to ban child labour, as this seems the logical consequence of a business policy usually developed after strong societal pressure. Nevertheless on further consideration such 'clean hands' may well be counterproductive because it does not tackle the child labour problem and its underlying causes. (2002, p.299)

'Western' solutions to dealing with child labour often involve boycotting goods made using child workers. However, in practice this often exacerbates the problem rather than providing a solution. In some cases, it may result in the eventual decline of the industry itself, leading to a further deterioration of the overall employment market and, as a result, increasing rather than decreasing the need for children to work (Gulrajani 1994). Many types of child labour are linked to parental poverty. Some commentators thus suggest that combating child labour necessitates developing macro-level policies to deal with poverty, including programmes aimed at generating and enhancing the employment and income of adults. Bans on goods produced by child labourers may also have the unintended effect of forcing children into other more exploitative forms of work. Hence, rather than eliminating child labour, such policies may simply displace child workers into similar or more abusive sectors. One of the most often quoted examples of this involved the boycott of textile goods in Bangladesh in 1996. Most of the 50,000 or so children thrown out of work ended up turning to crime or prostitution to survive (Guha-Khasnobis, Mehta and Agarwal 1999). As Gulrajani puts it, 'a ban or a boycott by external agents is no panacea for the problem of child labour' (1994, p.211). Moreover, Woodhead's (1999) research suggested that many girl domestic workers ironically aspired to work in garment factories. They saw garment factory work as preferable to their unpaid work in their own and other households and felt that moving to garment factory work was an indication of upward mobility and would teach them a skill which would be beneficial to them in adulthood. This again calls into question the appropriateness of boycotts for dealing effectively with child labour. As White puts it, 'any boycott or international sanctions must first select the right target; and second, ensure that the objective is one which the target group [that is child workers] would agree' (1996, p.825).

Education is often seen as a solution to child labour. The argument here is that if children are attending school then this by itself reduces their availability to perform work as well. However, this simplistic link between school and work is more complex than one which defines each in opposition to the other. In minority world countries for example, the introduction of compulsory schooling did not fully eradicate child labour, but rather changed the hours during which children became available for work, with children fitting in work obligations around school hours (Leonard 2004). Nonetheless, most commentators suggest that education is a crucial part of the initiatives necessary to reduce the potential for the exploitation of child workers. However, the education has to be affordable and relevant. Many families cannot afford to send their children to school. Even so-called 'free' education has all sorts of hidden costs, including books, travel, providing lunches, and so on. Many children often have to drop out of school and find work to support themselves or their families. Sometimes the education provided is inappropriate for the local environment in which the child resides, and parents and children may therefore see education as irrelevant and unable to provide them with necessary transferable skills to match their daily lives. As Ennew, Myers and Plateau point out, 'in many countries, schools serving the poor are so inferior and teach so little that children who might otherwise be perfectly willing to study leave and go to work' (2003, p.3). Some educational systems have attempted to provide a complementary balance between school and work by structuring the educational system around seasonal work demands, but such initiatives remain underdeveloped. The preferred option for the majority of working children (77 per cent) who took part in Woodhead's (1999) research was to combine work with school. This suggests that solutions to child labour are likely to be ineffective if child workers themselves are left out of the debate. Children's views of their working lives and how they perceive solutions to the issue are the subjects of the next section.

Hearing Working Children's Voices

Data on child labour is often based on quantitative measures which tend to ignore the input of children's voices into the research process (Woodhead 1999). Woodhead's research shows how children view work as an inevitable and necessary part of growing up. Rather than seeing children as passive victims of work practices, Woodhead advocates seeing children as active agents who 'shape their working life as well as being shaped by it' (1999, p.29). Hence, understanding child labour and how to deal with it necessitates asking children themselves what their work means to them and how their interests and rights could best be promoted (Boyden, Ling and Myers 1998). When children are asked about their work, 'they will tell you very clearly that they want to work and that the last thing they want is for

"Westerners" to take away their livelihood by means of legal bans or consumer boycotts' (Brazier 1997, p.9). As already outlined, when children were banned from the garment factories as a result of the Harkin Bill in 1993, the majority ended up in more hazardous work activities.

Many children subsequently interviewed found it difficult to equate their job losses with humanitarian concerns, given their subsequent relocation to more exploitative forms of economic activity than their factory jobs (Alam 1997, p.12). In the aftermath of the Harkin Bill, a number of working children's organisations emerged in many majority world countries calling for the right to work. Their main demand was to call for the regulation, rather than the abolition, of child work. In November 1996, they held their first global conference in India, where representatives of working children from 33 countries formulated ten demands, including the right to work, and a statement against the boycott of products made by children. Their final demand stated: 'We are against exploitation at work but we are for work with dignity, with hours adapted so that we have time for education and for leisure' (the ten demands are reproduced in the *New Internationalist*, July 1997, p.25).

Liebel (2003) argues that the emergence of these movements indicate that working children can competently speak up for themselves. His research reveals that the most consistent and recurring demand from child representatives from these organisations is the right to work. While recognising the potential exploitative aspects of their work, many children argue that properly organised work gives them the opportunity to learn essential skills. Liebel (2003) outlines a number of success stories where national governments and local administrations involved children in negotiations about child work. For example, in Nicaragua and Senegal, children selling a range of products on the street were treated with more respect by the police, who accepted their economic activities rather than stopping them from working. In Peru, city authorities drew up contracts which gave 'dignified' work to children over twelve years old, despite these children working under the recommended minimum age advocated by the ILO. Of course, these initiatives by themselves do not go far enough and only deal with one specific aspect of child work; but as Liebel concludes,

> children's organisations demonstrate through their own 'economic' praxis that work does not have to be put on a par with exploitation, that it does not inevitably stand in opposition to the needs of children to play and learn and that it can even contribute to promoting the personality development of the children. (2003, p.281)

In this vein, blanket prohibitions seem an inappropriate response, as they dismiss children's right to work.

Conclusion

Child labour should not be simply reduced to a 'for or against' issue. Such a simple dichotomy fails to capture the myriad of ways in which children work in majority world societies and the fact that their work often comprises a combination of positive and negative factors. As Ennew, Myers and Plateau point out: 'Work of the right kind can in many circumstances be quite beneficial to children ... [it can contribute] to self-esteem, human capital development, cognitive sophistication and even overall "happiness" and "contentment"' (2003, pp.11–12). Of course, not all works falls into this category, and this chapter mainly focuses on one form of child work, the production of commodities for export. Given that such a small percentage of children work in the export manufacturing sector, the importance attributed to this type of work in the international media may seem surprising.

Some commentators argue that minority world campaigners may hold ulterior motives, using this type of child labour as an excuse to promote protectionist policies. While this aspect of the issue fell outside the remit of this chapter, opening this small-scale example of child labour to further scrutiny reveals a number of misconceptions about child labour and its appropriate solutions. For example, the overwhelming focus on the exploitative aspects of such work may conceal its less negative elements. One child worker speaking of his work in the mines in Peru stated:

I want to make it very clear that work is not all bad. I didn't discover only exploitation in the mines. There were adults who really cared for us. We also had moments of gaiety, making a sport of racing each other in carrying the ore. There was joy in work. (Swift 1997, p.22)

This viewpoint adds complexity to the arguments around the issue of child labour. As Invernizzi and Milne point out, it leads to the somewhat uncomfortable position that 'exploitative work may offer a child a better income, better schooling opportunities or informal training that increases his or her chances of a better place in the labour market later on' (2002, p.425).

This suggests that understanding and dealing with child labour is a complex situation often resilient to seemingly well-intentioned solutions involving banning the practice and boycotting products made by child workers. Such initiatives, rather than solving the problem, could in practice make things worse. Unless appropriate alternatives are put in place, the removal of children from the world of work could lead them and indeed their families into more precarious economic conditions that in turn have a negative impact on current and future life chances. Indeed, many children work because of familial and community cultural expectations about their current and future economic contributions to their families and societies. Hence, dealing effectively with child labour demands economic as well as legal solutions.

While compulsory education is often seen as a panacea for child employment, working children themselves often argue for their right to work along with their right to an appropriate education. Rather than pitting one against the other, many children in majority societies see their complementary amalgamation as the best way forward. Incorporating children's voices into debates about child labour often demonstrates the fallacy of minority world solutions to the practice. Working children see legal bans as driving their economic activities underground, making abuses much more difficult to detect. Hence, they argue for rights in employment rather than protection from employment. They argue that the challenge is not to eradicate work itself but to change the conditions under which they carry out such work.

Boycotts are similarly dismissed as ineffective solutions. Indeed, many working children argue that such boycotts, rather than promoting their protection, make them vulnerable to more exploitative forms of employment. According to Hilowitz, rather than companies selling products not made by child workers, 'a more positive measure is a label indicating the company is engaged in activities to benefit the child workers employed in a given industry, thus alleviating some of the ill effects of work for the children concerned and sometimes their families as well' (1997, p.8). We are still a long way from a world free of child labour. Whether such a world is possible or indeed desirable remains a topic of heated debate. But in the meantime, given the reality of child workers, national and international policies should continue to explore the ways in which their working lives could be improved rather than simplistically assuming that bans, boycotts and education by itself will remove children from the labour market.

References

Alam, S. (1997) 'Thank You, Mr Harkin, Sir', *New Internationalist*, July, pp.12–14.

Bales, K. (2004) *Disposable People: New Slavery in the Global Economy*, University of California Press, Berkeley.

Bequele, A. and J. Boyden (1988) *Combating Child Labour*, International Labour Office, Geneva.

Boyden, J., B. Ling and W. Myers (1998) *What Works for Working Children*, Radda Barnen and UNICEF, Sweden.

Brazier, C. (1997) 'Respite and Respect', *New Internationalist*, July, pp.7–10.

Ennew, J., W. Myers and D. Plateau (2003) *The Meaning, Nature and Scope of Child Labour*, draft for the colloquium on 'Combating Abusive Child Labour', Iowa, July.

Guha-Khasnobis, B., P. Mehta and M. Agarwal (1999) 'Seen but Not Heard? Dealing with Child Labour', *Consumer Policy Review*, vol.9, no.4, pp.143–7.

Gulrajani, M. (1994) 'Child Labour and the Export Sector in the Third World: A Case Study of the Indian Carpet Industry', *Labour, Capital and Society*, vol.27, no.2, pp.192–214.

Hilowitz, T. (1997) 'Social Labelling to Combat Child Labour: Some Considerations', *International Labour Review*, vol.136, no.2, pp.1–19.

ILO (2006) *The End of Child Labour with Reach*, International Labour Organisation, Geneva.

ILO (2008) *Report of the Meeting of Experts on Labour Statistics*, 1–10 April, International Labour Organisation, Geneva.

Invernizzi, A. and B. Milne (2002) 'Are Children Entitled to Contribute to International Policy Making? A critical view of children's participation in the international campaign for the elimination of child labour', *International Journal of Children's Rights*, vol.10, pp.403–31.

Kolk, K. and R. van Tulder (2002) 'Child Labour and Multinational Conduct: A Comparison of International Business and Stakeholder Codes', *Journal of Business Ethics*, vol.36, no.3, pp.291–302.

Lee-Wright, P. (1990) *Child Slaves*, Earthscan Publications, London.

Leonard, M. (2004) 'Children's Views on Children's Right to Work', *Childhood: A Global Journal of Child Research*, vol.11, no.1, pp.73–89.

Liebel, M. (2003) 'Working Children as Social Subjects: The Contribution of Working Children's Organisations to Social Transformations', *Childhood*, vol.10, no.3, pp.265–85.

McDougall, D. (2007) 'Child Sweat Shop Shame Threatens Gap's Ethical Image', *Observer*, 28 October.

Myrstad, G. (1999) 'What can Trade Unions Do to Combat Child Labour?' *Childhood*, vol.6, no.1, pp.75–88.

Noguchi, Y. (2002) 'ILO Convention No.182 on the Worst Forms of Child Labour and the Convention on the Rights of the Child', *International Journal of Children's Rights*, vol.19, pp.335–69.

O'Donnell, O., E. van Doorslaer and F. Rosate (2002) *Child Labour and Health: Evidence and Research Issues*, ILO/UNICEF/World Bank, Understanding Children's Work Project, Florence.

Sancho-Liao, N. (1994) 'Child Labour in the Philippines: Exploitation in the Process of Globalization of the Economy', *Labour, Capital and Society*, vol.27, no.2, pp.270–81.

Standing, G. (1982) 'State Policy and Child Labour: Accumulation versus Legitimation?' *Development and Change*, vol.13, no.3, pp.611–31.

Swift, A. (1997) 'Let us Work', *New Internationalist*, July, pp.21–3.

White, B. (1996) 'Globalisation and the Child Labour Problem', *Journal of International Development*, vol.8, no.6, pp.829–39.

Woodhead, M. (1998) *Children's Perspectives on their Working Lives*, Radda Barnen, Stockholm.

Woodhead, M. (1999) 'Combating Child Labour: Listening to What the Children Say', *Childhood*, vol.6, no.1, pp.27–49.

Websites

Anti-Slavery Organisation	www.antislavery.org/homepage/antislavery/childlabour.htm
Child Labor India	www.childlabor.in
Child Labor Photo Project	www.childlaborphotoproject.org
Child Watch	www.childwatch.uio.no
ECLT	www.eclt.org
Human Rights Watch	www.hrw.org
ILO	www.ilo.org/global/Themes/Child_Labour/lang--en/index.htm
International Research on Working Children	www.childlabour.net
Save the Children	www.savethechildren.org.uk
Stop Child Labor Coalition	www.stopchildlabor.org
UNICEF	www.unicef.org

14

DEVELOPMENT EDUCATION AS AN AGENT OF SOCIAL CHANGE: THE THEORY AND PRACTICE

Stephen McCloskey

The end of the Cold War in 1989 heralded a period largely characterised by rapid globalisation, unfettered trade and the accumulation of increasing power and wealth by transnational corporations (TNCs). However, the apparent vanquishing of state-driven forms of economic growth by a reinvigorated capitalism in the conflict of ideologies underpinning the Cold War has not 'lifted all boats' in a tide of trade-driven prosperity. Many poor countries remain constricted in their growth and peripheral in the economic order that has underpinned global finance and trade over the past two decades. Indeed, the failings of contemporary globalisation were acknowledged by the United Nations (UN) in 2000 with the formulation of millennium development goals (MDGs) with their overarching aim 'to reduce by half the proportion of people living on less than a dollar a day' (www.un.org/millenniumgoals). These goals tell us that global poverty remains a persistent problem, particularly for developing countries.

Development education (DE) is a concept that emerged in the 1970s on the basis of work undertaken by missionaries and development organisations in the developing world. Its role is to contribute to the eradication of poverty through an enhanced understanding of the causes of inequality and injustice, both locally and internationally. DE has retained an important role in the post-Cold War era in supporting critical analysis of global poverty toward informing actions that will tackle underdevelopment in poor countries. The need for DE has arguably become even more acute in the current global recession, which could ultimately impact on aid flows to developing countries and reduce the volume of trade between countries in the global North and South.

The financial crisis has asked questions and challenged fundamental assumptions about the dominant free-market ideology that the world's leading economies have advocated as the basis for growth and development. As unregulated financial institutions have unravelled and created a contagion of market uncertainty that has spilled over into other economic sectors, there has been a growing clamour for public debate and action on how we engineer and manage development. Development education can support this public debate and provide the skills, values and knowledge needed to understand and act upon the major issues impacting on our lives. The action outcome of DE has become increasingly important in an era in which changes in consumer patterns toward sustainable lifestyles and social activism toward equality and justice have become essential rather than optional components of contemporary society.

This chapter examines the theory and practice of development education and its distinctive and radical model of learning. It assesses the contribution of DE in the formal, non-formal and tertiary education sectors and discusses the challenge of effectively measuring the impact of this work. It also outlines the policy environment in which development practitioners operate, particularly in Britain and Ireland, and considers the relationship between DE and environmental education (EE), within the scope of education for sustainable development (ESD). The chapter begins by focusing on some definitions of DE, before considering the educational philosophy of Paulo Freire, which provides the theoretical base of contemporary practice.

Defining Development Education

Defining development education can be problematic, as it involves capturing the range of components that comprise this broad and far-reaching pedagogical process. For example, do we focus on methodology (active, participative learning), the social and economic issues it addresses (trade, aid, conflict, etc.), the skills it engenders in learners (tolerance, respect, cultural awareness), the outcomes it intends (social justice and equality), the social relations it examines (rich and poor, developing and developed countries), the educational sectors in which it operates (adults, schools, youth groups etc.) or the tools it employs (teaching resources, training, information technology)? This problem is compounded by the various labels applied by educators to the methodology, content and process encompassed by DE. Alternatives include global dimension, global education, education for sustainable development, development studies and development awareness. In fact, some proponents of DE oppose the use of definitions, arguing that these can be counterproductive in limiting its terms of reference or that they anchor it in a particular point in history when it is a fluid, non-static process.

While accepting the limitations of definitions, they can at least point to the main parameters of DE activity and offer some guidance as to its aims. A commonly used definition is that framed by the UN, which states that development education is

> concerned with issues of human rights, dignity, self-reliance and social justice in both developed and developing countries. It is concerned with the causes of underdevelopment and the promotion of an understanding of what is involved in development, of how countries go about undertaking development, and of the reasons for and ways of achieving a new international economic and social order. (Osler 1994, p.51)

The Development Education Association (DEA), an umbrella organisation for DE organisations in the United Kingdom (UK), suggests that DE:

- explores the links between people living in the 'developed' countries of the North with those of the 'developing' South, enabling people to understand the links between their own lives and those of people throughout the world;

- increases understanding of the economic, social, political and environmental forces which shape our lives;
- develops the skills, attitudes and values which enable people to work together to take action to bring about change and take control of their own lives;
- works toward achieving a more just and a more sustainable world in which power and resources are more equitably shared. (www.dea.org.uk)

In its Development Education Strategy Plan (2007–11), Irish Aid suggests that

> [d]evelopment education aims to deepen understanding of global poverty and encourage people towards action for a more just and equal world. As such, it can build support for efforts by government and civil society to promote a development agenda and it can prompt action at a community and individual level. (Irish Aid 2007)

From these definitions we can discern the need to enhance understanding about development, address poverty-related issues, promote social justice and bring about change. The UN emphasises the role of countries in the development process, whereas the DEA focuses on people as agents of change, suggesting the importance of individual action and of taking responsibility for our lives. Irish Aid's definition encompasses both government and civil society as actors in the development process, reflecting the extent to which development NGOs and government agencies have become partners in the development process. The common themes that permeate most definitions of DE include:

- the need to encourage action as an outcome of the educational process;
- the local–global axis of education, involving both an understanding of development issues and our interdependence with other societies;
- the development of new skills, values, attitudes, knowledge and understanding that will inform individual action;
- the use of participative, active-learning methodologies;

- education as a visioning exercise toward social transformation;
- social justice, inclusion and equality;
- the need to inform practice with a developing world perspective.

The themes, concepts and issues addressed by DE have been largely derived from the philosophical thought and practice of Paulo Freire. His work has been a mainspring for development education practice since its emergence in the early 1970s, combined with that of missionary groups and development non-governmental organisations (NGOs) that have worked in developing countries. The next section examines the Freirean theory underpinning development education practice.

The Theory of Development Education

The seminal development education text is Paulo Freire's (1972) *Pedagogy of the Oppressed*, which was initially lauded primarily for its contribution to the illiteracy problem in Latin America. Indeed, Freire was the general co-ordinator of the National Plan for Adult Literacy in his native Brazil, but his educational philosophy had a methodology and praxis targeted at all socially oppressed peoples. What distinguished Freire's discourse on education from existing models was its assertion that learners could engage in a process of social transformation from oppression to liberation. Freire's radical philosophy struck a chord with dispossessed people throughout Latin America, where educational access was limited and poverty endemic. His work still resonates today in societies where educational provision represents more than the eradication of illiteracy, to support a more rounded and transformative concept of individual and communal development. His work frowns upon the dominant didactic model of education, in which students are mere receptacles of information delivered by the teacher. Freire advocated an active-learning approach to education through which students could engender a critical consciousness that would inform their future actions. He proposed that teachers should work with students 'in acts of cognition, not transferrals of information' (Freire 1972, p.47).

Development education also facilitates a process of problem-solving in which the students and teacher engage in dialogue and reflection that draws on their own experiences and 'strives for the emergence of consciousness and critical intervention in reality' (ibid., p.54). Freire's 'banking theory', whereby the teacher deposits information in the mind of the student as an incontestable, indelible truth, represented a negation of education 'as a process of enquiry' (ibid., p.45). Approaching education as a process of dialogue and enquiry enhances the capacity of the learner to develop values such as respect for the views of others. These values are complemented by the development of new skills that equip the learner to engage actively in society to effect change. Thus, the global-justice movement that emerged in the 1990s to challenge the international financial institutions (IFIs) which frame the rules of global commerce could arguably be described as DE in practice.

Angus McBrian (2001), an eyewitness to the high profile protests at the World Trade Organisation's (WTO) Ministerial Council meeting in Seattle in November 1999, suggested that 'the events in Seattle found their greatest success as an endeavour in development education'. The operations of the IFIs and their impact on poor countries are complex, technical and difficult to process into public campaigns. Nonetheless, the global-justice movement has engaged in what McBrian described as 'self-education' initiatives, involving 'teach-ins, workshops and seminars'. This methodology corresponds with the Freirean 'problem-posing education' and co-investigation in dialogue which resonates in the World Social Forum (WSF), established in 2001, and describes itself as

> an open meeting place for reflective thinking, democratic debate of ideas, formulation of proposals, free exchange of experiences and inter-linking for effective action by groups and movements of civil society that are opposed to neoliberalism and to domination of the world by capital and any form of imperialism, and are committed to building a society centred on the human person. (www.wsfindia.org)

The WSF promotes the core elements of DE practice – reflective learning, analysis and exchange, and social action 'centred on the human person'. While the relationship between DE and new social movements like the WSF has not yet been fully explored, the regional and global-justice organisations appear to be adapting Freirean concepts to their campaigning and education activities.

Reflective Action

Freire's work is noted for its articulation of the needs of the oppressed and those living in absolute poverty. He aimed to break what he described as the 'culture of silence' of those who were dispossessed through a union of theory and praxis. This process encompassed an analysis of the social relations and power structures (media, government, cultural elitism) which entrapped the masses in a state of domination. For Freire, the process of liberation should be characterised by the same principles and actions which underpin a transformed society liberated from the bonds of colonialism. The revolutionary process advocated by Freire involved reflective action encompassing measured and contemplative dialogue within the dominated class as part of a meaningful act of liberation. Freire regarded reflection without an action outcome as mere 'verbalism' and action without reflection as pure 'activism' (action for action's sake). Freire's concept of 'dialogical action' was influenced by Marx's 'dialectical materialism' and the assertion that philosophy's validity depended on how it informed action. As Karl Marx put it: 'Philosophers have only interpreted the world in various ways; the point is to change it' (Marx 1845, p.173).

Both Marx and Freire believed that the masses should participate in a revolutionary process to surmount the anti-dialogical praxis of the dominant elites. As Freire suggests: 'The unity of the elite derives from its *antagonism* with the people; the unity of the revolutionary group grows out of *communion* with the (united) people' (1972, p.140). The main concern of the ruling elite is to maintain the status quo of social relations by undermining any alteration to the social order. Freire cautioned against 'communiqués' or entreaties from the ruling class, offering to enter into dialogue with those they dominated. This was not dialogical praxis, but an attempt to quell the formations of action that threatened the power base of the elite. For example, the conquest of Latin America by colonial powers was followed by an equally oppressive neocolonial process of corrupt oligarchies and 'democracies' that were in fact executors of power bestowed by the old colonial masters. Thus, indigenous rulers in the main did not alter the social, economic and political forces that underpinned poverty and social exclusion. Freire, therefore, considered the revolutionary process as a liberating experience for both the oppressors and the oppressed, which based their relations on equality rather than domination.

Cultural Synthesis

Another key Freirean concept is that of cultural synthesis, which is also a dialectical process based on the notion that culture can either transform social reality or maintain the old hierarchical order. Freire described cultural synthesis as 'a mode of action for confronting culture itself, as the preserver of the very structures by which it was formed' (1972, p.147). Dialogical cultural action is based on relations of 'permanence' and 'change' that can be transcended through a new social structure. Cultural synthesis recognises the value of diversity and engenders an enthusiasm to learn from the values and traditions of others rather than imposing one cultural form on another. The colonial conquest of developing countries was often attended by a 'civilising' project intended to impose westernised cultures and faiths on indigenous populations. This was a process of cultural supremacy, not synthesis, and eradicated, rather than learnt from, indigenous traditions.

Placed in the contemporary context of globalisation, Freire's anti-dialogical theory of cultural domination resonates loudly in the economic activities of transnational corporations and developed countries. McDonalds, Starbucks, Nike and Coca-Cola are totems of a cultural invasion of developing countries that has accompanied economic dominance. The *Human Development Report* makes this point clearly when it states that 'today's flow of culture is unbalanced, heavily weighted in one direction, from rich countries to poor' (HDR 1999, p.4).[1] The cultural invasion of the global South from the global North creates an appetite for Western commodities and conjures up images of a superficially attractive path to development that masks massive levels of underlying poverty in developing and developed countries. The 2004 report states that '[c]ultural liberty is a vital part of human development because being able to choose one's identity – who one is – without losing the respect of others or being excluded from other choices is important in leading a full life' (HDR 2004, p.10).

Freire suggests that anti-dialogical action – cultural permanence toward social stasis – is constructed upon conquest, division and manipulation, while cultural action aims to 'supersede the dominant alienated and alienating culture' (1972, p.147). In this sense, we have witnessed increasing levels of cultural action in diverse settings around the world. As the HDR reports:

> In vastly different contexts and in different ways – from indigenous people in Latin America to religious minorities in South Asia to ethnic minorities in the Balkans and Africa to immigrants in Western Europe – people are mobilizing anew around old grievances along ethnic, racial, religious and cultural lines, demanding that their identities be acknowledged, appreciated and accommodated by wider society. (2004, p.10)

Thus, the theoretical underpinnings of Freire have found contemporary expression in the practice of new social movements in the developed and developing worlds that are challenging the divisive and disempowering domination of old elites.

---

1. The *Human Development Report* is produced annually and ranks countries on a Human Development Index (HDI) that provides a more rounded assessment of their social and economic performance over the previous year. The HDI is based on four main criteria: life expectancy at birth, adult literacy, combined gross school enrolment and gross domestic product (GDP). The aim of the index is to reflect the extent to which countries address the social and economic needs of their people rather than rely exclusively on the GDP criterion favoured by the World Bank and other international financial institutions. http://hdr.undp.org_20072008

Development Education Practice

In assessing the impact of Freire's educational philosophy on the activities of contemporary educational practitioners, Ann McCollum identified a significant gap between the theory and practice of development education. McCollum's critical analysis of the development sector, particularly in Britain and Ireland, concluded that the radical vision of Freire's work had been moderated by development educators to accommodate the dominant liberal ideology in the education sector. She suggested that 'Freire's ideas have been misappropriated within development education leading to dilemmas in relation to the theory and practice of development education which must be recognized and resolved' (1996). McCollum believed that the 'central assumption' of DE – that raising individual awareness of development issues would logically result in social action – was fundamentally flawed. Freire regarded education as an agent of societal change, whereas liberal education focuses on the development of the individual. McCollum argued that DE was not engaging with major social and economic structures and relations as advocated in Freire's radical social theory. DE lacked the 'conceptual space' to engage with the theoretical questions posed by Freire that underpinned action toward social transformation. Instead, development educators had embraced Freire's active-learning methodology without addressing 'the wider implications of the sociology of knowledge' (ibid.).

McCollum also identified problems within the wider operations of development NGOs that limited their impact as DE practitioners. She described the development community as speaking 'only to itself' and, thereby, limiting its influence within the education system and civil society. However, McCollum acknowledged the difficult context in which development NGOs have to operate. The DE sector in developed countries has been chronically underfunded, with government support normally representing only a small percentage of the overall development aid budget. In 1970, the UN set a target for developed countries of 0.7 per cent of gross national product (GNP) for overseas aid budgets and, almost 40 years on, most Western governments have fallen well short of this meagre contribution (with Scandinavian countries being a notable exception).

Contemporary Practice

So how has development education policy and practice moved on since McCollum's rather bleak assessment in the mid 1990s? In some respects the sector has made significant progress, particularly with regard to government support. From the 1970s to the late 1990s, DE was largely financed by development NGOs such as Oxfam and Save the Children, with limited funding also coming from government departments, trust funds and charities. Indeed, development agencies were largely instrumental in the establishment of some 50 development education centres (DECs) in Britain and Ireland from the 1970s onward, with the remit of delivering specialist DE services, such as resource provision and training workshops. The election of a New Labour government in 1997 resulted in the establishment of the Department for International Development (DfID) which superseded the Overseas Development Administration (ODA) as the ministry responsible for overseas aid, policy development and development education.

In November 1997, DfID published a White Paper which was the first 'definitive statement' by the British government on international development for over 20 years. The White Paper represented a renewed engagement by the government in international issues, following two decades of underfunding and a gaping policy vacuum. Indeed, DfID candidly accepted that

> [f]or much of the last 20 years, the UK government has attached little importance to development education work in the UK, leaving others, particularly the network of Development Education Centres and others in the voluntary sector, to take the lead in promoting greater awareness and understanding. (DfID 1999a)

Clare Short, the (then) secretary of state for international development, also commended the role of DECs in promoting DE, although she identified a need for strategic direction in the development sector:

> I want to pay tribute to the work of the 50 or so Development Education Centres spread around the UK. Often run on a shoestring, they have delivered both materials and expertise to many schools ... But DECs would be the first to admit that their reach and resources are limited. We have increased our support for their work but also need to look strategically at this area. (DfID 1999a)

Enabling Effective Support

The strategic focus of DfID's development education work has been most evident in the formal education sector, with the delivery of a new process called Enabling Effective Support (EES). EES was designed

> to provide teachers with more effective and sustained support to incorporate a global dimension into their teaching. It supports the development of locally owned strategies to achieve more comprehensive, high quality support to teachers for the delivery of the global dimension. (DfID 2002)

EES has been rolled out in nine regions in England, as well as in Scotland, Wales and Northern Ireland. The strategic component of the process signified a new approach to DE in the formal sector on the part of DfID, which included the development of partnerships with education ministries and key statutory bodies in each of the twelve jurisdictions.

EES has a two-phased strategy for delivery, with Phase 1 involving initial consultation and research 'to determine current provisions, needs, opportunities and activities related to the implementation of the global perspectives in each region' (DfID 2002, p.5). Research was commissioned in each region to assess the needs of teachers in respect of aspects of practice like continuing professional development (CPD) and access to quality resources on the global dimension. Phase 2 concerns the development and implementation of a strategy to enable the education system to respond to the challenges of a globalising society. The strategy in each region includes a planning framework 'to establish and communicate a clear agenda for the support of the global dimension' and provisions for the professional development of teachers. The strategy also creates a network of partners in the formal education sector – schools, curriculum authorities, education ministries, education authorities and NGOs – to ensure the effective delivery of an integrated package of support for teachers and schools.

The EES process has now been in operation for several years, and the regions have had variable levels of success in developing and delivering global-dimension strategies. The effectiveness of the process is contingent upon the receptiveness of statutory bodies to a global-dimension strategy and the general policy environment in each region. For example, the greater autonomy and legislative independence of the Welsh Assembly has been supportive of an effective policy framework in Wales for EES, whereas some of the other regions lacking this immediate policy access have found strategic delivery more challenging. However, even where existing structures and networks are not ideal for strategic policymaking, EES can support a practice-driven, bottom-up approach to the global dimension that can support the classroom practice of teachers. On balance, the development sector has favoured this more strategic approach from government to the global dimension as further integrating development education into mainstream formal sector practice.

Funding

The funding climate for development education over the past ten years has been decidedly mixed. In the United Kingdom, the DE budget has increased dramatically from a paltry £700,000 under the last Conservative government (1996–97) to £6.5 million in 2001/2 and £11.8 million in 2006 (www.deeep.org). Britain's total aid contribution, however, presently stands at 0.36 per cent of GNP, which is just over half of the UN's overseas development aid target. According to the Organisation for Economic Co-operation and Development (OECD) Development Assistance Committee (DAC) only five countries have reached the 0.7 per cent target of GNP for overseas development aid: Denmark, Luxembourg, Norway, Sweden and the Netherlands. Ireland's aid budget currently stands at 0.54 per cent of GNP, and prior to the recession was on course to reach the 0.7 per cent target by 2012. Ireland's DE budget in 2006 was €4.5 million which represents 0.67 per cent of the Irish overseas development aid figure (€665 million) and is two and a half times the sum for 2004 (€2 million) (www.dochas.ie).

While these increases in DE spending have been very welcome in the sector, there has been an increasing reliance on government support as development agencies have reduced their budgets for DE. Development agencies were the mainstay of DE for many years but appear to have derogated support for the sector to government agencies. Consequently, many DE centres have come to rely heavily upon government support, which leaves them vulnerable to a shift in policy, resulting in reduced funding for the sector. Moreover, NGOs may be more reluctant to critique a government agency that is also their primary funder. It is important, therefore, that development NGOs re-engage with the sector in terms of resourcing both their own DE work and that of external bodies like DECs. The current economic climate will ensure that development budgets across the developed world come under increased pressure and to shore up and diversify the sector's funding base, development NGOs need both to oppose any planned cuts in aid budgets and to increase their own DE spending.

Development Education Policy: Britain and Ireland

Since 1997, the British government has published three White Papers on international development (1997, 2000 and 2006) that made explicit reference to the need for strengthened awareness-raising across civil society, and in 2006 the Irish government published its first *White Paper on International Development*. Note the similarities in the messages contained in their policy statements on development education. The British government states that '[e]very child should be educated about development issues, so that they can understand the key global considerations which will shape their lives' (DfID 1997). The Irish government's

White Paper states that '[e]very person in Ireland will have access to educational opportunities to be aware of and understand their rights and responsibilities as global citizens and their potential to effect change for a more just and equal world' (Government of Ireland 2006).

The two governments have produced strategy plans to deliver results on their White Paper targets that make provision for more strategic interventions in the education system through interdepartmental dialogue and co-operation. In the case of DfID, it published a strategy paper, *Building Support for Development* (1999b), which set out the department's strategic aims for DE. These included:

- reversing the decline in DE spending;
- reaching out to new sectors in securing their support for development awareness – trade unions, business, church and faith groups, etc.;
- promoting DE resources in education sectors (schools, youth groups, community organisations, etc.) more effectively;
- influencing schools' curriculum review processes in England and Wales, Scotland and Northern Ireland;
- enlisting the support of other government departments for DE.

Building Support for Development concentrated DfID's work around four main sectors: formal education, the media, business and the trade unions. Part of this process involved awarding Strategic Grant Agreements (SGAs) to UK civil society organisations 'for whom development is not the main focus, but who have the potential to work constructively and strategically with DfID in helping to reduce poverty' (www.dfid.gov.uk). Recipients of SGAs have included the Trade Union Congress and UK Black and Minority Ethnic Civil Society; they aim to enable recipients to make a more effective strategic contribution to international development. In addition to the SGAs, DfID supports DE work through a UK-wide Development Awareness Fund (DAF) and mini-grant schemes that operate in England, Scotland, Wales and Northern Ireland.

Thus, DfID has delivered on many of its key targets outlined in the 1999 strategy paper. It has engaged new audiences, enhanced financial support for development, become more strategic in its focus and, through EES, enhanced delivery of the global dimension in the schools sector. More negatively, DfID has yet to secure the co-operation of other key ministries in adopting a more integrated approach to development. Government development policies should prioritise environment protection; enhance financial support for development to the required UN level of 0.7 per cent of GNP; reduce spending on defence and tighten enforcement of arms export controls; enforce ethical investment criteria; and ensure a more explicit requirement for the study of international development within the statutory schools curriculum and in teacher training programmes – in short, a 'joined-up' approach to sustainable development that has the full support of appropriate ministers and civil servants. As a relatively new department and a 'junior partner' in government, DfID perhaps lacks the political clout to ensure effective co-ordination in the delivery of an international development agenda across government departments. However, with respect to development education, DfID has considerably advanced the policy and practice environment for the sector in comparison to previous governments.

With regard to the Irish context for development education, Irish Aid has followed up publication of the White Paper with a DE strategy for the period 2007–11, titled 'Promoting Public Engagement for Development'. The strategy has four major components:

- strengthening coherence between DE and national education;
- contributing to high-quality DE through strengthened support for DE practitioners;
- supporting the further integration of DE in formal and non-formal education programmes;
- ensuring that DE initiatives raise public awareness and understanding of the underlying causes of global poverty.

In identifying targets for the new strategy, Irish Aid commissioned a review of the 2003–05 strategy, which pinpointed areas for specific action. These included strengthening individual and community capacity in the DE sector; enhancing the representation of adult and further education in DE; addressing 'the paucity of research in development education'; continuing the professional development of teachers and other educators; supporting the integration of Black and Minority Ethnic (BME) communities in DE; and exploring 'new ways of supporting educators to effectively integrate development education into their work' (Irish Aid 2007). With regard to delivery mechanisms for the new strategy, Irish Aid is promoting links with the broader government aid programme, prioritising a partnership approach, and maintaining levels of flexibility to respond to new challenges and opportunities.

DfID and Irish Aid are therefore operating in similar contexts, with strategies that aim to broaden support for development education in government and civil society, employing strategic mechanisms for delivery. Both departments are junior partners of more influential foreign office ministries (Department of Foreign Affairs in Ireland, Foreign Office in the United Kingdom) and are therefore likely to feel the spending squeeze in an economic downturn. However, recent White Papers, strategy plans and increased budgets have enhanced their standing in mainstream formal education and drawn non-traditional deliverers of DE into the sector. The next section considers the impact of DE in the formal and non-formal education sectors.

Formal and Non-formal Education

Development education practitioners have made significant headway in enhancing awareness about development issues in the formal and non-formal sectors, particularly over the past decade. Development agencies, DECs and statutory education bodies have developed models of good practice in training provision and resource production that encourage educators to incorporate development issues into their teaching practice. Increased funding of the development sector in recent years has enhanced the professionalism of the services provided by NGOs and enabled them to promote their work more effectively through information technology. Moreover, the widespread recognition within the education sector that globalisation necessitates the development, from an early age, of a global perspective among young people has added weight to the argument for the increased resourcing and practice of DE.

Development educators have traditionally focused their activities on the formal (schools, colleges, universities) and non-formal (youth groups, community organisations, adult education, trade unions, women's groups, etc.) education sectors. Formal-sector work can comprise the continuing professional development (CPD) of teachers, initial teacher education (student teacher training), resource provision, workshops with school students, and advocacy work aimed at integrating DE into mainstream curricula and education practice. Activity in the non-formal sector is less constrained by statutory curricula and targeted at a wide range of groups in civil society that have an interest in broadening the global perspective of their constituents. The methodology applied in both sectors is based on the Freirean active-learning approach, although the content of training events can be tailored to meet the needs of target groups – for example, trade unions are likely to be most interested in the impact of trade and globalisation on workers in developed and developing countries.

The limitations of DE practice have often resulted from a lack of clarity as to how this form of education relates to and benefits learners and what the concept actually means. The sources of this confusion include the breadth of DE content, which can overwhelm the learner; the various labels pertaining to DE, which can dilute its impact; the notion that development issues have a global context that is somehow removed from the learner's own experiences and reality; and the concern that development education is an additional subject area to be foisted on to already overburdened teachers and educators rather than an area of study that complements their teaching practice. Of course, the misperceptions of learners can often result from the failings of DE practitioners to adequately promote their work, strategically align their activities to mainstream education needs and build alliances with statutory education bodies. Development NGOs have acknowledged weaknesses in their practice, but can point to some of the mitigating factors discussed above – inadequate funding, a fragmented policy environment and limited windows of opportunity to introduce a global dimension in education practice. Also, within the operations of leading development agencies there may be competing priorities for their resources (campaigning, fundraising, overseas aid, as well as DE).

A significant and positive development within formal education in Britain and Ireland that has created new opportunities for the study of development issues has been the introduction of citizenship education into the statutory curricula. Citizenship facilitates the study of local and global aspects of development and, as a statutory component of the curricula, has also been introduced into teacher training and the in-service training of practising teachers. As a new area of the curricula in the two countries, citizenship has required the production of new resources, including materials addressing its links with international development (see, for example, www.bigpic.biz). Development NGOs have a new foothold in schools, in addition to traditional carriers of DE, such as geography and religious education.

More negatively, citizenship education is required to tackle a wide range of issues, such as racism, cultural diversity, conflict, homelessness, drug abuse and development, with an equally broad number of civil society groups competing for the attention of schools, teachers and curriculum planners. Moreover, among senior management and decision makers in the formal sector, and possibly among some practitioners, the perception may gather strength that DE has a new home in the curriculum. This position frustrates the long-held assertion of development educators that DE can support teachers in addressing aspects of all subject areas in the statutory curriculum, something that our globalising society demands. The DE sector needs to make this case vociferously to curriculum managers and government education departments, to ensure that a global dimension is introduced into the practice of teachers at all levels and in all subject areas of formal education.

Part of the process of enhancing the status of DE in the formal and non-formal sectors lies in creating new opportunities for the study of international development and DE in the tertiary sector.[2]

Tertiary Education

When referring to development education at third level, this includes opportunities to study international development issues which are clearly an important component of DE. Doug Bourn suggests that although DE at third level is becoming increasingly well supported by government agencies and policymakers across the European Union,

> most of this activity has been based around the practice of a range of NGOs and, while there has been a greater level of activity within higher education linked mainly to teacher training or deepening the study of development issues across a range of degree courses, there has been no independent body of educational research in development education. (Bourn 2007, p.31)

Bourn suggests that this lack of independent research focus has meant that DE 'has minimal academic profile' compared to related 'adjectival' educations such as environmental, human rights or citizenship education.

However, two recent initiatives in Galway and London are aiming to address this lack of academic profile for DE at third level. The Institute of Education at the University of London launched a Development Education Research Centre (DERC) in 2006, funded, inevitably, by DfID. The DERC aims to 'act as a hub for generating issues and areas for knowledge generation, new thinking and quality output on development education' (Bourn 2007, p.34). DERC activities include helping to tackle the perennial issue of demonstrating the value and impact of DE on target groups. The DERC will also develop a 'community of

2. *Policy and Practice: A Development Education Review*, Centre for Global Education, Belfast, issues 1–7, 2005 – 2008. This is the only development education journal currently in production in Britain and Ireland and carries articles on issues central to contemporary development education practice in Ireland, Europe, North America and the developing world. A sample of articles is available from www. centreforglobaleducation.com.

researchers engaged in development education' and offer the first ever master's degree course on DE in the United Kingdom.

The Development Education and Research Network (DERN) was established in 2005, with similar aims to the DERC, at the National University of Ireland (NUI), Galway. The DERN aims 'to promote DE and enhance networking between researchers and academics interested in development and education issues' at NUI Galway (www.nuigalway.ie/dern). The network aims 'to contribute to capacity building for development education' and 'promote an interdisciplinary approach to development issues in teaching and research'. The DERN believes that research on development issues suffers from a '10/90 gap', meaning that 90 per cent of the research funding in the world goes to solving the problems of the richest 10 per cent of its people. Addressing this gap, by supporting 'greater equality in knowledge partnerships', is a key DERN objective.

Clearly, both these initiatives have great significance for DE in helping to establish the academic standing of DE by commissioning high-quality research, publications and articles on aspects of policy and practice. Bourn considers research in DE as essential in 'strengthening public confidence in, and support for the fight against global poverty' while also 'raising standards in educational attainment' in development education. Khoo, Healy and Coate (2007) have raised concerns about the current research landscape faced by development education practitioners, arguing that it goes against DE values and intrinsic humanism. They ask how the 'narrow instrumental' approach to education found in 'academic capitalism' will coexist and integrate with the more egalitarian and co-operative modes of working central to DE practice. Development educators will have to combat this instrumental view of knowledge that has attended the injection of new research funding in higher education. The research initiatives at Galway and London offer new possibilities for research practice that will build the case for strengthened DE delivery in all sectors of education, by demonstrating the value and need for a global dimension in our learning. The next section considers the importance of evaluation in providing evidence of the impact of DE practice on its target groups.

Evaluation

One of the main challenges for development educators is in assessing the effectiveness of their practice and identifying appropriate methodologies to measure its impact on learners. Development education aims to instil values and attitudes in the learner that should be reflected in attitudinal and behavioural changes consistent with a social justice agenda. It should also result in the development of skills such as critical literacy skills, facilitation and training skills, and group-work skills. However, some of the outcomes of DE are not immediately evident and require time to gestate. For example, attitudinal change may only evolve over a sustained period of time and can be difficult to capture effectively through evaluation. Nonetheless, this is an area of activity that assumes increasing importance as DE demonstrates its value to learners and the wider education system. McCollum argues that evaluation has often suffered from the pressured working environment of NGOs, in which the emphasis has been on 'getting the job done' rather than assessing its contribution to stakeholders. She suggests that '[t]here has been inadequate development in areas such as measuring intangible performance parameters, measuring organizational effectiveness and judging synergetic factors in effectiveness' (McCollum 1999).

DE practitioners are acutely aware of the need to assess their work thoroughly; to provide evidence that they offer value for money to funders; and, most importantly, to deliver results on the intended learning benefits of their work for target groups. Initiatives launched by practitioners in this area include the 'evaluation of the impact of DE activities' devised by members of the Development Education Exchange in Europe Project (DEEEP). DEEEP is a European Union-wide network that aims 'to raise awareness, [and] educate and mobilise the European public for world-wide poverty eradication'; its members are drawn from DE networks in all EU member states (www.deeep. org). DEEEP's evaluation work has included e-discussion groups, workshops and regional seminars that enabled practitioners and experts to present and discuss an analysis of methodologies used to evaluate DE activities. The outcomes of this work have included the development of a toolkit to support members in their organisational practice (available at www.deeep.org/ evaluation.html).

A lot of contemporary development education work is funded through three-year project cycles; this often frustrates meaningful evaluation because of the limited 'conceptual space' available to reflect on project activities. Three-year periods also limit the capacity for longitudinal studies that can measure attitudinal or behavioural change through qualitative consultations over an extended timescale. McCollum argues that regular discussion with target groups and partners in education, combined with constant reference to 'long-term goals' and 'ultimate objectives', will inform a meaningful evaluation process. Moreover, evaluation techniques and approaches should reflect the active-learning and participative methodologies underpinning DE. The active participation of learners in the evaluation process is equally important to their engagement with DE activities – they are part of the same continuum.

Development NGOs, therefore, need to evaluate their work as part of a broader, ongoing organisational review process, to ensure that activities correspond with their aims and objectives. They also need to avail themselves of research grants, to support in-depth studies of work carried out with specific target groups. The emergence of the DERN and DERC research networks at the universities of Galway and London will support the gathering of evidence-based learning on DE practice and, hopefully, increase the number of research partnerships between universities and development NGOs. The next section considers the sometimes uneasy partnership that DE has developed with environmental education (EE) in a different area of practice and learning – education for sustainable development.

Education for Sustainable Development

The concept of education for sustainable development dates back to the Brundtland Commission's report in 1987, but it really gathered momentum after the 1992 United Nations Conference on Environment and Development (UNCED) in Rio de Janeiro. One of several ESD definitions states that:

> Education for Sustainable Development is about the learning needed to maintain and improve our quality of life and the quality of life of generations to come. It is about equipping individuals, communities, groups, businesses and Government to live and act sustainably as well as giving them an understanding of the environmental, social and economic issues involved. It is about preparing for the world in which we live in the next century, and making sure that we are not found wanting. (DFEE/QCA 1998)

The significance of ESD for development education is its conscious aim of addressing environmental and human development concerns in a holistic, educational context. Proponents of ESD suggest that environmental and development organisations share common concerns with regard to the sustainability of the planet and its people, and therefore make natural bedfellows in the field of education. Development and environmental groups also share the pedagogical practice of participative learning and encourage active citizenship in promoting sustainability. There is also some overlap in the content of environmental education and development education – challenging unsustainable models of economic growth, promoting the sustainable use of natural resources, and, of course, addressing the causes of climate change, etc. – that lends itself to a more complete understanding of sustainable development issues. In contrast, some development educators have argued that ESD is not a partnership of equals, and that the more public-friendly environmental message eclipses or minimises the importance of human development. They also argue that ESD is not a simple hybrid of EE and DE and that adopting such a perspective can traduce their respective agendas for change.

Therefore the triangular relationship between DE, EE and ESD has often been an uneasy one (Hogan and Tormey 2008), with the competing but related interests of DE and EE staking out their claims to ESD, and with DE suggesting that sustainable development has unduly gravitated toward environmental causes at the expense of societal interests, or has prioritised the environment over human development. Tensions arising from the contested ownership of ESD have sometimes undermined collaboration between development and environmental practitioners aimed at preventing the denudation of the environment and its consequent exacerbation of poverty levels, especially in the developing world.

More recently, however, we have witnessed an increasing level of co-operation between environmental and development NGOs at policy and practice levels. A significant factor in this collaboration has been the urgency attached to the issue of climate change, which is now globally recognised as endangering the sustainability of the planet and threatening the development of all societies, with poor countries most vulnerable to the effects of global warming. While climate change was perhaps initially considered to be primarily an environmental concern requiring action from environmental agencies, this view has shifted as the full global scale and impact of the problem has emerged.

For example, in 2008 Trócaire, the Irish development agency, adopted climate change as the theme of its Lenten campaign, stating that 'while rich countries continue to consume and use energy levels beyond what is fair and sustainable, the greatest impact is being felt by poorest people who are least able to cope' (www.trocaire.org/lent). So climate change is now considered a development issue as well as an environmental one, and has prompted environmental and development NGOs to work together in alliances and coalitions on climate change to carry out advocacy for policy changes aimed at reducing global warming and carbon emissions.

Development and environmental NGOs are also collaborating on activities and events as part of the United Nations Decade on Sustainable Development (UNDSD) from 2005 to 2014. The main goals defined for the Decade of ESD (DESD) at a national level are to provide an opportunity for refining and promoting the vision of and transition to sustainable development through all forms of education, public awareness and training; and to give an enhanced profile to the important role of education and learning in sustainable development. An International Implementation Scheme (IIS) has been put in place for the DESD, based on extensive consultation with national governments, NGOs, the United Nations' agencies and various specialists. The challenge for local government departments, NGOs and civil society groups is to determine the extent to which the decade impacts on local audiences through events, publications and educational programmes until 2014. With the emergence of climate change as an issue of both national and international importance, ESD now has a timely opportunity to present the importance of individual and communal activism in addressing climate change through activities organised under the auspices of the DESD.

Conclusion

The global character of the financial crisis that has impacted so severely on economies around the world reflects the extent to which decisions and actions taken globally have a local resonance. It underlines the interconnections between nations that have resulted from globalisation, and signposts a future that will make increasing demands of our knowledge and understanding of the global forces that shape our lives. Development education, therefore, has attained greater importance as an educational process and means of learning about the world than at any previous stage since its emergence in the 1970s. The importance of DE is based partly on its capacity to support an analysis of social relations and to nurture the learning of attitudes, values and skills that can inform action toward social justice and equality. It is also based on an active-learning methodology that engages the learner as a participant in the educational process, rather than as a receptacle of truth from a more informed source. The Freirean concepts that inform contemporary DE practice are manifest in some of the popular responses that have challenged neoliberalism and socioeconomic inequalities – such as the global-justice movement and the World Social Forum.

DE is also permeating mainstream education curricula and tertiary education, albeit at a frustratingly slow pace. It has been encouraging to chart the increased policy recognition and financial support for DE from government bodies – which must be part of both a top-down and a bottom-up approach to building support for DE. However, it has been disappointing to chart the declining support for DE in the development NGO sector; this trend needs to be reversed to ensure that DE has the breadth of financial support required for it to thrive at a practice level. Critical to the process of enhancing the practice base of DE is its increased academic profile at third level, with more opportunities for the study of DE and international development in higher education institutions. DE needs a stronger research base and more academic funding to measure its impact on learners, particularly in effecting behavioural change toward more sustainable lifestyles and social justice initiatives.

The post-Cold War period has regrettably exacerbated rather than narrowed the poverty gap between the North and the South. It has been a period during which respect for human rights and international law has weakened, ethnic conflict has been on the march rather than abating, the number of refugees has increased rather than dropped, privatisation has advanced at the cost of public services, neoliberalism has led poor countries into economic weakness and debt, and the natural environment has come under unprecedented threat from unsustainable consumption. This is a period that demands active citizenship and social responsibility to meet these global challenges. Development education can enable us to fulfil this responsibility and pay our way.

References

Bourn, Doug (2007) 'Building Academic Support for Development Education', *Policy and Practice*, vol.5, Autumn, Centre for Global Education, Belfast.

DfID (1997) *Eliminating World Poverty: A Challenge for the 21st Century,* a White Paper on International Development, Department for International Development, London.

DfID (1999a) 'Education and Our Global Future', a speech by Clare Short, secretary of state for International Development, at the Annual Conference of the Secondary Heads Association, Brighton, 24 April, DFID, London.

DfID (1999b) *Building Support for Development: Raising public awareness of international development issues,* a Department for International Development strategy paper, London.

DfID (2002) 'Enabling Effective Support: Responding to the Challenges of the Global Society: A Strategy of Support for the Global Dimension in Education', Department for International Development, London.

DFEE/QCA (1998) 'Education for Sustainable Development in the Schools Sector', a report to DFEE/QCA, London, 14 September.

Freire, Paulo (1972) *Pedagogy of the Oppressed,* Penguin Books, London.

Government of Ireland (2006) *White Paper on Irish Aid* (2006), Dublin.

Hogan, Deirdre and Roland Tormey (2008) 'A Perspective on the Relationship between Development Education and Education for Sustainable Development', *Policy and Practice,* vol.6, Spring, Centre for Global Education, Belfast.

HDR (*Human Development Report*) (1999) 'Globalisation with a Human Face', United Nations, New York.

HDR (2004) 'Cultural Liberty in Today's Diverse World', United Nations, New York.

Irish Aid (2007) 'Development Education Strategy Plan 2007–2011: Promoting Public Engagement for Development', Irish Aid, Dublin. www.irishaid.gov.ie/Uploads/Dev_Ed_final.pdf

Khoo, Su-ming, Carol Healy and Kelly Coate (2007) 'Development Education and Research at Third Level', *Policy and Practice,* vol.5, Autumn, Centre for Global Education, Belfast.

Marx, Karl (1845) 'Theses on Feuerbach', in D. McLellan, *Karl Marx: Selected Writings,* Oxford University Press, Oxford, 2000.

McBrian, Angus (2001) 'The Battle in Seattle: Mass Protest as Development Education', *The Development Education Journal,* vol.7, no.2, Development Education Association, London, March, pp.32–3.

McCollum, Ann (1996) 'Bridging the Gap between Theory and Practice', a paper presented to the Network of Development Education Centres and Groups (NODE) conference, *Development Education in Ireland Today,* Dublin, 25 May.

McCollum, Ann (1999) 'Evaluating to Strengthen Partnership: Engaging Schools in Development Education', Development Education Centre, Birmingham.

Osler, Audrey (ed.) (1994) *Development Education: Global Perspectives in the Classroom*, Cassell, London.

Regan, Colm et al. (2006) *80:20: Development in an Unequal World*, 5th edn, 80:20, Dublin.

Websites

Centre for Global Education	www.centreforglobaleducation.com
Children in Crossfire	www.childrenincrossfire.org
Citizenship Education	www.globaldimension.org.uk
Comhlamh	www.comhlamh.org
Cyfanfyd (Welsh Development Education Association)	www.cyfanfyd.org.uk
Department for International Development	www.dfid.gov.uk
Development Education Association	www.dea.org.uk
Development Education Exchange in Europe Project	www.deeep.org
Development Education Ireland	www.developmenteducationireland.org
DICE Project	www.diceproject.org
Dochas	www.dochas.ie
Global Dimension	www.globaldimension.org.uk
Global Dimension in Schools	www.globaldimensioninschools.org
IDEA	www.ideaonline.ie
IDEAS (International Development Education Association of Scotland)	www.ideas-forum.org.uk
Irish Aid	www.irishaid.gov.ie
Teachers in Development Education (Development Education Centre, Birmingham)	www.tidec.org
The Big Pic	www.bigpic.biz
Trócaire	www.trocaire.org

15

CONCLUSION: DEVELOPMENT IN THE FACE OF NEOLIBERAL ECONOMIC STRATEGIES

Gerard McCann

On 1 January 2009 the British Chancellor, Alistair Darling, announced that the global economy was facing its most serious crisis since the beginning of the First World War. The contraction of the global banking system, a mass rise in unemployment, unprecedented stock and share fluctuations, spiralling national and personal debt, and the forced recapitalisation of key economic sectors across the world signalled the beginning of a global recession that many economists expect to be as deep and as wide as the slump that hit the global economy in the 1930s (Wade 2008, pp.5–21; Brenner 2006, p.ix). The effects have been pervasive and disruptive, and the implications of this grinding halt to the process of globalisation will take years to overcome. As with previous slumps in the Western market system, the effects will reverberate across the globe, affecting developing countries and the economic peripheries as well as core economies in a cycle of debt, reduced trade, industrial collapse, stress on society and political instability. Arguably the long term implications of the recession will include the frustration of global development strategies, resulting in the political and financial commitments of development agents being undermined or reduced.

This chapter attempts to examine some of the factors which have accentuated the global recession. It assesses systemic reasons for this economic breakdown and locates key facets behind some of the dysfunctional aspects of globalisation that have intensified the crisis. It focuses particularly on the ideological premises of a system which, by its very nature, propels the economies of many countries towards systemic shock or collapse; and it provides evidence to suggest that the current crisis is, to an extent, the logical outworking of neoliberal dominance of global economic governance (Harvey 2007, pp.183–206; also George 2000, pp.27–35). Moving from these theoretical premises, the chapter looks at the implications of the neoliberal approach to human development, and outlines a case for more integrated democratic and sociological interventions in development policy. Finally, it draws from commentaries on the crisis by organisations such as the United Nations and the World Bank, and engages with macroeconomic theory to assess the possibilities for development in the midst of a reintegrating global market system.

Building the 'Spontaneous Order'

The economic system that has come under such strain recently has been the construct of a distinct and highly prominent school of economic theory which, since the 1980s, has come to shape a vision of human development dependent on market fluctuations and entrepreneurial activity. Neoliberalism has its origins in the classical liberalism of the eighteenth and nineteenth centuries, when economists such as Adam Smith, David Ricardo and Thomas Robert Malthus attempted to harness the energies of global commerce – built largely on industrial investment, imperial conquest and slavery – to design a governance model for societies which prioritised the needs of certain financially profitable elements. Smith in particular introduced commercial enterprise as formative within society. His 1776 *An Inquiry into the Nature and Causes of the Wealth of Nations* was to herald a philosophical departure in the emerging study of political economy and economics in general. This text provided a scientific analysis of economic shifts across the globe and set out the rationale and conditions necessary for the progressive expansion of the market system, with profitability as its driver. In his theory of economic and human development, government was to become the 'invisible hand' which would only intervene in socioeconomic development when prudent and profitable to do so; that is, governments are obliged to let the economy take its own course without interference or obstruction to commercial development. For Smith the objective of every state was to increase the wealth and power of the 'nation' (Smith 1776, II.v.31). By 'nation' Smith played on the tensions between the state and the commercial agents within any region, with his interpretation of wealth specifically meaning 'produce', or commodities. Wealth is therefore made up of commodities, and this could be quantifiable in terms of national productivity. This method of economic development was a snub to the landed classes who retained 'inactive' wealth and a spur to the emergence of a commercial class who were naturally predisposed to manage society. Smith's definition of development was eventually to emerge into our understanding of gross domestic product (GDP), which is used in the measurement of global development to this day, although honed down to the calculation: consumer spending, plus business investment, plus government purchases, plus net exports, equals GDP. Thus the greater the GDP the more developed a society becomes.

A further significant contribution that Smith made, both to our understanding of this political economy and to its practice, was in the break-up of the production process. This he called the 'division of labour'. Working with a model of commodity production similar to that of Ricardo and Malthus, Smith saw that the more productive a society is, the more functionally divided the labour is – output and revenue (income) can be increased if the workers can produce different parts of the commodity in different locations (Smith 1776, I.i.6–7). What emerges from this system of commodity production through the division of labour is a 'natural value' for the produce, a price. Within a fluid and competitive economy, in which various commercial interests are providing similar commodities across disparate regions, the profitability can be measured by a 'natural' interaction which mediates towards the maximisation of profit and its accumulation, with minimum outlay. In the global system of commerce, natural and human resources can be sourced in one region (usually colonies) and wealth value can be created through commodity production in another (usually the European commercial powers). Ultimately, what is provided by Smith is a theory of wealth and how to create it, with the legacy of this theory being its dominance in global commercial practices through the mantra of 'free trade'. This perspective was to become the basis of laissez-faire economics, in which market forces would drive society forward, and the invisible government would busy itself with war or the local infrastructure. The free market was to become the foundation of the political economy of western Europe and northern America, and through forced industrialisation and colonisation it was to provide 'scientific proof' of progress as designated by the more profitable regions and states (Vaggi and Groenewegen 2003, pp.103–16).

Once the philosophy of a market-driven society had been defined, this signified the arrival of a predatory commercial class, who informed their profiteering with a principle of right – a belief system that placed entrepreneurialism and wealth creation as primary motivating factors in societal and global development. This meant essentially that development was to become synonymous with the generation of financial wealth. In the mid twentieth century a school of philosophers grouped around the Mont Pelerin Society set out to reinvigorate this classical liberal approach to economic development, with a mixture of concepts promoting 'openness', freedom and the right to acquire wealth. They held that the disasters of the 1930s and 1940s were a result of governments trying to control the natural acquisitive inclination of individuals by closing down society and suppressing entrepreneurialism. Around this philosophy Friedrich von Hayek was able to gather together the significant architects of modern economic liberalism, including Karl Popper, Milton Friedman, Ludwig von Mises, and the guru of the monetarist revolution in Britain, Keith Joseph. As the mission statement of the society asserts, authoritarianism is a result of 'a decline of belief in private property and the competitive market; for without the diffused power and initiative associated with these institutions it is difficult to imagine a society in which freedom may be effectively preserved' (www.montpelerin.org/mpsAbout.cfm; Thorsen and Lie 2006, pp.11–13).

Their opposition was to be found in the interventionist and humanist ideals of 'social' market economists John Maynard Keynes (1936) and John Galbraith (1958), who the 'open' market economists believed were advocating a form of authoritarian state planning. Keynes had argued that economic development should move from a stable society forward and not from the monetary system backward, believing that managing employment and inflation, and alleviating poverty were central to economic growth. This would mean a high level of governmental involvement in the economy. For the economic liberals, the strong state and the open market system were seen to be in conflict; and where the state was active in the economy the neoliberals envisaged a stifled or 'closed' society, of which the oppressive Soviet bloc could provide a myriad of examples. For the neoliberals, the 'laws' of the market were an efficient enough regulatory framework within which an economic system could develop. As Karl Polanyi stated, on the formation of neoliberalism:

> Free enterprise and private ownership are declared to be essentials of freedom. No society built on other foundations is said to deserve to be called free. The freedom that regulation creates is denounced as unfreedom; the justice, liberty and welfare it offers are decried as a camouflage of slavery. (www.montpelerin.org/aboutmps)

Hayek's *The Constitution of Liberty* (1960) was to signal the beginning of a new era of economic liberalism, and with his adherents being elevated to some of the most powerful positions globally, the neoliberal hegemony started taking shape. Hayek's theory of the commercial cycle advocated a 'spontaneous order' in which society would repeatedly adapt and change to market conditions. From the 1970s onwards, adherents of the liberalised system emerged in positions of economic and political power across the globe – becoming directors of dozens of transnational corporations (TNCs) or leaders of the major political parties; they included a sequence of presidents of the United States and a number of British prime ministers. Indeed, Margaret Thatcher was famously to declare at a cabinet meeting that the *Constitution of Liberty* was what she believed in. The economic theorists were also backed up with social and political theories emanating from Chicago University and a school led by Leo Strauss and the neo-conservatives, who brought forward a vision of the future which was uncluttered by government and fixated with fundamentalist Christian morality and monetarism. Hayek was to receive the Nobel Prize in economics in 1974, followed by his colleague Friedman in 1976.

By the end of the 1970s, neoliberal strategies of economic development were well entrenched across the Western world; this was to be reflected in their increasing dominance within those institutions that had the role of shaping development strategies worldwide. The flourish of neoliberal activity also brought forward dozens of supporting agencies, each extolling the virtues of the free market and advocating the rollback of the state. The Adam Smith Institute (founded in 1976), the Institute of Economic Affairs (founded in 1955, revived in 1975), the Centre for Policy Studies (founded in 1974), the World Economic Forum in Davos, the Paris Club, the Heritage Foundation in Washington, to mention a few, were all established to concretise the theories of a progressively liberalising market with competition at its core. Across the Western world, governments were by choice to act on the ideological underpinnings of this alternative means of development, breaking from the social-market model that had dominated global economic development since the 1940s. Across the developing world this message was to be increasingly enforced in practice through the operations of the various international financial institutions (IFIs). The pattern of governmental action was to become similar the world over – emphasising commercial freedom and individuality as rights, dismantling unionised labour relations, cutting taxes, deregulating corporate operations, prioritising financial interaction in policy design, privatising public utilities, and attempting to dissolve welfare provision into market forces. A particular facet of this hegemony was the highlighting of the financial sector (banking, stock exchanges, venture capitalists, 'the City') as key agents of this model of economic development.

As the global political environment adapted to neoliberal ideas, the institutions engineering global economic development also changed. Another Nobel Prize winner for economics (2001), Joseph Stiglitz, in *Globalization and its Discontents*, noted that by the mid 1980s the key global institutions had come under the influence of the neoliberals and had set about systematically removing Keynesian (social-market) strategists and thinkers. After the 'purge', policies on development were reviewed, and a new model of development was progressively introduced: 'Free markets were the solution to the problems of developing countries' (Stiglitz 2002, p.13). The Adam Smith Institute became an advisory support to the World Bank, informing its *Global Development Finance* report, monitoring and listing hundreds of privatisations around the world (George 2000, pp.30–1). The realignment of the global economy can be seen in the dramatic manner in which the International Monetary Fund (IMF) and the World Bank in particular, under the guise of 'structural adjustment', began to apply the liberal model to developing regions. The liberalisation of trade was to become the focal point of this adjustment, but it also contained a litany of attendant policies which were to debilitate many developing countries for decades. Debt repayment schemes, coupling aid and trade with Western concepts of freedom and liberty, supporting compatible leaders (including China's Deng Xiaoping and Augusto Pinochet of Chile), facilitating access by TNCs, deregulating and taming public expenditure, all came to symbolise ways in which the market could adjust to the new world order. The effects of this type of restructuring were felt across the globe; and with the advent of the new hegemony the most noticeable, quantifiable evidence of market-driven development policies became the increasing divergence between rich and poor:

> In Latin America the top 10 per cent of wage-earners increased their share of total income by 10 per cent while the poorest 10 per cent saw their income drop by 15 per cent, wiping out what meagre improvements

they had made in the previous decade. Income inequality also grew in Thailand, Indonesia, China and other Asian nations even though the region enjoyed healthy economic growth throughout the decade. In sub-Saharan Africa the situation was worse; after two decades of IMF and World Bank structural adjustment not only is income inequality growing but average per capita incomes are falling. They are now lower than they were in 1970. (Ellwood 2001, p.98)

Freeing Markets as a Means of Development

Since the 1980s the various theorists and adherents collectively grouped around the often opaque ideology of neoliberalism set about reintroducing the methods of classical liberalism to stimulate economic growth and wealth. Primary to the strategy was the preference for a commercial elite and zeal for market competition. As with earlier incarnations, the new generation of economic liberals brought with them a concept of political economy that is market-fixated and formative in the integration of concepts such as individual freedom, democratic intent, liberty and globalisation. Of this new ideology, David Harvey, in *A Brief History of Neoliberalism*, commented:

Neoliberalism is in the first instance a theory of political economic practices that proposes that human well-being can best be advanced by liberating individual entrepreneurial freedoms and skills within an institutional framework characterized by strong private property rights, free markets, and free trade. (Harvey 2007, p.2; also George 2000, pp.27–35)

Anna-Maria Blomgren defines neoliberalism in a more flexible manner:

Neoliberalism is commonly thought of as a political philosophy giving priority to individual freedom and the right to private property. It is not, however, the simple and homogeneous philosophy it might appear to be. It ranges over a wide expanse in regard to ethical foundations as well as to normative conclusions. At the one end of the line is 'anarcho-liberalism', arguing for a complete *laissez-faire*, and the abolishment of all government. At the other end is 'classical liberalism', demanding a government with functions exceeding those of the so-called night-watchman state. (Blomgren, cited in Thorsen and Lie 2006, p.12)

Ultimately, from the perspective of the neoliberals, the mechanism of civic and state management has to be redesigned in a manner that would enhance and protect a particular interpretation of freedom. The functionality of markets and the circulation of finance were to be elevated to become the lifeblood of a money-driven society. As a consequence, the role of government has been reduced to intermittent intervention when deemed necessary for the protection of neoliberal policy development in areas such as finance, commerce or security. Internationally, the role of governments should be to protect the interests of the market and the freedoms that this style of governance could, in theory, bring. In practice this method of economic management was to be sold worldwide as the answer to underdevelopment and, by the mid 1990s, became the consensual and dominant form of governance and policy among the most powerful states and IFIs.

Increasingly, as the system of neoliberal political economy rolled out, governments withdrew by stealth from the historic social and economic supports that were best typified by the Keynesian tradition in the United Kingdom and the *dirigisme* of France, their national health systems and key protected industries. In developing countries it meant asset-stripping public resources and changing economic structures, focusing on debt repayment, trade and complying with the demands of the IFIs. Since the 1980s and crucially during the 1990s and the advent of accelerated globalisation, Western governments began withdrawing from investment in health, education, housing, infrastructural building and key state-supported industries such as energy and telecommunications. The state was to be utilised by the increasingly influential neoliberal lobby (often under the tutelage of TNCs) to release public assets to the 'potential' of the free market. It meant that governance and policymaking procedures were progressively transformed to give the private sector access to previously unassailable market possibilities. The core policies that accompanied this ideology – premised by calls for individual freedom – revolved around the practices of *privatisation, cutting taxation* and *deregulation*. The target and victim of this assault was the public space that in many countries had, in a very real sense, underpinned not only social protection mechanisms such as health care and third-level education, but also cultural antecedents – communitarian structures such as trade unions, faith organisations, and voluntary societies. If an organisation or section of the community did not have a market-oriented function, it remained superfluous to this vision of a globalised society.

In the post-Cold War era, country after country, from the social market economies of the European Union (EU) to the centrally planned communist regimes of China and Vietnam, came to endorse some of the most aggressive forms of neoliberal economic engineering. The methods of extending markets and commodity production were to be generally accepted as a natural way of integrating economies across the globe. Over the past two decades, globalisation has increasingly gravitated towards maximising the demands of the neoliberal lobby and the institutions directing its formation. Interdependence in global market systems was to become a key objective of this dominant interpretation of globalisation. In practice this would mean working to eradicate trade restrictions and barriers to transnational commercial activity; the promotion of information and communication technology (ICT), with Internet access increasing from 180 million stations in 1998 to 500 million by 2002, and further exponential increases thereafter (Siebert 2000, p.8); the costs of communication and transport going down year after year (World Bank 1995, p.25); securing intellectual property rights; a consensus on the methods of market expansion coupled with the dissolution of Cold War tensions; opening new markets in India and China; policy orchestration by financial institutions; the structural adjustment of economies around the globe to comply with ease of commercial access strategies; the emergence of highly influential TNCs emboldened by foreign direct investment (FDI); prioritising the finance sector; and finally, a patchwork of agreements and treaties which would act as staging posts for further expansion.

Collectively this network of policies and technical interventions would characterise globalisation in its neoliberal guise.

By the mid 1990s, with the consolidation of monetary economic policies, TNCs and the financial sector were working largely unchecked across the globe as agents of development or, as they saw it, 'wealth creation'. The structural aspects of the system began to evolve, together with a series of global initiatives which sought to adjust the globalising economy into a more functional network. The raft of deregulation legislation which swept the global economy in the early 1990s was compounded by the launch of the overseeing World Trade Organisation (WTO) in 1995. Monetarism also became evident in the activities of various global economic networks, such as the North American Free Trade Agreement (NAFTA), economic partnership agreements (EPAs), the Doha Development Round, structural adjustment programmes (SAPs), the Lisbon Agenda, and the Cotonou Agreement, which reshaped EU development policy towards a market bias (Dinan 1999, pp.548–56; Flint 2008, pp.22–3, 145–7). The adaptation process, often shaped around TNCs' strategies, was notable because policies tended to prioritise deregulation, privatisation and governmental compliance and served to facilitate competitive advantage on a global stage – with other economies being forced into this orbit. In responding to this global economic realignment, the USA was to introduce the defining statement of the neoliberal consensus, reasserting its leadership and plotting the refinement of the process through the so-called 'Washington Consensus'. This was an initiative devised in 1989 by John Williamson to assist in the expansion of corporate interests globally (Wade 2008, p.6; Williamson 1990; Flint 2008, pp.58–61).

The 'consensus' encapsulated the neoliberal economy by advocating a redirection of public expenditure priorities towards key financial sectors, fiscal discipline, interest rate liberalisation to 'free up' money, competitive exchange rates, liberalising inflows of foreign direct investment, deregulation, aggressively privatising public assets, securing property rights, and the all important trade liberalisation. As developed countries signed up to this agreement, the IFIs set about a progressive implementation of a similar structural adjustment plan for developing countries. The extent of operations represented the highest level of global financial influence by the advocates of neoliberal policies. From the position of the developing countries, the new consensus would mean that in order to qualify for aid and participation in the global market they would have to change their economic systems and traditions. This would become a prerequisite for financial assistance in the form of aid, loans or trading opportunities. For example, trade tariffs were to be reduced, even though in some of the poorest countries, such as Gambia and Cape Verde, this would mean a 20 per cent reduction in spending on public services, health care and education (Oxfam 2006, pp.4–5). In the attempts to restructure Ghana, the country experienced a 40 per cent reduction in primary school attendance. With the privatisation process, 350,000 people lost their jobs in Uganda. Price rises were symptomatic of the process. After an attempt at currency manipulation in Sierra Leone in 1986, prices for stable goods rose by up to 300 per cent. In Uganda inflation rose to 300 per cent (Flint 2008, pp.60–1; Jameson and Wilber 1996, p.50). The pattern was the same across the developing world. While countries such as China were in a position to integrate their economies forcefully into the new global system, other regions – such as South America – elected to concentrate on the development of their national economies with a greater focus on regional development. Sub-Saharan Africa in its attempt to adapt fell into an immiseration process unseen historically by the people of that impoverished continent. Indeed, the US think tank Global Financial Integrity (GFI) reported that by 2008 the volume of capital flight (financial outflows) from developing countries had been rising at an astounding 18 per cent per year, to almost ten times the aid budget for all developing regions (c. $900 billion per year). In assessing the situation for developing countries, Raymond Baker of GFI stated: 'Illicit financial flows siphon revenue out of poor countries, robbing them of much-needed assets and stunting economic development' (www.gfip.org; *Observer Business and Media*, 30 November 2008, p.2).

In practice the restructuring of the global economy – through 'adjustment' in some regions and 'shock therapy' in other regions – brought about obvious differentials in wealth and opportunity. This was most notable in regions that indulged in the most aggressive forms of economic liberalisation. Russia, for example, whose political elite, at the behest of oil-rich 'oligarchs', forced the country's population into a socially catastrophic 'gold rush' that was to see life expectancy for Russians drop by one year per year throughout the 1990s. United Nations' figures showed that inequality doubled between the years 1989 and 1996. The richest 20 per cent of Russians received an income eleven times that of the poorest 20 per cent. Barter was reintroduced across the economy and, as Stiglitz noted, 'Russia's transition has entailed one of the largest increases in poverty in history in such a short span of time (outside of war and famine)' (Stiglitz 2002, p.182; *The Nation*, 4 October 1999; Ellwood 2001, p.105). The extraordinary elevation of the Chinese market system onto the global stage, irrespective of very visible authoritarian credentials, accompanied one of the greatest migratory shifts of population in human history from rural to urban economies. Indeed, the Chinese Economic Council has continued with plans to build 200 new cities for 200 million people within 25 years, while profiling the new policy 'wealth is good'. Whereas in western Europe the dismantling of the social market and welfare systems signalled the arrival of neoliberal practices, in other areas of the globe the depth and speed of change has been highly destructive. No more so than in the states of sub-Saharan Africa, where countries attempted to comply with structural adjustment programmes (SAPs) and debt repayment schemes, yet were left vulnerable, with their public amenities being opened up to venture-capital initiatives and asset-stripping on a scale not known since the height of colonial rule. Viewed at a macroeconomic level, the disparities have been obvious and stark:

> [T]he income gap between the fifth of the world's richest people living in the richest countries and the fifth in the poorest was 74 to 1 in 1997, up from 60 to 1 in 1990 and 30 to 1 in 1960 ... the world's 200 richest people

more than doubled their net worth in the four years to 1998, to more than $1 trillion. The assets of the top three billionaires [were at that stage] more than the combined GNP of all least developed countries and their 600 million people. (UNDP 1999, p.3)

The influence of those sympathetic to liberalising policies on global economic management ensured the reconstruction of some of the most dynamic economies as well as many of the most vulnerable. The neoliberal formula decoupled social development from economic opportunity, the latter being implicit in the process of globalisation. Examples of the effects stretch across developed and developing countries alike. Military engagement in Iraq in 2003, for example, falsely activated by the suspicion of 'weapons of mass destruction', led to one of the most vulgar drives at market shock treatment, which served to create new and highly profitable market opportunities. This included the entrepreneurialism that accompanied the new business of 'homeland security', private security, and conflict reconstruction industries. In Afghanistan the Bush administration's strategy for development was transparent: 'You can receive millions of dollars helping the anti-Taleban forces ... This is enough money to take care of your family, your village, your tribe for the rest of your life' (Klein 2008, pp.305, 298–307). Between 11 September 2001 and the end of 2006, a staggering $457 billion was released from the US federal budget for private contractors involved in homeland security industries (ibid., p.301). In comparison, total global foreign aid went down from $106.8 in 2005 to $103.9 billion in 2006 (http://ictsd.net/i/news/bridgesweekly/7583/).

Zambia, like a number of African states which faithfully tried to apply IFI stipulations on market restructuring, went from being one of the wealthiest regions of sub-Saharan Africa, with one of the highest standards of living, to being one of the 20 poorest countries on earth; this had catastrophic effects on the population. Mozambique and Kenya, among others, suffered similar fates (Moss 2007, pp.58, 66). To participate in this patronised global economy, developing countries were to be reshaped by the IFIs in a manner that would strategise development through the deepening intervention of commercial interests from the West. This often brought an accusation of 'neocolonialism' against the institutions that were engineering the policies of structural adjustment. The process could be seen across the IFIs' work: freeing capital markets as a prerequisite to membership of the WTO and the IMF; priority being given to financial management, through the auspices of the banking and financial sector; an approval of monetarism as a method of economic management; hyper-interest on debt repayments to Western states and institutions; debt relief subjected to the opening of markets; protected products – such as coffee beans, cocoa beans, copper, cotton, etc. – released to the 'open' global market. Each of these practices militated against development: 'Macroeconomic policy and macroeconomic instability would be one major explanation of volatility, and the way that monetary, fiscal and exchange rate policies affect investment and demand, as well as external shocks such as variations in the terms of trade' (Thirlwall 2003, p.183).

Even with relief plans and the adaptation of development policies there were neoliberal qualifications. The Brady Plan in 1989, which sought to get financial institutions to write off 35 per cent of debt, was subjected to the usual sequence of structural reforms and bound the 18 participating developing states to financial and institutional tie-ins. That was to cause the Mexican economic collapse of 1995, the Brazilian collapse of 1998 and the Argentinean collapse of 2001 (Harvey 2007, p.75). Interestingly, the Argentinean situation was the culmination of corporate mismanagement, IMF and World Bank pressure and misguided administrative attempts at compliance to the stipulations set by these two global agencies. The indigenous economy also fell victim to one of the biggest corporate scandals in history, perpetrated by the directors of the USA energy company Enron. Enron, with its nepotism and influence at the highest levels of political power in the USA, had been given pay-off over its support for the Bush administration in the early 1990s. This included the tactical deregulation of the energy market together with pressures to ensure market expansion at IFI level. The result was Enron accessing Latin American energy sources, including those of Argentina, and drawing capital and finance away from the indigenous economy towards the Enron core in Houston, Texas. The weight and pressure of this 'profit repatriation' destabilised the regional economy, significantly contributing to economic collapse of the Argentinean economy. Eventually the Enron magnates were prosecuted for fraud on a massive scale, while Argentina still struggles to recover. With structural adjustment Brazil fared no better, as it moved into crisis in 1998 the IMF enforced public spending cuts that amounted to one fifth of the national budget. Even emergency food supplies were affected by this austerity and caused some of Brazil's poorest communities to fall into even deeper poverty, yet $50 billion was spent trying to maintain monetary policy (Stiglitz 2002, pp.198–199). Developing world debt, another implication, went up still further: 'from $580 billion in 1980 to $2.4 trillion in 2002 ... In 2002 there was a net outflow of $340 billion in servicing this debt, compared to overseas development aid of $37 billion' (Harvey 2007, p.193).

Global Recession

In the summer of 2008 the global financial system suffered an immense systemic shock which began in the loan/property markets of the southern states of the USA and reverberated at an ever increasing velocity across the global market system. Arguably, not since the 1930s has such an extensive network of sectors and economies been affected so quickly and so pervasively. The conventions of the neoliberal approach to global development, as manifested through the auspices of the various IFIs and strategic agreements emanating from initiatives such as the Washington Consensus, immediately came into focus and placed a question mark over the nature of this system of economic management, the role of government in global economic development, the extent of power of the finance sector in the disparate economies around the globe, and the autonomy of corporations in both economic and human development issues. In effect, the depth of the slump in the global market system mirrored the aggression and intrusion of monetarist policies. While the process of globalisation signalled the consolidation of a particular model of economic power with all its patronage, it also represented the height of neoliberal global management and influence. However, the weakness of this hegemony could also be located from this point forward.

The mechanism that has underwritten the roll-out of the free market in the twentieth century has been operating within the auspices of the Bretton Woods Accords (1944), the agreement that had originally been designed to stabilise the global market system in the volatile aftermath of the Second World War. The Bank of International Settlements, the International Monetary Fund, the World Bank, and the additional World Trade Organisation were to become the hubs of free market expansion and strategy. Through this network and circulation of ideas the system of free trade was to be engineered in such a manner that it would ensure the free flow of capital, goods and movement for those who were capable of facilitating market growth. Since the early 1990s the IFIs drew developing countries to the system while attempting to bring various policies for development into line with orthodox market growth strategies (See Bello, Bullard and Malhortra 2000). As the former adviser to the International Monetary Fund, Jeffrey Sachs, commented about the authors of this system in the *Financial Times*: 'It defies logic that a small group of 1,000 economists on 19th Street in Washington should dictate the economic conditions of life to 75 developing countries with around 1.4 billion people' (Sachs 1997). This comment from an insider highlighted the structure of the neoliberal hegemony, emanating from a professional and entrepreneurial elite who were almost exclusively focused on financial management and wealth creation. The most notable aspect of the IFIs' system as it evolved was the role of private financial institutions and in particular financial speculators, the banking system and activities aimed at opening markets dependent on credit, loans, derivatives, hedge funds and sub-prime mortgages. Immediately prior to the recession public finance and political representatives were being utilised to assist private finance and corporate strategies, while scores of developing countries and vulnerable industries were brought to the brink of collapse for not complying, structurally adjusting or fulfilling debt repayment obligations.

As well as the realignment of governments to become compliant with corporate financial strategies, a symptom of this new world order was the systemic crises that would periodically affect the global economy. In its process of readjustment the cyclical nature of globalisation and its contagion would become apparent. An adverse cause in one element of the financial sector could see effects ripple out across the globe, impacting on microeconomies and the macroeconomy alike. Other examples of the cyclical volatility of the system came with the break-up of the Exchange Rate Mechanism in Europe in July 1993 – which brought about the collapse of a UK administration, the destabilisation of all European currencies, and billions being made by speculators on the collapse of the system and misfortune of all connected. Indeed, the financier George Soros made $1 billion alone during this particular cycle. The raft of investments (financial shifts and stock exchanges) in New York in mid 1995 that initially caused the collapse of the Mexican economy, crucially multiplied its effect across Latin America and then as an implication it infected economies as diverse as Thailand and Poland (Stiglitz 2002, p.57; Harvey 2007, pp.94–6). The Asian economic collapse of 1997–98 was an indication of things to come: rapidly adjusting economies in South Korea, Thailand, and Indonesia – under pressures by the IMF to liberalise – disintegrated into political and economic breakdown. Interestingly, the countries that selectively engaged with IMF strategies, Malaysia and Singapore, were to an extent cushioned from the devastation that affected the rest of the so-called 'Tiger' economies. As Joseph Stiglitz observantly noted in *Globalization and its Discontents*, it was financial corporations that were in patronage to the IMF that were to become the ultimate beneficiaries of the destabilised Asian economies:

> The IMF first told countries in Asia to open up their markets to hot short-term capital. The countries did it and money flooded in, but just as suddenly flowed out. The IMF then said interest rates should be raised and there should be fiscal contraction, and a deep recession was induced. Asset prices

plummeted, the IMF urged affected countries to sell their assets even at bargain basement prices ... The sales were handled by the same financial institutions that had pulled out their capital, precipitating the crisis. These banks then got large commissions from their work selling the troubled companies or splitting them up, just as they had got large commissions when they had originally guided the money into the countries in the first place. (Stiglitz 2002, pp.129–30)

Crisis and systemic shock as a method of opening up market opportunities have become a standard method of releasing financial opportunities. This method of economic 'development' has become implicit in the neoliberal system of globalisation, with the 1987, 1993, 1998, 2001 and 2008 stock market crashes forewarning of the cyclical nature of this system. The Western economies were always vulnerable to economic slump, in which opportunities revealed themselves at each contraction, but developing countries have remained particularly susceptible to the fluctuations.

Global economic contractions and the process of contagion are nothing new and are symptomatic of free-market development. With the dominance of the system residing within two economic cores, the USA and the EU, any contortions within these economies will reverberate outward. Representing some 50 per cent of global trade, these regions have a controlling influence on the fortunes of markets and countries around the world. Consequently, 'downturns' in these economies are infectious throughout other less robust economies, including the weak and exposed economies of the developing world. Robert Brenner, in *The Economics of Global Turbulence*, puts this into perspective with the comment that, in comparison to the 1950s and 1960s, recent years have seen 'an era of slower growth and increasingly economic turbulence ... marked by deeper recession and the return of devastating financial crises absent since the Great Depression' (Brenner 2006, p.ix). For him, profitability has become more focused and financially targeted, and downturns have become more extreme as the globalised system has evolved. If anything, the 1997–2007 period, with its sustained growth in

Western economies, was abnormal in post-war history in that it was positively reacting to structural adjustment and seemingly manageable as a process. What was notable about this period in the Western states was the growth of the so-called 'knowledge economy', scientifically and culturally based, and driven through the revolution in information and communications technology (ICT). In effect, for a period, the Western states had a competitive advantage and could project their design for economic growth onto other compliant economies – China and India being the most noticeable examples of emerging economies that have become inextricably linked to Western growth rates. Other countries, particularly former colonies of EU powers in sub-Saharan Africa, have not been able to participate during that same period and have, more often than not, recoiled into underdevelopment in the face of various adjustment strategies. By 2008 all 'low human development' countries, the poorest regions on earth, were in Africa (22 of them) – with Ethiopia being the only one that was not a former colony of EU powers (UNDP 2007, pp.231–2).

In September 2008 the inadequately named 'credit crunch', which sparked a global recession, can be seen to be a systematic implication of an ideologically informed model of economic development. In the run-up to this recession, financial industries which would have been profiled as champions of the neoliberal economic philosophy were to become the focus of the crisis – banking, derivative markets, and loan markets. This can be seen with New York's Bernard Madoff's 'Ponzi' investment scheme, which fraudulently 'lost' a staggering $50 billion on one front, while city bankers in four banks in London alone – Goldman Sachs, Morgan Stanley, Merrill Lynch and Dresdner Kleinwort – carved up £6.4 billion in personal bonuses to exploit the volatile economy on another front (*Observer Business and Media*, 21 December 2008, p.1). In one month (November 2008), President Bush in the USA committed $800 billion to the banking system as capital support, and the British prime minister, Gordon Brown, provided £600 billion in a 'rescue plan' for British banks. The Confederation of British Industry (CBI) responded with a calculation that the recession in the United Kingdom would leave one in ten unemployed, with 600,000 jobs to be lost in 2009 (www.cbi.org.uk). Ultimately the global economic system as it has evolved has left economies worldwide open to rapid and networked disintegration – yet the warnings were there. In June 2007 the Bank of International Settlements stated in its annual report that 'years of loose monetary policy have fuelled a giant global credit bubble, leaving us vulnerable to another 1930s slump' (Wade 2008, p.7). The response from the IFIs has also been predictable:

> Just as the IMF gives short shrift to the concerns of the poor – there are billions available to bail out banks, but not the paltry sums to provide food subsidies for those thrown out of work as a result of IMF programs – the WTO puts trade above all else. (Stiglitz 2002, p.216)

Furthermore, the rapidity of the disintegration has exposed the IFIs as wholly inadequate in an environment in which finance-based theories of economic development have become ineffective and destructive. This has been very noticeable with the recapi-talisation of banks and key industries on an unprecedented scale, and a return to Keynesian-style governmental intervention, in an attempt to stabilise economies against collapse. Even the neoliberal giants of the USA and the EU have had to return to almost socialist-style planning, a 'new deal', to manage their way through a recession that has the real potential of becoming a global depression. The Bretton Woods institutions, while moving to assure the financial markets, have emerged helpless and obstructive as agents of development. Their 'downsizing' or replacement has subsequently become a key question in global economic development and arguably the biggest hope for those vulnerable economies around the globe which have been victims of the economic engineering. John Monks, the general secretary of the European Trade Union's council, was more targeted in his assessment, commenting that '[t]hey must never be allowed to forget the damage they have caused' (Monks, quoted in Brockett 2009, p.10).

For developing countries the effects of the financial crisis in the USA and the EU will be long-lasting and destabilising. With the expansion of protectionist policies in the developed economies and possible resistance to financial assistance initiatives (aid), the international development environment will in sequence also contract. As with previous slumps, countries will attempt to protect indigenous employment and trade by restricting inward movement of goods, people and services. This will reflect on developing regions through a rationalisation of trade flows, restrictions on finance and capital, reduction in investment (by 50 per cent between 2007 and 2009, according to the World Bank), and curtailment of aid and technical support as the developed countries work to make their own economies viable. In January 2009 the World Bank released its projection for developing countries caught in the current cycle:

> The recent food and fuel crises have already pushed millions back into poverty and hunger. Sharply tighter credit conditions and weaker growth are likely to cut into government revenues and their ability to invest to meet education, health and gender goals, as well as the infrastructure expenditures needed to sustain growth. The financial crisis now threatens to shrink emerging markets' access to trade and investment, and each 1 percent drop in growth could trap another 20 million in poverty. (World Bank 2009, www.worldbank.org/html/extdr/financialcrisis/)

Ultimately, for international development, there will be an adverse impact on poverty relief plans and the goals that had been set prior to September 2008 – particularly the already faltering United Nations millennium development goals (MDGs). While the United Nations call is for realignment towards the MDGs, the World Bank has pessimistically called for 'safety nets' for the poorest countries until the richest countries can discipline their economic growth (ibid.).

Conclusion

The global economic system and development policies such as structural adjustment programmes have been dominated by ideologically driven strategies for the past 25 years. In terms of global development, the activities of the Western governments and the financial 'rulers' have resulted in a distinctly aggressive method of economic management, and as a consequence they have overseen the disintegration of an evolving consensus on global development policies. This break-up can be witnessed with the emergence of alternatives and increasing resistance to Western hegemony. A social democratic alternative – most prominent in Venezuela, Bolivia, Brazil, Ecuador and Chile – has come to dominate South America, with an attempt at non-aligned economic policies, indigenous economic growth and rural regeneration. In geopolitical terms, arguably, this alternative has become the first substantial 'adjustment' away from the neoliberal process of globalisation. Other resistance has come from various Islamic states which have recognised that neoliberal economic practices are wholly incompatible with the theological *mores* of their economic traditions.

Further, in terms of practical development strategies, tension remains between neoliberal policies and progressive, socially focused initiatives such as the millennium development goals – specifically when the MDGs are juxtaposed with practices encouraged through schemes such as the Washington Consensus, the IFIs' trade rules, or aggressive market-adjustment initiatives. This matrix of policies, attached to a process of economic globalisation, has resulted in a global debt-repayment crisis, capital outflow from developing countries at the highest levels ever, the reduction of aid budgets, the rationalisation of technical support, the damaging liberalisation of tariffs and trade, and a raft of cultural and political compliances driven through the IFIs' regime. These have collectively and systematically debilitated development for dozens of the poorest countries on earth. With the global recession exposing the weaknesses of neoliberal strategies, the various attendant policies can be seen to be counter-developmental and exploitative on a grand and global scale.

Theories about a 'spontaneous', 'open', or 'free' market as a primary catalyst for human development go back as far as Smith and Malthus. The effects of such structural systems of human development were divergent then and remain so. At each appearance of this political economy (economic liberalism) there have also been some very considered counter-points – Marx and Utopian Socialism flagging up the early alternatives, Keynes and Galbraith in the mid twentieth century, and Bello, Sen and Sachs at least opening up the current debate (Sen 1981, 1999; Sachs 2005; Bello, Bullard and Malhotra 2000). To emphasise the parallels in the debate, the original critique of political economy may shed some light on the current manifestations of this economic liberalism. Social economist Karl Marx, in addressing an economic breakdown in the 1880s, provides an insightful commentary on the current crisis: 'In a system of production, where the entire continuity of the reproduction process rests upon credit, a crisis must obviously occur – a tremendous rush for means of payment – when credit suddenly ceases and only cash payments have validity' (1894, p.490). This will result in 'the entanglement of all peoples in the net of the world market ... with the constantly diminishing number of the magnates of capital, who usurp and monopolise all advantages of this process of transformation' (1887, pp.714–15). In terms of globalisation these crises can be recognised as being elements indicative of a peculiar economic system – market-driven as opposed to socially driven.

Invariably, economic strategies as well as progressive social policies are necessary for recovery and international development. The current mechanisms and theories that have brought the world into global recession obviously no longer serve the purpose of facilitating development and urgently need to be adjusted in their own right. This demands an informed rethinking of global development programmes as they stand and suggests a need for another more *humane* model of development, another possible future. Furthermore, with the systemic break that has arrived with the global recession, there is an opportunity for political leaders globally to redesign development policies away from the current flawed model dominated by neoliberal schemes and to work towards genuine global development strategies – including the MDGs – which are actively social, economically integrated and pro-poor.

References

Bello, W., N. Bullard and K. Malhotra (eds) (2000) *Global Finance: New Thinking on Regulating Speculative Markets*, Zed Books, London.

Bello, Walden (2002) *Deglobalization: Ideas for a New World Economy*, Zed Books, London.

Brenner, R. (2006) *The Economics of Global Turbulence*, London and New York.

Brockett, James (2009) 'More State Bail-Outs on Cards', *People Management*, 1 January.

Dinan, Desmond (1999) *Ever Closer Union*, Palgrave, London.

George, Susan (2000) 'A Short History of Neoliberalism', in Bello, Bullard and Malhotra (2000), pp.27–35.

Ellwood, Wayne (2001) *The No-Nonsense Guide to Globalisation*, New Internationalist Publications, Oxford.

Flint, Adrian (2008) *Trade, Poverty and the Environment*, Palgrave Macmillan, Basingstoke.

Galbraith, J.K. (1958) *The Affluent Society*, Houghton Mifflin, Boston.

Harvey, D. (2007) *A Brief History of Neoliberalism*, Oxford University Press, Oxford.

Hayek, Friedrich von (1960) *The Constitution of Liberty*, Routledge, London.

Jameson, K.P. and C.K. Wilber (eds) (1996) *The Political Economy of Development and Underdevelopment*, McGraw-Hill, New York.

Keynes, J.M. (1936) *General Theory of Employment, Interest and Money*, Macmillan Cambridge University Press, Cambridge.

Klein, Naomi (2007) *The Shock Doctrine*, Penguin Books, London.

Marx, Karl (1887, 1974 edition) *Capital*, vol.1, Lawrence & Wishart, London.

Marx, Karl (1894, 1974 edition) *Capital*, vol.3, Lawrence & Wishart, London.

Moss, Todd (2007) *African Development*, Rienner, London.

Oxfam (2006) *Unequal Partners*, Oxford briefing paper, Oxford.

Sachs, J. (1997) 'IMF is a Power unto Itself', *Financial Times*, 11 December.

Sachs, Jeffrey (2005) *The End of Poverty: Economic Possibilities for Our Time*, Penguin, Harmondsworth.

Sen, A. (1981) *Poverty and Famine: An Essay on Entitlement and Deprivation*, Oxford University Press, Oxford.

Sen, A. (1999) *Development as Freedom*, Oxford University Press, Oxford.

Siebert, H. (2000) *The World Economy*, Routledge, London.

Smith, Adam (1776) *An Inquiry into the Nature and Causes of the Wealth of Nations*, Methuen, London.

Stiglitz, J. (2002) *Globalization and its Discontents*, Norton, New York.

Thirlwall, A.P. (2003) *Growth and Development*, Palgrave, Basingstoke.

Thorsen, Dag Einar and Amund Lie (2006) 'What is Neoliberalism?', University of Oslo. www.statsvitenskap.uio.no/ISVprosjektet/neoliberalism.pdf

UNDP (United Nations Development Programme) (1999) *Human Development Report*, Oxford University Press, Oxford.

UNDP (2007) *Human Development Report*, Palgrave, Basingstoke.

Vaggi, Gianni and Peter Groenewegen (2003) *A Concise History of Economic Thought*, Palgrave, Basingstoke.

Wade, Robert (2008) 'Financial Regime Change', *New Left Review*, vol.53, pp.5–21.

Williamson, John (1990) 'What Washington Means by Policy Reform', in John Williamson (ed.), *Latin American Adjustment: How Much Has Happened?* Institute for International Economics, Washington, D.C.

World Bank (1995) *World Development Report*, World Bank, New York.

Websites

Bretton Woods Project	www.brettonwoodsproject.org
Centre for Global Development	www.cgdev.org
Global Financial Integrity	www.gfip.org
History of Economic Thought	http://cepa.newschool.edu/het/
International Trade Centre	www.intracen.org
McMaster History of Economic Thought	www.mcmaster.ca/economics/
Montpelerin	www.montpelerin.org
Stiglitz Commission	www.stiglitz-sen-fitoussi.fr/en/
Third World Network	www.twnside.org.sg
UN Trade and Development	www.unctad.org
World Development Movement	www.wdm.org.uk
World Trade Organisation	www.wto.org

CONTRIBUTORS

Paul Hainsworth is a senior lecturer in politics at the University of Ulster. His specialisms include international human rights, the extreme right and European integration. He is active in Amnesty International and has a long-standing commitment to the democratisation process in Timor-Leste. He is editor of *The Extreme Right in Europe and the USA* (Pinter, 1992) and *The Politics of the Extreme Right* (Pinter, 2000). His most recent book is *The Extreme Right in Western Europe* (Routledge, 2008).

M. Satish Kumar is the director of QUB–India Initiative and teaches at the School of Geography, Archaeology and Palaeoecology, Queen's University Belfast. He previously taught at Jawaharlal Nehru University, New Delhi and the University of Cambridge. His recent publications are *Colonial and Postcolonial Geographies of India*, co-edited with Saraswati Raju and Stuart Corbridge (Sage, 2006); and *Globalisation and North-East India: Some Developmental Issues*, co-edited with Amaresh Dubey, Nirankar Srivastav and Eugene D. Thomas (Standard Press, New Delhi, 2007).

Madeleine Leonard is professor of sociology in the School of Sociology, Social Policy and Social Work at Queen's University Belfast. Her main research interest is in the sociology of childhood, particularly in creative and participatory methods of including children in the research process. She is particularly interested in children's experiences of growing up in divided societies and has carried out research in interface areas in Belfast; she plans to extend this focus to other divided cities, such as Nicosia and Jerusalem. Recent articles include 'Segregated Schools in Segregated Societies: Issues of Safety and Risk' (2006), in *Childhood*, vol.13, no.4, and 'Teenagers Telling Sectarian Stories' (2006), in *Sociology*, vol.40, no.6.

Chrispin R. Matenga teaches development studies at the University of Zambia. He has also been head of the Department of Development Studies since 2005. He is active in policy and action research, specialising in tourism and poverty, child labour, community-based natural resources management, and corruption.

Gerard McCann is a senior lecturer in European studies and geography at St Mary's University College, Queen's University Belfast. Formerly the chair of the Centre for Global Education, he is director of the Global Dimension in Education project (SMUC) and co-ordinator of a number of partnership initiatives with colleges in Nairobi (Kenya), Lusaka (Zambia) and Bethlehem (Palestine). He has written extensively on the European Union's economic and development policies.

Stephen McCloskey is the director of the Centre for Global Education, a development non-governmental organisation. His publications include *The East Timor Question: The Struggle for Independence from Indonesia*, co-edited with Paul Hainsworth (I.B. Tauris, 2000). He is also managing editor of *Policy and Practice: A Development Education Review*, the first development education journal published in Ireland.

Joanne McGarry is Trócaire's aid and accountability policy and advocacy officer. She works on issues of donor governments' aid commitments, aid effectiveness, and accountability. Prior to this she worked on Trócaire's west Africa programmes. She has an MA in development studies from University College Dublin. Recent articles include 'Ireland Using its Influence for Positive Change in Accra' (Trócaire, 2008).

Anna Morvern is an immigration adviser at Law Centre (Northern Ireland) and chair of the Refugee Action Group. She obtained a BA (Hons) in modern languages from Oxford University and went on to do a master's degree in human rights at the University of Essex before training as a lawyer. She specialises in legal applications involving human rights and European law and frequently acts for men, women and children who are claiming political asylum.

Ronaldo Munck is head of internationalisation and social development at Dublin City University and visiting professor of sociology at the University of Liverpool. He has taught in Latin America and in South Africa. His recent books include *Globalisation and Contestation: The New Great Counter-Movement* (Routledge, 2007) and *Contemporary Latin America* (Palgrave Macmillan, 2008).

Nessa Ní Chasaide is the co-ordinator of the Debt and Development Coalition Ireland (DDCI) and has worked in the non-governmental sector for over ten years. She has previously worked with Trócaire in Dublin and in Kenya, Oxfam Ireland, and Dóchas, the umbrella body for development NGOs in Ireland. DDCI is a national network of development organisations, religious congregations and trade unions that work for juster relationships between rich and poor countries; it campaigns for an end to the financial exploitation of impoverished countries, in particular through campaigning for debt cancellation and an end to unjust resource flows from the global South to the North.

Denis O'Hearn was trained as an economist and sociologist at the University of Michigan, where he received his Ph.D. in 1988. He worked for a number of years in the Sociology Department at the University of Wisconsin–Madison, where he was associate professor, and joined the Sociology Department at Queen's University Belfast in 1994. He has been Fulbright professor of sociology at University College Dublin (1991/92) and visiting scholar at several universities in the United States, Europe and Japan. He has been on the board of the *Centro de Estudos Sociais* in Coimbra, Portugal and the board of experts of the *Esercizio di Valutazione Nazionale della Ricerca* in Italy.

Andy Storey is a college lecturer in the Centre for Development Studies, School of Politics and International Relations, University College Dublin. He previously worked at the Development Studies Centre, Kimmage Manor, and for the development agency Trócaire. He has published extensively on issues of European political economy and trade policy and on wider development issues, including aid, conflict and migration.

Maeve Taylor is the policy and training project leader of Banúlacht. She has represented Banúlacht and Network Women in Development Europe (WIDE) at a number of United Nations conferences on gender, development and trade issues. She has a master's degree in human rights law from Queen's University Belfast and is a member of the Advisory Committee of the Women's Human Rights Alliance. She is the author of Banúlacht's 2004 publication, *Looking at the Economy through Women's Eyes* and has taught a course entitled 'Women, Economy and Society' as part of the MA in women's studies at the Women's Education Research and Resource Centre, University College Dublin.

INDEX

Compiled by Sue Carlton